C000259069

THE FLYING PENGUIN

More Stories of a Freelance Motorcycling Journalist

FRANK MELLING

Melling

A Collie Press Book

To Bess With Love

Copyright © Frank Melling, 2016

First published in Great Britain in 2016 by:
The Collie Press
Manley Lane, Manley, Cheshire WA6 0PB.

Copyright © Frank Melling, 2016
The right of Frank Melling to be identified as the author of this Work has been
asserted by him in accordance with the Copyright, Designs and Patents Act 1988.
Cover artwork by Mark Jarvis of Motografix:
The Boiler House, Alma Road, Rotherham S60 2HZ

Text and Design © Frank Melling

Layout by Geoff Fisher

Whilst every effort has been made to ensure the accuracy of this book, the author
and publisher cannot be held responsible for any errors, omissions or inaccuracies.
Unless otherwise indicated, opinions expressed herein are those of the author of the
book and do not necessarily represent the views of persons or companies
represented.
A CIP catalogue record for this book is available in the British Library

ISBN 978-0-9527987-3-6

Printed and bound by CPI Books UK, Croydon, CR0 4YY

Praise for The Flying Penguin

"A Penguin in a Sparrow's Nest", the first part of Frank Melling's autobiography was brilliant.

The second part is even better. The stories are incredible – funny, sad and unique all told by someone who really knows how to write.

And there's a lot about me in it too which is great!

Jim Redman MBE – Six Times World Champion

*****

I couldn't name anyone I revere as a hero, but I'm always inspired by the quiet dignity and tales of a life well fought that emerge from those who glide just below the surface of personal fame – and who hold their values and family far dearer than money or stardom.

This is one of those stories, enhanced by a narrative interwoven with motorcycles, racing, the turbulent founding and success of one of Europe's largest biking events and the passion to succeed against others' expectations.

"The Flying Penguin" continues where "A Penguin in a Sparrow's Nest" left off, charting the rise, fall, rise, fall, and rise again of Frank Melling. But it's much more than that. The book is as much a social narrative on recent British history, teaching, troubled youth and the determination to transform nascent ideas into well executed success as it is about the people who have helped, hindered, supported and sacrificed as they move in and out of one man's life story.

Few of the famous names that grace best-seller charts have had such an interesting life, and almost none could write their own story with the engaging warmth, honesty, and generosity that Frank has. He should have called it 'To Be Frank: the honest story of a more than ordinary man.'"

Richard Newland - Deputy Editor MCN

*****

Frank Melling tells a mean tall story. You'd seek him out on Friday night, pint in hand, to hear ripping yarns about being black-flagged on Sammy Miller's Norton Kneeler, or staring down the wrong end of a Colt 45 barrel in backwoods Missouri.

The twist to this second collection of postcards from a riding life is that Frank's tall stories turn out to be true. Spanning three decades, Frank beguiles the reader with traumatic near-death experiences, the emotional upheaval of discovering your soulmate, and the story behind the immensely successful Thundersprint - and why it eventually ended.

Broken bones, broken bikes, broken relationships – all precariously balanced on the knife-edge of a freelance journalist's permanent state of financial insecurity.

Out of the occasionally all too real fires of experience emerges if not a phoenix then certainly a Flying Penguin...

Rowena Hoseason – Editor Real Classic Magazine

Acknowledgements

THIS part of the book is very important to me because although I have written "The Flying Penguin", it has truly been a team effort.

The most important people behind this book have been you, the readers – and that's not just me being polite!

When Carol and I both wanted to produce "A Penguin in a Sparrow's Nest" we were told by all the experts that the book would never work commercially and that we were wasting our time and money. The book had the wrong title, the wrong content and it was known as absolute fact that self-published autobiographies were lucky to sell a couple of hundred copies. As I am writing this we have just passed the 2,000 sales figure so, from the bottom of my heart, thank you for buying our book!

Along with good sales, came a lot of requests for the second part of my story. We were very moved by these and I was personally gratified that anyone would want to read more about a clubman racer who can touch type and tell stories.

With the strong sales record of the first "Penguin", and the enthusiasm from readers for more stories, we set out to produce "The Flying Penguin".

This book is, necessarily, very different from "A Penguin in a Sparrow's Nest." At the start of "The Flying Penguin" I am not a penniless sixteen year old living in a Council House but a 38 year old who had enjoyed considerable success. I was, however, penniless once more!

So, this story begins with one of the lowest points in my life and then goes on through mad days of importing bikes from America, working with some of Britain's most serious young criminals and concludes with the Thundersprint – the biggest event of its type in the world.

It was a real adrenaline ride and I hope that you will enjoy reading the stories as much as I have enjoyed writing them.

I had such a good team helping me with "A Penguin in a Sparrow's Nest" that I couldn't imagine changing it. My long-time friend, Peter Wilson, went through the early drafts of the manuscripts with the same meticulous, insightful care as he had done with the first book and Harry Moffatt made many useful observations which were woven into later versions of the text.

We desperately wanted both "Penguins" to be high quality productions – the equivalent, or better, than anything produced by the major publishers. For this reason, we persuaded Mark Jarvis to produce a second front cover design for us and Geoff Fisher to typeset the manuscript.

We stayed with CPI simply because, as one of Britain's biggest book printers, they always produce top quality publications. After all the work which Carol and I had put into the book, we didn't want to look at something which wasn't satisfying for us both.

And now to Carol. I keep referring to "we" not out of any sense of political correctness, or even parodying the way racers now refer to "us" not doing so well or "we" won a race. No, it's nothing like this at all!

Carol is the key part of my life all day, every day, and when she is absent I miss her terribly. She is my wife, best friend, soulmate and business partner and, in the case of the two "Penguin" books, also my editor – and in this role our relationship becomes very complex.

On the one hand, as my wife and friend, she can see how hard I have worked writing a chapter of the book and clearly wants to be sympathetic and supportive. However, as my editor she demands the best that I can do – even when this means multiple re-writes!

Her skilful hand has made both books tighter and more readable in a way that no other editor could achieve. If you enjoy "A Penguin in a Sparrow's Nest" then you will be taking pleasure from Carol's work as much as mine.

Thanks again for joining me on this journey. Perhaps one day I might write the stories which haven't made it into the first two books.

Contents

Preface

In which we find our hero in a rather tricky position . . .

Fate is Inexorable - But Freelancing is Very Good for the Health

I finished my post graduate course and couldn't wait to get back to school. I badly needed a break, so my wife and I planned a fantastic trip through Europe. At least, I thought that we had planned it. She was planning something even more impressive – and memorably so too!

On the final day of term, she gave me a big kiss and said she was looking forward to me coming home in the evening. I left school as soon as I could after the sherry and cakes and counted the seconds until I could be with her.

When I arrived home, her car wasn't there which I thought was rather unusual but there was a note. It was brief and to the point. It said that she knew that I loved her but she no longer loved me so she had left me - forever.

It was a devastating blow.

My first concern was for her safety so I spent the next few days just trying to find her and make sure that she was well. She was, so that was good.

All divorces are sad and, from my point of view, this one was no different.

I am constantly restless and hard work at best, and impossibly fidgety and irritably dissatisfied at worst, so I can understand why she wanted a new life. However I was, and I still am, sad that she felt she had wasted seventeen years with me when I would have preferred her to be happy from the start with someone else.

Her departure hit me very hard, in so many ways, and there is no point in recounting them here.

Eventually I couldn't manage another day of sadness so I decided that I would end my life. It wasn't an irrational, spur of the moment decision but rather a case of arriving at the end of the line emotionally, physically and intellectually.

It wasn't a cry for help either because I didn't want any help from anyone.

I just wanted to stop going to sleep on a tear soaked pillow and waking up the following morning with the feeling of infinite emptiness which was life without my precious wife.

I had nothing left to give, even to myself: I was just an empty shell.

In those days, Valium used to be given out very freely and my Mum had numerous bottles of this powerful sedative. She also had industrial quantities of really powerful sleeping tablets. Over a week, claiming that I couldn't sleep, I acquired a good supply of these narcotics from Mum and I also scrounged some from one of my colleagues at school who was suffering from depression.

I laid all the tablets out on the dining room table along with a bottle and a half of whisky. I didn't write a suicide note or leave anything at school. Nor did I tidy the house or try to leave things in any order because I didn't care what anyone thought.

As I got ready to take the pills and drink the whisky, the phone rang. I still don't know why I answered it. Maybe it was just an automatic reaction, from a lifetime of answering calls.

It was Jeff Clew from Haynes. I had nearly finished a book for them – but not quite. I had been very ill for some months and it wasn't so much that I wouldn't finish the last chapter but that I couldn't. I had nothing to say to anyone except that I was very, very sad and no-one wants to hear this. My typewriter's dust cover hadn't been moved since the summer and why should it? A writer needs something to give the reader – ideas, passion, information, opinions but something - and I had nothing.

The bulk of the manuscript and photographs had been with Jeff for some months and the book was nearly ready for production. Jeff was sympathetic but he had problems too. Haynes had paid me a generous advance against future sales and now, quite reasonably and fairly, Jeff wanted his book – and immediately too, because he was getting some serious stick from the upper echelons of management.

I was stuck in a corner with no way out. Here was someone who was, quite literally, pleading for my help. He was desperate. What could I do? To put my needs before his was unthinkable and so, in a few seconds of confusion, I agreed to get Jeff out of his corner – and, without knowing it, me out of mine at the same time.

Once I had given my word, I was trapped by the code of the freelancer: never let anyone down, no matter how much effort it takes. It was all the way back to promising a test report on the bike which won a TT for my third article – and delivering it.

Why did I agree? That's more difficult to answer. First, as I have said, it's in the DNA of every thoroughbred freelancer never to let an employer down. A freelancer only stays employed by being reliable.

Then perhaps I felt wanted and needed by someone, so that was a factor too.

Kindness also had a part to play. I couldn't see someone in a mess I could fix and not help.

Maybe it was a combination of all these and more but I pushed the tablets to one side for later, made a cup of coffee and started work. Just before midnight, I faxed the chapter to Jeff - and then fell fast asleep without even getting undressed.

The following morning, I saw the tablets and whisky - but also the faxed sheets and I knew why I should stay alive. For the freelancer, every day is a new day and the next job is always round the corner.

I'm glad that I did do the job for Jeff because I was about to climb aboard another adrenaline ride which was the second part of my life.

Yes, Fate is inexorable - but freelancing is very good for the health!

For Ibby – My Baby With the Pointy Head

Who absolutely insisted on being in a second book

1

Things Can Only Get Better

As a child I used to sit on the long seat at the back of the bus with my Mum and listen to the stoic working class women discuss what was, by modern standards, a brutally tough existence. Their conversations were peppered with the folk sayings that kept them going.

"Never look a gift horse in the mouth."

Or, translated, "Mrs. L's new man friend is a stoker on the trains at Dallam Loco Sheds and, can you believe it, he brings her free anthracite home in his gas mask bag?"

"Every cloud has a silver lining" was another good one.

"The old man's buggered off with that cleaner from Greenings and good riddance too – she's as common as muck…"

However, the most common adage was the one which most puzzled me: "Things can only get better."

Better than what? I didn't know anything more than the cloistered existence of a working class kid in a northern industrial town and so the idea of getting better, or being better, was an alien one.

But, after leaving school aged 16, things did get better for me – much, much better. In fact, by 1985 I was pretty certain that things couldn't get any better at all. I was a very successful author and journalist and travelled the world as a writer and motorcycle racer.

In my teaching career I was an extremely young Head of Department and had been marked out for further promotion.

I had an intelligent, pretty wife whom I worshipped and I lived in a large detached bungalow in a very upmarket Cheshire village.

All this was a long way from the sink Council Housing Estate where I grew up with an alcoholic father. At 38 years old, I was sitting with a big smile on my face and looking forward to the next batch of successes which were sure to follow.

If things could get any better, I couldn't see how.

Then my lovely wife left me, without any warning, and I became so ill that I got within touching distance of ending everything. You can read this part of the story in the last chapter of "A Penguin in a Sparrow's Nest". It's also at the start of this book if you haven't come across it already.

My first concern was whether my wife was safe and, I hoped, even happy now that she was without me. I think that she had a somewhat less charitable view because she left me flat broke.

Better still, this was one week before that month's direct debit payments had to be made and so I was in a rather tricky situation. I sat at home, catatonic with grief, and just over the horizon was a genuine tsunami of financial demands – I hadn't a penny to pay them. As the Chinese curse goes, "May You Live in Interesting Times."

And they really were!

Of course, what I needed was the support of the Midland Bank, the Halifax Building Society and the trade suppliers who provided me with goods to sell. And, with equal predictability, everyone saw disaster ahead, followed by certain failure - and abandoned me.

I had been a close friend, or thought I had been friends, for a long time with the head of one of the big motorcycle trade suppliers. He summed up the situation very succinctly. "Listen Baby Boy, you can ring up for sympathy – but don't ask for any money or credit. I'm not running a charity."

And so it was with almost everyone. The Midland Bank cancelled my overdraft – and immediately too.

The Halifax Building Society threatened to re-possess my house if I didn't pay my mortgage on time.

One of my best customers for Griffin helmets rang the factory, told them how ill I was and said that they should stop supplying me and let him have the franchise instead. Of course no-one wants to back the horse with three broken legs, so they agreed.

There was a whole truckload of problems but, on a positive front, I did lose a lot of weight very quickly!

Not only could I not write professionally, I couldn't write at all. I remember trying to compose a letter to my solicitor about the impending divorce and not being able to start the first sentence – and this, from someone who had produced a shelf full of books and hundreds of feature articles!

I also couldn't spell. In fact, this isn't quite right. I could spell but then I had to check that every word was correct with a dictionary. From being fluent and confident with 1000 words, just getting half a dozen sentences on the page was an epic struggle.

Yes, things could only get better – and on every front too because, for sure, they couldn't get any worse!

*****

For the first two or three weeks I ate very little and just used what was in the cupboards, because I didn't care about anything. One night, I had a tin of pineapple rings on a round of toast so you can see where I was at gastronomically!

Eventually, I ran out of tins and so I took myself off to Marks and Spencer with the intention of replicating what my wife used to buy. I wandered round the store like the lost soul that I was and, when I arrived at the checkout, the bill came to over £20. It was like having a Taser shot in both eyes! First, I didn't have £20 and secondly, if I did have this much money the Midland Bank and the Halifax wanted first dibs on it. In every way, I was a long way down the food chain!

What was worse was that the cashier was a young girl, barely older than the ones I was teaching, and she looked at me as if I was a 38 year old bloke who had just been sent on his first independent food shopping venture.

With overt contempt, she took my shopping from me – whilst the queue of ladies behind me drilled holes in the back of my head. Men carried bags and followed their womenfolk at a respectful distance - and this is what happened if you let them dabble in grown ups' work.

For a couple of weeks, I was on short rations but there are only so many ways in which toast and marmite are better than nothing. Interestingly, or perhaps even bizarrely, the first step forward came via a packet of "Batchelor's Savoury Rice" alluringly displayed in the corner of a Chester delicatessen.

Before my wife had left me, we used to eat out a lot and I was very fond of Chinese restaurants and rice. No doubt to attract the gullible, like me, the packet showed a delicious looking plate of rice with bits of vegetables in it. It was all that I could do to stop drooling.

I can't remember the price of the rice but it was horrendously expensive – something in the region of 25p. As I drove home, I kept a close eye on the rice in case it tried to escape through the window. With so much of my hard earned money invested in it, there was no way I was going to let the little rascal out of my sight. If there had been a mouse trap to hand I would have had it on the seat to clonk down on the rice if it tried to make a run for it.

When I got home, I read and re-read the packet and then followed the instructions to the letter. I even dug around in my race kit bag, and found my Heuer Trackmaster stopwatch so I could get the timing right to the second.

I had a measuring cylinder, for calculating two-stroke pre-mix, in the garage so this was forced into service to measure precisely 350ml of water – plus, of course, a hint of race oil for added bouquet.

I couldn't bear to look at the pan when I emptied the contents of such a valuable packet into boiling water. This had to be madness. Boiling water destroyed things – not made them edible. Still, self-discipline took over and I did as the packet said and stirred in the rice.

No expectant father was more nervous than me as the seconds ticked by towards the magic 15 minutes. At 14 minutes and 59 seconds, I whipped the pan from the stove and poured the contents into a colander.

The rice was all yellow and sort of, well, ricey and the whiff of racing two-stroke in the background was emotionally re-assuring, so I took a very tentative taste on the edge of the spoon I had used for stirring and, to my utter amazement, it was edible.

In fact, this does not do justice to the finished product. It wasn't merely edible it was rather nice – and a lot better than pineapple rings on toast!

I liked the rice a lot and, surprisingly, every time I cooked it the finished product tasted fine. The problem was the cost. 25p a packet was just too expensive to eat regularly.

My saviour came in the form of the wildly exuberant, not to say highly eccentric, Keith Floyd and his first food programme, "Floyd on Fish". Until Floyd, cooking shows had been very serious, pedantic, almost "Open University" programmes which involved a lot of measuring and weighing and checking and timing. Then Floyd came along and chucked ingredients about and sloshed things into pans with an immense amount of passion and unbridled joy. I watched and I thought that Floyd could have been a motorcycle racer. He truly was one of us and the only difference was that he cooked instead of raced.

Inspired, and there is no other word for it, by Floyd's energy and delight in preparing food I bought a packet of plain rice at a fraction of the cost of the Holy Batchelor's Savoury Rice and cooked it by feel, rather than following a recipe. To my surprise, I found that I had the knack of being able to cook and so now I could have a plate of rice and some grilled tomatoes. Add a sprinkle of salt and pepper and a blob of mayonnaise – clearly with an added spoonful of Castrol "R" for that piquant edge - and here was a meal worth eating. Just as good, it was at a price I could afford.

Boiling rice and grilling tomatoes was only the start. Since I am the world's worst mechanic, and have never been any good at the traditional "man crafts", cooking was a bizarre experience. Without anyone teaching me, I found that I could cut and chop easily and the spoon in the pan became an extension of my hand. It felt really odd - almost as if someone, or something, else was doing the cooking and I was a by-stander.

The vast majority of things I tried to cook worked really well and I also found that cooking from "quick sale" ingredients was a cheap way to live – and I really do mean cheap with a capital "C".

*****

There is no point in describing the last stages of the divorce. It was horrible and there is nothing else to say. The final act of the tragedy was the court hearing. In the 1980s, "Clean Break Divorces" were in vogue and nowhere was this more apposite than in our case.

I had done my best as a husband but it hadn't been enough to earn my wife's love or respect so a clean break was the best way forward – although it certainly wasn't the most fun I have had.

After the final court hearing, my solicitor took me back to his office and politely asked for a cheque before I left. Clearly, along with everyone else, he didn't think that I was much of a bet for the future!

I went home alone and unlocked the door to a silent, empty house.

Sleep was nearly impossible so eventually I took myself off to my surgery for some help. My own GP, with whom I had a good relationship, wasn't in but I saw the duty doctor. He was as kind as he could be within a five minute appointment but he had better things to do than to listen to a sad man, maundering on and on and on about how miserable he was.

Clearly, the answer lay in a bottle so he gave me some super-duper strength sleeping tablets so that, in his words, "You will get a good night's rest and feel better in the morning."

In fact, for me, the opposite was true. After three nights I could barely stand up in the morning and even washing was a huge effort.

I'm not saying that all sleeping tablets are wrong for everyone but my experience is that you really do have to approach them with extreme caution because they can easily cause another set of unforeseen problems entirely on their own.

It was at this point that motorcycle racing saved me or, more accurately, the mind-set which comes from racing enduros. Here's what happens when you really do see Saint Peter opening the gates to the after-life – close up and in full colour.

*****

In the open circuit enduros which I used to ride in the 1970s, riders were often faced with tough, life-threatening decisions. Let me give you an example of something which actually happened to me – and it's not an exaggerated story, or a pub tale, but completely and totally factually accurate.

At the time, I was sponsored by Alan Clough Motorcycles, a Honda dealer in Stockport. Because I was generously supported, I had to ride at events which I would normally avoid. One of these was a winter enduro which was held in late October or maybe even November – I can't remember exactly when. Certainly, it was a foul day – freezing cold with iron grey sheets of sleet, marching in battalions across the Welsh moorlands where the SAS train.

I always rode with goggles, regardless of how bad were the conditions, but in this case I was passing slower riders very frequently and they were throwing up clouds of liquid mud - so much so that I just couldn't see a thing.

There was nothing else to do but drop my goggles and then turn my head away, as I passed the rider in front.

Deep in the Crychan Forest, I did just this - and missed the blind corner which followed. The next thing was that I had flipped over an earth bank and was ricocheting down through the trees, completely out of control.

Eventually, I crashed heavily into a rocky stream with my head three-quarters under water and the bike on top of me.

Here's the situation. I am almost, but not quite, unconscious with the Honda lying across me. The water is choking me because, with the bike on top, I can't get my head clear of the stream bed. It's now snowing and I am shivering very severely and in a lot of pain. I actually just want to relax, shut my eyes and give up. That's the easy option – but not one which I can take. I have to survive.

So, with a huge amount of effort I lever the bike off my body and somehow roll and drag it down to a hard shale, forestry road which I can see just a couple of hundred yards beneath me. There is no "Phone a Friend" or "Ask the Audience" option. The choice is very stark: get to the road or die in the forest. It is a wonderfully cleaned up version of life without any of the unnecessary add ons.

Bless its 200cc mechanical heart, the little Honda fired up after two or three kicks and there was a glimmer of hope again.

By this time, I was shivering so badly that I could barely hold on to the handlebar grips. I was also lost, and the sleet was becoming heavier. It was a completely 50/50 choice whether to head left or right on the shale road - but left looked slightly downhill so I turned the Honda this way.

Five minutes later, in a second stroke of utter good fortune, I came across a forestry worker's cottage. There the man's wife gave me a rough towel to dry myself off and allowed me to stand naked before her log fire, whilst she fed me scalding hot tea and dried off my riding gear on her Aga.

Later, Russ Foulkes – my loyal and long serving pit crew - and I had a laugh at the mess I had got myself into and how completely unimpressed the lady of the house must have been with my cold, shrunken man bits.

I could only agree with Russ on every count. Regardless of how I looked, I had survived. No support group, mentor or NHS hotline. If you are in the forestry drowning, and on the brink of hypothermia, you are either going to stay there, and eventually leave in a body bag, or get yourself out. There are no other options.

There is a wonderful American racing expression which has been one of the driving forces of my whole life. It's this: "When the flag drops – the bull***t stops."

Against the odds, I had got myself out of the Crychan and lived to tell the tale. Now, I had to do the same thing after the divorce and it was going to be a lot harder than drowning and freezing to death in a Welsh Forest.

2

Wyrd Bið ful Aræd – Fate is Inexorable

IF this book were a novel, we would be at the point where the hero picks himself up from the floor, dusts himself down and walks straight into the arms of a stunningly beautiful girl who, in my case, would also be a motorcycle racing fan dreaming of meeting a freelance journalist.

Unfortunately for the story, I wasn't a hero and the mere thought of speaking to a girl of any sort terrified me. I was also very much an ex-journalist who couldn't string two sentences together. Other than these few challenges, things were fine. However, I was lonely and I did need some companionship.

Throughout my life, there had always been dogs around so I thought that a canine companion might fill the empty void. I didn't give the process much thought. After all, a dog is a dog is a dog. They wag their tails when they're happy and sit on the couch with you to be stroked whilst you watch TV. It's about as simple as this - and simple was what I needed.

In the classifieds section of the Chester Chronicle there was a farmer advertising Collie dogs for sale. I didn't know anything about Collies except that they were black and white and the picture I had seen in the school reference book showed a happy looking dog with a big, pink tongue. At the time, a happy dog with a big pink tongue was about all I needed or wanted.

The dogs were advertised for £25 which was a horrendous amount of money for me but my teacher's salary had just gone into the bank and, with a month of frugal living, I thought that I could just about scrape together enough funds to buy one.

I set off for the farm, which was high in the hills above the Welsh border town of Flint. The farmer had two working Collies and the pups were their off-spring. The father was a big, powerful lad full of verve and confidence. The mother was much slighter, with an oddly thoughtful face. Exchanging looks with a dog who was clearly studying me was a bit of a strange experience.

The pups were weaned and all six of them were housed in a loose box at the end of the stable block. They say that dogs look, and behave, like their owners – or vice versa – so the big, confident Collie dog set off down the yard following his equally large and loudly spoken boss. I was neither big, nor confident, nor noisy so I followed in silence behind them.

When we arrived at the loosebox five of the six pups were bouncing up and down as if they had been feeding on a whole range of illegal narcotic substances. The farmer scooped up a large, muscle bound male pup who immediately tried to escape and join his doggy Dad. This, explained the farmer, was the pick of the litter.

I didn't like refusing the lovely pup but I knew that this wasn't the dog for me. The farmer picked up the sub-text of the silence and hauled out a lovely, blue merle dog pup for inspection. Blue Merles have blue eyes, are considered to be physically attractive and folk tales say that they are also highly intelligent.

However, while the farmer did his best to help, something very, very strange was happening.

In the far corner of the loosebox, standing well back from the other pups, was a small bitch. She wasn't nervous or timid but simply seemed to want to distance herself from the other pups. She made very strong, direct and sustained eye contact with me. If this had been a Disney film, streams of little stars would have been travelling between us.

At that point, I knew that something special had happened. However, just what this special thing was I didn't understand at the time.

The farmer was bemused and, to be fair to him, did point out that the little pup was the least desirable animal in the litter. However, he didn't debate with me for long because no doubt he felt that if I was sufficiently dim to ignore his advice and reject the quality dogs, then it was going to be a big problem off his plate. Now, he wasn't going to be left with a second-rate pup on his hands when all the good stock had been sold.

He whisked the little pup out of the loose box and put her down on the yard. She immediately ignored him and looked at me with eyes which were disconcertingly intelligent. You will have seen pictures of the way dolphins look: well, she had a dolphin face.

We set off down the yard towards my car and the pup trotted alongside me, in a way which would have won the obedience award at an amateur dog show.

The farmer felt sorry for me having the second-rate pup and so let me have her for £15.

I had a brought an old towel with me because pups are invariably car sick on their first journey, or have a toilet accident, so I spread the cloth on the passenger seat and put the little dog on it. She lay down as I reversed out of the yard then wriggled across the seat until she could put her head on my knee – and promptly went to sleep. This was not how things were supposed to happen.

When we arrived home, I got her into the back yard as soon as possible because she had been a long time without having access to a toilet and I thought she must have been bursting: I wasn't wrong. She relieved herself very quickly and then started an inch by inch inspection of the large garden. In the end, I needed the bathroom so I left her to it.

I came back to the kitchen and there was the pup, along with a freshly killed mouse by way of a house warming gift for me. She stood back from the present and her face split almost in half with such a cheeky, cheerful grin that I burst into tears at the sight of such happiness. I might be sad but Bess, for that was now her name, certainly wasn't.

She sat on the kitchen floor whilst I cooked my tea and by the end of day she was even beginning to grasp the concept of being house trained. There were mistakes because she was only a puppy but her intelligence was amazing. I have never shared a house with a dolphin, or a mountain gorilla, but whatever Bess was, she certainly wasn't a dog - she was something much further up the ecological tree.

We washed up together and then sat down to watch TV, also together. She sat next to me and I stroked her head as it rested on my knee. The silky softness of her fur, the calm, deep breathing and her sweet, oaty, puppy smell combined to envelop us in a bubble of peace and safety. After so many nights, and days, of sadness I suddenly felt sheltered and protected. My limbs became heavy from the relaxation and I looked at the pup with wet eyes. Maybe, just maybe, this was the first hint of pre-dawn light on the horizon.

Eventually it was bed time so I took Bess into the garden. She immediately got the idea of why she was there and after a couple of minutes we both headed back into the house. I didn't have a basket for her but had made a large bed in the kitchen, out of a fleecy quilt. My wife had been particularly fond of it so I had no hesitation in giving it to Bess!

I put a little soft toy on the quilt for company, along with a flavoured chewy stick in case she needed something to gnaw on in the night. Finally, I half-filled a breakfast bowl with water and then dipped my finger in it and let Bess lick the liquid so that she was certain of where she could have a drink.

The last thing was to kneel down next to the quilt, make sure that she was comfortable and give her a kiss on her forehead. She snuggled down and put her tail around her head. I closed the door as quietly as I could, tiptoed to the bathroom and went to brush my teeth.

It had been an emotionally exhausting day but I was happier than I had been for months. Even my lovely new pup was playing her part by settling down peacefully. After so many sleepless nights, I was actually looking forward to getting into bed.

I began brushing my teeth – and then the noise began.

First, it was a sobbing, soprano howl – like a wolf serenading the moon. I carried on brushing. Within a minute, the sobbing had a half-bark built into it. Now, it was a wolf with a complaint about the moon – and a serious one too!

By the time I was undressed, a wail had been added to the complaint. In fact, there was a full operatic libretto coming from the orchestra which now seemed to be sat on the fluffy quilt where my dog had been a few minutes previously.

In principle, Bess' reaction was fairly standard. A lot of pups get upset for a few minutes on their first night away from their brothers and sisters but then they settle down and sleep the deep, peaceful sleep of puppies.

What made this complaint so spectacularly different was the range, volume and determination of the performance.

Regardless, I was determined to master the situation once and for all: permanently and forever. She was the dog, I was the human and she was going to do what she was told. Tough though it might be for us both, that was that!

Bess must have had the same thoughts – but from a somewhat different perspective. She needed to tell me what was happening, and what was going to happen. Clearly, howling and barking was not getting the message across. A change of tack on her part was needed.

My bungalow was a big, posh house and the Master bedroom was some considerable distance from the kitchen. Even so, I heard the boom of the first impact as if I was right outside the kitchen door. Crash! Boom! Thud! And then, fifteen seconds of silence. The dog was trying to batter down the door! I was utterly freaked out. My lovely new dog was going to kill herself trying to reach me.

Three attacks were all that was needed before I broke. I ran across the hall, through the dining room and opened the kitchen door. There was Bess, panting heavily, and getting ready for the next assault.

She looked up at me with a face of sheer exasperation. How could I have been so careless as to close the door? And why hadn't I heard her calling to me? Was I deaf? She didn't quite tut and shake her head but I had seen the same expression on the faces of managers faced with incompetent staff so many times before.

"Humans…You know how it is. Can't live with 'em and can't live without 'em!"

I was still going to win this one though. I decided that I would let Bess come into my bedroom just for five minutes and then it would be back in the kitchen where she was going to live.

It had been a long day, a very long day indeed, so I just rested my eyes for a few minutes…

When I woke up, the morning sun was streaming through the curtains and Bess was sat beside me – smiling and wagging her tail.

There had been no accidents in the night and, as she proved on so many occasions during the next seventeen years, she had been as right over where she should sleep as she would be over all her other decisions.

Bess wasn't a dog – she was a furry person and from now on, where I slept then so would she.

*****

The other tiny flicker of light in a dismal landscape was my passionate belief in the democratisation of literature. It is really odd to write this but despite the problems with my finances, day to day living and the fragile state of my head, I still couldn't let go of the one idea which, more than anything else in my life, had been a guiding beacon.

Books, reading and writing had taken me from the most abject poverty to a lot of success. I believed that literacy was the most powerful tool our species has – and I still do today. Instead of Social Workers, Support Groups and BBC programmes on the need for mentors, true social mobility comes through literacy: full, complete fluency in the written and spoken word so there is no area of knowledge and human experience which can't be reached and touched by every single person, rich or poor, in the world.

Literacy leads directly to equality of opportunity and I despair when I hear someone say that they don't read.

There is a 19th Century saying that I am now going to plagiarise. It's this:

Give a man a fish and you feed him for a day. Teach a man to fish and you feed him for a lifetime.

Here's my version.

Give someone literacy and they can work out how to fish for themselves - and with no intervention from the State and its services.

Regardless of the mess I was in personally, I still could not let go of the belief that I had a duty to let the kids from the challenging school in which I taught enjoy the benefits of full literacy. This was more than an aspiration, it was a quasi-religious tenet. The kids had the same right to literacy as they did to clean drinking water and free health care: it was that important to me.

So that is my philosophy and it's all very well and good. However, I didn't want to write an academic paper on the democratisation of literature or even teach a course on the subject. What I wanted was action.

Thinking and talking about ideas is easy: putting them into practice is a lot harder - but I soon had a plan.

I decided to produce a class magazine with my bottom set English kids. I chose this group deliberately because they were the least able in terms of literary skills – and yet had most need of literacy.

They would write, edit and design their own magazine. In doing this, I would empower a group of young people who, in normal circumstances, would never get within a million miles of exercising control over the written word.

The easy option would have been to do the magazine with the brightest children, who could have undertaken the tasks necessary to make a publication with the least effort. But I didn't want the easy option: I wanted to push the democratisation of literature out to the whole school population. And I was determined that it would be successful!

The first thing was to get some funding because for sure my wallet was still eerily empty! My Head Teacher was a scientist with not much interest in literature, or me, but he was kind enough in a distant sort of way, and gave me £50 to produce his idea of what a class magazine should be. If the project cheered me up a bit as a by-product, then it was £50 well spent.

I need to digress slightly at this point and explain how class, and school, magazines worked at the time. They came in three main flavours. The first was the most common: a collection of the kids' work usually laid out on wall display boards and often tied in with a parents' evening. I had made hundreds of these since I started teaching.

The second option was reproduced on a Banda machine. This was a fascinating piece of kit – and one which would get today's teachers banged up in a high security jail for ten years.

The Banda, also known as the Ditto machine in America, was invented by Wilhelm Ritzerfeld in 1923. It was a loose relative of the copper plate etchings which had been around for centuries.

There were two parts to printing off copies. The first was the master page on which you wrote or even typed if the school had access to one of the big, Olympia office typewriters. Beneath the master sheet was a piece of purplish coloured paper which looked rather like a sheet of carbon paper – but somewhat thicker.

The pressure of writing, typing or even drawing on the master sheet transferred ink on to the shiny back of the master – but as a mirror image. There was no way of correcting mistakes and so Bandas were fine for producing class work sheets but you can imagine what the results were like from kids who weren't exactly gifted at writing!

Once you had a master, the fun really began. The actual Banda machine was mainly a small drum with a lovely, cast aluminum handle. The master was carefully – extremely carefully – clipped into the drum so that it sat precisely at 90 degrees to it.

At the bottom was a pad which, in a very Goldilocks way, had to be given just the perfect amount of Banda fluid. Too much and the text would smudge: too little and the reproduction would be weak. But, just right and you would get legible copies of what you had written, or drawn, in purplish ink on sheets of plain paper.

The actual mounting of the Master, wetting the fluid pad and then turning the Banda handle with a slow, accurate and methodical timing was way beyond my skill set so, like any entrepreneurial 19th century industrialist, I brought in child labour. Eleven and twelve year old girls were always the best for Banda jobs – small fingers, neat and patient: what could be better? All over Britain, such fine young tradespeople were knocking out worksheets by the hundreds of thousands!

Of course, these highly skilled artisans needed to work undisturbed and I recognised this. My clerical staff were allowed to operate the Banda in my small stockroom, with the door tightly closed for security and peace.

Here's where things get interesting. Banda fluid was a 50/50 mix of two forms of industrial alcohol – methanol (the fuel used for speedway bikes) and isopropanol. So, there are the lovely girls working diligently away in a sealed room without any ventilation, sloshing industrial alcohol on to a pad and then taking deep breaths. Problems? What problems? Little wonder my workers always staggered out with smiles on their faces!

A somewhat better job could be done with a Roneo duplicator. A Roneo master was not as easy to make as the Banda master because it had to be cut with a typewriter. The typewriter ribbon was lifted out of the way and then the keys were struck very hard to cut the master. The problem was that school secretaries, the only people capable of typing quickly and accurately, despised the teaching staff and so even Heads of Department had to crawl into the school office on their knees and then oblate themselves before the typing deities.

I found the whole exercise distasteful and, even if I had zipped my mouth tightly shut, which I rarely did, the finished results were still tacky. What I wanted for the kids was something which looked like a real publication.

Photocopying was about but it was expensive and not common in schools.

Unfortunately for me, £50 was not going to buy a professional publication for a number of interesting reasons. It seems almost impossible to imagine now but, 31 years ago, the use of computers was very restricted. For example, 1985 was a whole four years before the invention of the internet by Sir Tim Berners Lee.

There were a lot of computers around but, in schools, their use was dominated by Maths teachers to whom you had to apply for permission to use the machines. In my eyes at least, computers were posh adding machines and tools for working out timetables.

The only useful thing I had seen a computer do was Word Processing. This is where you can type something on screen and then correct it. Word Processing was vastly better than applying blobs of Tipp-Ex – another satisfyingly toxic substance for the little ones to sniff if they got tired of being stoned on Banda fluid or Evostik – to words and then typing over the resultant thick, white blob.

You could correct mistakes with a word processor but the programmes we had in school were crude things and the coarse, wobbly green text hurt my eyes to a savage degree.

Newspapers and books were made by what was called "Hot Metal" typesetting. This system quite literally used molten lead which was then cast into letters to form words – hence the name "Hot Metal".

The whole process was very much a craft skill, involving complex decisions based on years of experience, and applied to everything from how many lead "pigs" needed to be melted for the huge Linotype machines, to deciding how a journalist's or author's typed words would look on the page. The latter skill fascinated me. A skilled compositor could glance at a page of typewritten words – called copy – and "cast it off" by eye, calculating exactly how much space it would take on the page. It was an unbelievably clever skill which took thousands of hours to learn.

Typesetting was rigidly, militantly controlled by two trade unions: the NGA (National Graphical Association) and SOGAT – (The Society of Graphical and Allied Trades).

No-one except card carrying members of these two unions was allowed "On the stone" (the actual area where the typesetting was done). In fact, journalists sometimes used to pass their copy through a hatch to the typesetters. On one side was the NUJ (National Union of Journalists) card holding journalist and on the other, the card carrying NGA or SOGAT member. Unions really did have publishing by the throat and exploited their monopoly ruthlessly.

Hot metal typesetting was also 100% male dominated. It was hard, hot work and women were effectively banned from it. Girls could be journalists but the real work of making newspapers and books had to be left to men.

The older I get the more I am convinced by the ancient Norse concept of fate. It's the title of this chapter: Wyrd Bið ful Aræd – the Old English translation of "Fate is Inexorable". You just can't avoid fate.

Take a moment to think about what happened next in this story. It's October 1985. A teacher wants to produce a real magazine for, and with, his kids but has no money or experience. The job was, quite literally, impossible. Not merely difficult or challenging but just not possible with a £50 budget. It's a cul de sac with no way out.

In July 1985, Aldus had launched Desk Top Publishing with their iconic Pagemaker programme. This programme simply dropped a nuclear bomb on existing publishing practice – it was that important.

The new system was called Desk Top Publishing because you could make a publication from the computer on the desk where you worked. Nothing in the history of printing was so important in the democratisation of literature. Now, anyone could make a publication to professional standards.

Copy – the journalists' words – were entered into Pagemaker and then they could be arranged in columns, just like hot metal typesetting. The size of the type could be adjusted instantly, pictures added and big, bold titles put across the top of the page. In fact, Pagemaker could do everything that hot metal typesetting could do – but without any of the SOGAT or NGA trade skills. Instead of five years of training to become a fully trained compositor, four weeks would transform a competent typist into a reasonable typesetter.

To the utter horror of the male dominated trade unions, women – who were often trained secretaries with excellent touch typing skills – could sometimes set a page faster than a man who had been through a five year trade apprenticeship. It was instantly ground zero for hot metal typesetting.

The first publisher in Britain – and probably in the rest of Europe too – to use Pagemaker was the Messenger Press which was based four miles from my school. The Messenger Press was the child of Eddie Shah, a free-wheeling entrepreneur with a long, successful history in the publication of local newspapers. He had an equally extended and challenging record of going head to head with the print unions and so when Pagemaker arrived he saw the instant fix for all his problems.

Mr. Shah had also imported a colour press from America so that, for the first time ever, a newspaper could have a full colour front page. No other British newspaper offered this. The colour reproduction was very poor – so much so that it was mockingly referred to as "Shahvision" – but it was light years better than black and white images.

Free from union control, anyone could make a newspaper – and I did. Fate? Good fortune? Sheer chance? I don't know. But what is certain is that I was in the precise centre of the perfect publishing storm and with equal certainty I was the first teacher in the world to use Desk Top Publishing in education.

Not that it was easy. I would go down to the Messenger Press after school had finished and these highly skilled, ex-hot metal tradesmen would teach me how to make a newspaper. They taught me about leading, point sizes, cross-heads, fonts and a vast amount more.

They treated me with a wonderful mixture of utter contempt – how could such a f***wit be allowed to teach when I was too thick to wipe my own bum – and derision for my lack of understanding of the technicalities of printing. But there was also affection for how hard I tried and respect for what I was trying to achieve.

I might be told to make the tea, and have stale bread rolls thrown at me when I made mistakes, but I was listened to respectfully when I explained the importance of literacy.

Perhaps most importantly of all, no-one mentioned my divorce or the hard time I was having at school.

I also took the kids into the Messenger Press so that they could decide where a story should go on the page and which pictures should accompany it.

This was the fire in my soul. No longer would an exclusive elite control the publishing process but ordinary kids from ordinary backgrounds would be given the power of decision.

This was what the democratisation of literature really meant.

Two weeks before Christmas, I stood in the cold and damp at the base of the press, housed in a basic industrial unit on the outskirts of Warrington, and saw the very first publication, written, edited and typeset for children by children, skid noisily into the despatch tray. The magazine was called "My

Christmas" and, even now, I rate this crude little publication as one of the highlights of my life. Publishing was now for everyone – rich or poor, genius or common person.

Not since the first printed page appeared in 1440 had anything as important happened in the transmission of human knowledge. I was at the centre of the revolution and felt deeply grateful.

It had been a long five months but suddenly the light had come on. Now, it was just a matter of getting the rest of my life back on track – but this time there was no computer programme to help me sort out the mess.

3

Kick the Tyres and Light the Fires (With Apologies to Top Gun): We're Off!

I sat back at the end of Christmas Day and felt rather pleased with myself. The Midland Bank and Halifax were off my back now that they knew they would get paid – it's strange how these financial institutions only want to help when you don't need it – and, with my Mum's help, the house was presentable in a sort of man way: neat and clean but with no homely touches.

My Mum had taken my wife leaving me very badly and so I was extremely pleased, and proud, that I had made a traditional Christmas Dinner for her. As Mum, Bess and I sat down to eat our turkey, I couldn't help but think how much better things were now than in July.

Not that the sun was shining everywhere. In particular, my three car garage was a very bleak and empty place. During the worst time, when I was penniless, the motorcycling hyenas had really attacked me and all my bikes had gone at fire sale prices. So had a lot of the spare parts and even the little Myford lathe which I had owned for 20 years.

The turning point came with my pillar drill. This was made by the British Meddings company – still manufacturing superb machine tools in Devon today – and was a thing of beauty. A particularly vicious scavenger slunk in under the garage door and offered me £5.00 for it. I told him where I would stick the pillar drill, and in no uncertain terms too, if he didn't leave immediately.

Although it didn't feel like it at the time, the jackal had done me a great favour.

At my amoebic level, I felt just the same as Churchill did after the Battle of El Alamein - and he really could capture complex and important ideas in just a few words:

"Now this is not the end. It is not even the beginning of the end. But it is, perhaps, the end of the beginning."

I was solvent; still in my own house; had cooked Christmas dinner for my Mum and made a wonderful magazine for the kids I taught. I wasn't a loser any more. From now on, I was going on the offensive.

*****

Writing had been my life since I left school aged sixteen. I had written everything from feature articles to very successful books, an important film script and tens of thousands of words for schools and teachers. Now, as I went into my study, it seemed like a lifetime since I had tried to write anything outside of utter necessity.

At the time I produced my articles on a huge, Hermes electric typewriter which had an early form of Word Processing built into it. There was a tiny LED strip which showed eight or so words as they were typed and any mistakes could be corrected as you wrote – hugely better than Tipp-Ex or an eraser.

The machine was a big, heavy beast almost the size of a large tea tray. It was covered with a translucent grey cover which had not been removed for months.

I actually sidled up to the typewriter nervously, as if it were hibernating. Quietly, to avoid startling the sleeping beast and have it run off, I pulled my chair up to the desk where I had written so many articles. Very tentatively, I lifted the cover off the machine.

It sat there, black and silent – almost accusingly, because I had neglected it for so long.

The tension was palpable. I felt like a character from a fantasy film, entering the dragon's den and looking at the sleeping reptile. All my adult life I had been a writer – someone who was very good with words and now I doubted, very deeply, if I still was. It was far more than just a question of writing: the issue was whether a huge part of me had died in the sadness of the divorce.

Magazines all over the world had paid for my stories and many tens of thousands of people had bought my books. Then, I couldn't write. The shock was immense and truly traumatic.

I looked at the Hermes, afraid of switching it on for fear of discovering that I still couldn't create words. The fear of failure stared me in the face and I was frightened.

The Hermes was a beautiful piece of Swiss, precision engineering. The power switch eased into position smoothly, silently and effortlessly. Inside, the motor hummed almost noiselessly into life. The keys clattered momentarily as the beast woke from its deep sleep and the tiny green display flicked on: then there was nothing but silence and stillness.

It was like walking across one of those tiny, fragile, wobbling rope bridges spanning a ravine of infinite depth. If I didn't begin typing then I would be stranded forever, on one side, never able to write again. If I did type, and the ideas refused to transform themselves into words and the sentences wouldn't build from those words, then I would still be stranded.

For a writer, it was a genuinely frightening moment.

The Hermes required only the lightest pressure on a key to make a letter. I rested my fingers on the home keys – the middle line of keys on a keyboard where everyone who can touch type begins. Now, I had to stand outside myself and let my writer's mind type whilst I watched as an interested, and very concerned, bystander.

I touched the first key and the letter I had asked for appeared. Then another, and another, and even more. Without thinking or planning or effort, there were some sentences about how I met Bess.

It would be more dramatic if I said that I struggled with the ideas and words but this would also be a lie, because I didn't. My fingers floated over the keys, and the verbs and adjectives flowed on to the page. Full stops came without thinking – colons split sibling ideas without thought.

I could write again - but the next chasm to cross was just as challenging.

*****

Just before Christmas, I had attended an evening course about reading material for the least able teenagers. This was a very challenging subject since there were, and are still, a lot of eleven year olds who are functionally illiterate. Reading ability is assessed by a measure called "Reading Age." This compares the ability of a student against a notional average for their age group. For example, a very bright 10 year old can have a Reading Age of sixteen years – that is she reads as well as the average sixteen year old.

At the other end of the scale, we had a good sprinkling of kids who were coming to us aged eleven with a reading age of seven or less. In practical terms, these pupils were illiterate.

The snag is that you can't give students of this age, who have just started their "Big School", reading books about teddies and elves – not unless the teddies wear bandanas and mirror sunglasses, and the elves carry stun guns!

I had written a very successful series of books aimed at older students with literacy problems, and I was at the course to hear what else was happening in the world of reading material for less able kids.

Afterwards, we all went for a drink in the college bar and a couple of teachers came across to meet me because they were using my books in their schools. To be honest, I was rather flattered that they wanted to speak to me.

One lady teacher was particularly attentive. She was bright and enthusiastic but without being pushy. She was also quite pretty – just the sort of woman whom I found attractive.

I had many faults as a husband but one of them was most definitely not a wandering eye. In the sixteen years I had been with my wife I had never, ever, strayed from the path of monogamy – not even once.

Now I was single again and being shown more than passing attention by a lady who ticked all the boxes.

We sat and chatted about teaching and books for half an hour and then she delivered the killer line: "My house is on the way back home for you, do you fancy a coffee?"

It was the most polite, discreet and courteous invitation – but one which was also pellucidly clear.

From the outside, the effect must have been interesting. I immediately became an inarticulate clod. In fact, if I had applied for the job of village idiot I would not have been appointed - on the grounds of being too stupid.

She smiled encouragingly and I responded with a stream of drivel, consisting largely of, "Errr, yes. That would be great but, no, I mean, thanks no. Yes, I do mean thanks, but no, and my dog's in the car, and she gets stressed and she wants to go home now and I should go home now as well and…"

No wonder she gave up in exasperation.

There was a whole package of problems. First, I was desperately, achingly frightened of being rejected. The thought of arriving at the teacher's house, asking for a coffee with milk and then finding out that she thought everyone who didn't drink their coffee black was sub-standard would have destroyed me.

Then, once I got near anything approaching social conversation, I became tongue tied and a nervous wreck.

Last, but far from least in terms of importance, for the first time since I was thirteen years old my bloke bits had no interest in girls.

We didn't exchange phone numbers or any other contact details. I simply fled out of the bar as if pursued by the hounds of hell and didn't calm down until I got back to my car and had given Bess a hug.

I liked girls a lot. I liked them as friends. I liked them as colleagues. And I liked them in all the other ways they deserved to be liked too.

The colleagues bit was still sound but everything else was a chaotic, emotional quagmire and only time was going to help sort out the mess.

*****

In fact, it was a good thing that girls didn't rate in the list of priorities because I was pretty fed up with being broke. The breakthrough came, as it always had, through writing. I received a letter from an Australian magazine which was running a feature on BSA motocross machines. They had read the story I had written years ago about the John Banks Cheney BSA and wondered if I would sell it. In pre-internet days, material tended to stay country specific so it was easily possible to sell the same piece to multiple magazines. I had made a lot of money doing this over the years.

I re-worked the story a little and then sent it off in a big envelope. Six weeks later, a cheque arrived and I was back in business. I could write professionally again - and this was an even greater relief than finding out that I still liked girls!

The biggest challenge was that 1986 was an awkward time in the history of motorcycling – or more particularly my little sliver of motorcycling history. The date needs putting into perspective. At 39 years of age, I was old for the bikes which were current at the time and classic racing was very much in its infancy. In fact, Alan Cathcart, Dick Linton and Steve Linch had only founded the Classic Racing Motorcycle Club seven years earlier, in November 1979.

Classic motocross and trials did exist but this too was at an early stage. In fact, the whole classic bike movement was, in many ways, quite amateurish compared to its present state.

In short, I was having difficulty finding the right orbit for tiny planet Frank in what looked like a new, and very strange, galaxy.

The obvious step was to ride enduros again, which was the discipline where I had achieved most success, and once more on a Suzuki, the marque I knew so well. There had been some friction in the Crooks family and now Eddie, who had been my sponsor for so many years, had opened his own shop just down the road from the iconic Crooks-Suzuki premises in Crellin Street, where I had spent so many happy times when I was younger.

Eddie sourced an RM250 motocross machine for me and the idea was that we would convert this into full enduro trim if I liked it. Eddie was as kind and supportive as ever but this was not 1978 when we had ruled the enduro world together with the wonderful Suzuki PE 250.

We were both older and the world had changed. If you should never meet your hero then, a million times more, you should never try to relive your past.

I ran in the new Suzuki but didn't feel good on it. The bike was a massive step forward over the last dirt bike I had raced seriously and I wasn't using it properly.

I pretty well predicted what was going to happen – and it did. I took the bike to a Welsh Hare and Hounds event – like an extended motocross race – and had a miserable time. I ran mid-field but this was a huge disappointment because when I had stopped riding enduros just five years earlier, I would have expected to finish near the top of the entry.

The reasons were clear. First, I couldn't make the best use of the bike. It handled vastly better than anything I had ever ridden off-road before and I just wasn't able to make the mental adjustment.

I was also hugely unfit. By this I don't mean that I was unfit for a 39 year old – but rather that I was on a different planet compared to the 20 year olds I was racing against. Enduros are an intensely physical sport, pushing every part of the body to the outer limits, and when I rolled the bike up to my car at the end of the day I just felt like death. This was no fun!

I phoned Eddie and he wasn't surprised. I had paid for the bike and Eddie was no longer my sponsor but, regardless, he was kind. He told me to get the Suzuki sparkling clean and he would put it in his showroom for me and let me have the money, less a small commission, when the bike sold.

I duly spent a week getting the Suzuki nice and shiny and ran it up to Eddie on Saturday morning. We didn't say much because he knew as much as I did that an old bloke had tried to go racing against youngsters – and had failed. Cut the bovine excrement. That's what had happened and that's all there was to it.

Then, with no warning, in through the showroom door flew the Good Fairy – as she has done so often in my life – and gave me a lovely present.

As I was drinking Ed's coffee, he introduced me to one of his customers who knew my name from having read my books and articles. Incredibly, he owned a Cheney BSA – and one which had done only four meetings from new.

His house was near to Eddie's shop so I went round to see the bike and, even with a lifetime of buying bikes, I was surprised. First the Cheney was in large bits in the loft of the house so I had to grope around in the dark to see what I was buying. Not that I needed much persuasion because what was there, in between the joists, was an almost brand-new Heanes Thumper.

This bike needs a little bit of explanation, as is often the case with anything Eric Cheney did. That Eric, I was actually privileged to call him "Uncle Eric", was genius is beyond dispute. For my money he was the greatest of all the artisan British chassis designers of the 1960s and early 1970s. Eric felt, rather than understood, a motorcycle chassis in a remarkably intuitive way - just as a top chef simply senses precisely the right amount of seasoning to put in a dish and a sculptor becomes part of the marble being shaped.

By some remarkable combination of an engineer's knowledge, a craftsman's eye and a metallurgist's sense of how steel tubing will behave when bent and welded, Eric produced the best motorcycle chassis of his day.

I worked with, and occasionally for, Eric for many years and one of the saddest moments for me is that I never wrote his life story. I pestered Eric relentlessly for years to help me with the detail – the dates, times and places – so that I could put them into a narrative and, just as he finally agreed, what should have been a very minor operation proved to be fatal and this colossus amongst motorcycle designers died: I cried when I heard the news.

Genius though Eric was, and I will use that word both literally and advisedly again, Cheney was not a great businessman. In fact, he had a view of business which left many of us frustrated at the missed opportunities – and more than a few customers seriously out of pocket.

Eric's primary problem was an incredibly low boredom threshold. Give him a new challenge and Eric would work 25 hours a day to solve it. Ask him to make a production item which would pay the bills and his eyes glazed over with lack of interest.

In 1973, Eric had joined forces with John Banks in a bid to win the 500cc World Motocross Championship – at the time, the world's premier dirt bike competition. Without wishing to become too commercial, you can read the full story in the prequel to this book – "A Penguin in a Sparrow's Nest."

The bike was the JBR – the John Banks Replica – and it was the best handling motocross machine of its time. With the support of a major factory, I still remain convinced that Banks and Cheney could have won the 1973 World Championship.

The results were astonishing for a private effort – but nowhere near good enough to become #1 in a world where Grands Prix must be won week in and week out. However, the team did win the British 500cc Motocross Championship – the last all British effort to achieve this distinction.

Following Banks' success, customers were banging on Eric's door demanding replicas of the works bikes. Even Eric couldn't entirely ignore the demands and so he did build a few clones of Banks' works bike. No-one will ever know how many true JBR replicas Eric made but it wasn't very many. I would be surprised if there were many more than 25 or 30. I had one myself and they really were stunning pieces of kit – a true GP bike which you could, more or less, buy from Eric – but only if he liked you and the planets were lined up in the right astrological order.

Eric lived at Church Crookham, in Hampshire, and his near neighbour was Ken Heanes – a very interesting character. Ken was an excellent motocrosser and, arguably, Britain's finest ISDT rider in the 1950s and '60s. He also owned one of Britain's biggest Triumph dealerships in Fleet, Hampshire.

Ken was highly regarded at Triumph and was considered to be a smart businessman, which he was. To say that he was a factory insider is something of an understatement. Heanes had a palatial house, complete with indoor swimming pool and grand piano, overlooking the South Downs. It was called Meriden – after the home of the Triumph factory near Coventry – and one of Ken's house guests was the Triumph riding film star, Steve McQueen.

In 1973, the BSA Group – part of which was Triumph – was desperate for income. Three years earlier the idea of selling engines, or any other parts for that matter, produced by Triumph or BSA to a third party would have been absolute heresy. In fact, anyone suggesting it would have probably been shot at dawn in the works car park at Armoury Road.

But things were different now. Not only were all the BSA Group motorcycles old fashioned but there had been a number of immense management blunders. For example, BSA Group Managing Director Lionel Jofeh had purchased 100,000 Dutch Anker mo-ped engines for the ridiculous Ariel 3 – an abomination which was little more than a motorised child's tricycle, aimed at an utterly non-existent urban commuter market.

With this catastrophic project, he robbed the Group of both capital investment and engineering resources. Additionally, the engineers were badly and chaotically managed. The Group engineering centre at Umberslade Hall – popularly known on the shop floor at both BSA and Triumph as "Slumberglade Hall" – was out of touch with the needs and aspirations of its motorcycling customers and the Group Engineering Director, Bert Hopwood, was nothing more than a very average designer who carried with him a sack full of political agendas.

Finally there were militant unions and, as one trade supplier to BSA recently told me: "There was more stuff being nicked out of the back door than there was being sold legitimately through the front."

In short, it was a mess.

I had a walk-on part to play in the saga because, in a very odd way, I was highly regarded at BSA. Because of my writing, BSA Group PR Manager, Reg Dancer had managed to get a works BSA built for me after the Competition Shop had closed.

I was careful, extremely careful, not to assume or even pretend that the bike was given to me in recognition of my riding ability. I was at the time, and remain to this day, a competent club racer and that is all. Therefore, I was always grateful for BSA's help and expressed my gratitude whenever I could.

In parallel with this clear vision of my riding ability I was not overawed by anyone at BSA. Because I was not a motorcycling superstar, I represented BSA's customers – the sort of bloke who worked hard and went without things in order to buy a new Triumph or BSA.

I was also respected for having a good commercial brain and understanding the motorcycle industry. I felt extremely honoured that the views of such a young man – for I was only 23 years old – should be given such credence by senior figures in the motorcycling industry. But they were, and so I did my best to always be completely honest and objective when my views were sought.

My opinion was asked for, on an irregular basis, regarding a number of BSA Group projects and one of them was the idea of selling B.50 motocross kits to Eric Cheney and Alan Clews. On one of my visits to the BSA factory at Small Heath, I was summoned into the office of the BSA Works Manager Al Cave (Mr. Cave to you young Frank, and don't you forget it!) for a meeting with Reg Dancer and Mr. Cave himself.

The idea had begun with Ken Heanes. He wanted BSA to produce 1000 BSA B50 motocross kits for Eric Cheney to build into his Cheney John Banks Replica frames. Heanes would fund the whole project but in staged payments.

The concept was practical and sensible. BSA would produce 100 kits at a time and Ken would pay for them, cash up front. Eric would make the kits into complete bikes, ready for the track. Ken would sell them and everyone would make a nice profit. It was a perfect idea, in that it would provide immediate cash flow for BSA whilst requiring no investment from the company because all the parts provided for Heanes would be absolutely standard, production line items.

The bikes – to be called the Heanes Thumpers, complete with a Disney licensed picture of Thumper the Rabbit – would sell like chilled water on a hot beach because the Cheney JBR was the best handling chassis of its day.

Despite everything looking sound on paper, BSA were still nervous and their angst had a lot to do with the fact that Eric Cheney was involved in the equation. As I have said, I worshipped Eric for his genius but he was also a very wayward character.

BSA had helped him in an informal way for many years and he had produced some stunning BSA engined bikes which had, on occasions, beaten the factory machines. The problem was that you couldn't tell Eric to do anything – not ever, for any reason - no matter how sound and sensible. If what he wanted to do coincided with what you needed, then he was the dream craftsman. Equally, no amount of logical argument, common sense, pleading or threatening would get him to complete a job if he didn't feel moved to do it.

I am all too well aware of my own faults – most of which are predicated on having a mouth which is sometimes bigger, and more active, than my brain. However, it has always been one of my core beliefs that if my opinion is sought professionally then I should do my utmost to provide an honest, objective and balanced response. You might not like, or agree, with what I have to say but my comments will be the very best I can provide.

When I was asked about the idea of providing Eric with 1000 engine and cycle part kits, I just could not say to Reg and Mr. Cave that this would be a sound commercial decision. Much as I admired "Uncle Eric", as only a true acolyte could, I was certain that there would be a manned mission to Mars before Eric would buckle down to making such a long production run of a single bike.

I was then asked about CCM – Clews Competition Motorcycles. Again, I would claim some credit for my honesty and professionalism. I didn't much like Alan personally – nor did he like me. However, I did admire him hugely for his vision and determination. I suggested that the best way forward with the project would be to let Clews have 500 kits for CCM and Eric the other 500 for the Thumpers.

I wouldn't even have suggested that Eric should have 500 kits except for the fact that Heanes was managing the project – perhaps micromanaging is more accurate. Ken would be responsible for buying the Reynolds tubing and delivering the kits. He even offered to hire a welder to help Eric. In short, Cheney's main role was to supervise the whole job and sit back whilst the money rolled in. This would have been wonderful – except for the fact that Eric was at the centre of the whole scheme.

The Thumpers really were nice motorcycles and Heanes had done a very clever job in making their production possible. The key part of the bike was the JBR frame – a magnificent, single down tube creation, fabricated from Reynolds 531 – the best cold drawn, seamless tube in the world for racing motorcycles – and then bronze welded and nickel plated. Goodness me, one of these should be in the Louvre alongside the Mona Lisa.

The bike I was looking at, in the loft, retained the slim, stylish Cheney petrol tank and saddle, and even the eccentric rear wheel chain adjusters were there. Money was saved by using standard B50 MX forks, instead of the solid billet items on the high specification JBRs, and the hubs were from the BSA B50 instead of exotic magnesium items.

Hand-made items such as the front mudguard bracket and the Magura clutch and brake levers were ditched in favour of standard BSA parts. Critically, the engines were absolutely standard rather than having the 200 hours Eric once told me he spent on each of John Banks' motors.

The bikes were sold, ready to race, at the killer price point of £495. Depending on the precise specification, a rider could easily spend more than double this on a full specification JBR Cheney so the Thumpers were a guaranteed sales success: nearly.

Of course, even the best designed and built arch will collapse without the key stone and, with equal predictability, Eric became bored with making the same bike and just earning lots of money. No-one – not even Eric – ever knew how many Thumpers he actually made but he once told me that it was around 125. However, it is important to remember that to Eric, 125 was not a unit of fixed empirical value but was merely indicative of being a lot – more than a few but less than a huge number. It could have been 75 or 150 but certainly it was a small number.

Clearly, it drove Heanes bonkers with frustration but that was the standard state of mind for everyone who came into contact with Eric – including me – so there was nothing new there!

I was grateful that I had not allowed personal feelings to get in the way of behaving as an objective professional commentator. BSA sold the vast proportion of the B50 kits to Alan Clews who was everything that Eric wasn't in terms of being a ruthlessly determined businessman. The kits played a huge part in the growth of CCM, and Alan used his slice of good fortune wisely, so it was a happy ending all round.

For historical accuracy, BSA struggled to provide all that they had said they would produce so Clews' engines largely came in the form of kits of parts.

Now I too had been given a huge slice of good luck cake because, thirteen years after they had ceased production, I was being offered what was effectively a brand-new Thumper.

I didn't get much of a welcome – any welcome in fact – from the vendor's wife but that wasn't an issue. We agreed a price which was at the top end of what I could afford but it was very much a seller's market because my tongue was hanging out for the Cheney!

The chap agreed to bring it part of the way to me and we met at Lancaster Services, on the M6. I was grateful that he would bring it this far south because I was on short rations again after the purchase, and the money saved on fuel was very useful.

The bloke off-loaded the bike; I paid the wife and they left. It was time for another one of the lessons life can teach you, if you will listen.

I had spent some considerable time in Libya as a teenager so I had a very open minded approach to people who have a different skin colour to me or worship whatever brand of God gives them peace and succour.

The absolute truth is that there are some people with black skins who are violent, manic criminals – but there are an equal number of whites who are dishonest psychopaths too.

There are Muslim terrorists who kill without thought, and plenty of Christians who have slaughtered innocent people in the name of Christ.

I have always believed that the person inside should be judged by their actions – not by the exterior labels put on to them by their skin colour or faith or anything else.

Even so, I was about to have my beliefs tested in a very real way. The trailer I had at the time was an awkward thing to load a bike on to single-handedly and as I struggled to lift the Cheney on to it, a good number of well-dressed white people walked past and pointedly looked the other way.

Next to me was a very dodgy looking Transit van, finished in the much loved white-and-rust paint job. Naturally, the front wing was in the obligatory pink primer and where the off-side indicator should have been was a fetching area of brown parcel tape.

Leaning out of the window was a huge, shaven headed black man with a broken nose, which had set badly, and a seriously battered face - complete with lumpy scar across one eyebrow. He fixed me with a long, cold, hard look.

It was only out of passionate love for my new Cheney that I didn't just drop the bike and sprint for the safety of the café, to avoid being robbed and beaten to death – both of which were certain to happen in the next few seconds.

Slowly, he unwound his enormous frame from the torn seat of the Transit and, with a liquid but deliberate amble, he came across to me.

The voice was a soft baritone. "Wassup man, you strugglin' a bit?" Then his face split into the happiest smile I have ever seen on a member of the human race.

I explained that I was and, in a couple of seconds of bulging biceps, he lifted the bike on to the trailer and then held it whilst I lashed everything down.

I thanked him profusely and he was utterly dismissive. His response was interesting and I learnt a lot from it, "If you can't help someone, what's the point in bein' 'live?" And then he was gone in a cloud of diesel smoke - and rust, obviously.

Now I had Bess for company, food to eat – and a Cheney. What could be better?

Well, viewed objectively, quite a lot and I needed to take some action – and fast too.

4

Thank You Mrs. Thatcher

IN some ways, the late 1980s was a wonderful time to be alive because things could be done and achieved. This is one of the reasons In Our Own Words was able to thrive and succeed. It was also a time of immense change – sometimes for the better and sometimes for the worse.

I have very mixed feelings about Margaret Thatcher. On the one hand she did much to destroy British manufacturing and this breaks my heart. As a nation, we can't survive by selling Chinese made waterproof coats for pets, and synthetic food at pizza chains. We have to be an innovative, highly skilled country which takes in raw materials and manufactures the best possible products for sale on the world market.

Mrs Thatcher felt that casting, turning and milling were 19th century activities and were valueless in the 1980s. This was a travesty of the truth and helped drive the country towards the benefit obsessed, risk-averse culture we have now.

That she was able to push through this highly philosophical agenda was due, entirely and completely, to the militant trade unions who exploited weak and lazy management.

As a young man I worked, and I use this word in the loosest possible way, on the construction of the Fiddlers Ferry Power Station at Widnes. There was a rarely a week went by when one of the unions was not on strike for something. Any excuse, no matter how trivial or petty, was good enough to call out one or other of the innumerable unions on site and, once the pickets were in place, no other worker would cross the line. In short, it was chaos.

For both philosophical and practical reasons, Mrs. Thatcher pushed forward a programme of privatising the state owned behemoths which dominated the British landscape – and some truly were giants.

In her memoires she said: *"It (privatisation) was one of the central means of reversing the corrosive and corrupting effects of socialism.*

"Just as nationalisation was at the heart of the collectivist programme by which Labour governments sought to remodel British society, so privatisation is at the centre of any programme of reclaiming territory for freedom."

The big idea was that these enormous, monolithic companies which were burdened with crippling working practices and incompetent management would have to face life in the modern world – or go out of business.

At the same time, ordinary people would become share owners and, as such, part of a capitalist society where everyone could invest in wealth generators without actually doing any of the work – a concept I have always found distasteful. Yes, make money - but do so because you have got up early, gone to bed late and worked hard in between. This is the only fair way to earn a living.

Finally, the government would have a huge windfall which it could invest for the benefit of the country.

Only the first aim was realised. The government did not invest in Britain but used the money to buy votes and keep the Tories in power.

Nor did the man in the street become an investor. On the contrary, he became a speculator.

Regardless of how I felt about the privatisation programme, or the Thatcher government, I did see a chance to make some fast money, and with the approval of the government too, so I got seriously stuck into the process of buying privatisation shares because, for sure, I needed any available funds a lot more than Whitehall did!

In many ways, it was a bit of a wild-west time. Share purchases for the state companies were limited to one application per person and, as the privatisations became ever more popular, some people became greedy. Keith Best was MP for the Isle of Anglesey at the time. He submitted multiple applications in false names and was inevitably caught out. He was duly banged up for four months and whacked with a whopping £4,500 fine.

Risking a jail sentence seemed to be a deeply unattractive way of making money so I just did my homework for every privatisation, to optimise the number of shares I could legitimately buy. I invariably succeeded in getting everything which was available to me – and legally too.

Interestingly, by this time getting capital for my share speculation was no problem because I was back in favour with the Midland Bank. That's capitalism red in tooth and claw. Need help, seem like a loser and out you go over the stern - and good luck with avoiding the sharks. Start to look like a winner again and you're back on the Bank's Christmas card list. Is there any surprise we are all cynical about banks and bankers?

*****

Things had settled down at school but it was not a happy time. The number of pupils wanting to transfer to our school was dwindling at a terrifying rate and anyone with half a business brain could see that the writing was well and truly on the wall – and in large, fluorescent letters! Closure was a dead certainty.

But, like the beachcomber who goes out in the pouring rain, gets soaked, ends up freezing cold and then stumbles across a gold and diamond studded bracelet which the waves have just washed up, for me things were about to get better – very much better indeed.

First, my Head Teacher funded a second magazine which, by a sheer fluke, we both agreed on in terms of style, presentation and content – but for completely different reasons.

He wanted an example of what a progressive, switched on school he had and so the more impressive the publication the better. I too wanted a bigger magazine but one which was more inclusive and brought far more kids into the project.

He put up the money, gave me a little bit of time off teaching during the Christmas Term to go down to the Messenger Press and I became more experienced, and so faster, at making magazines.

The publication was called "My Christmas Term" and it was a success from every point of view. Now I wanted to make a third magazine – but on a totally different scale.

Teachers grumble a lot – often justifiably – about work load and stress but in the late 1980s they also enjoyed an unbelievable amount of protection in terms of job security. My school was shrinking in size and was over-staffed. An easy fix was to give me two days a week away from teaching whilst I job shared with another teacher, who also wanted a part time role.

A lot of this happened in Local Authorities all over the country and there was plenty of abuse of the system. Instead of teachers taking these sabbatical periods to do useful things, there were those who simply took the time as an extended, and paid, holiday away from the classroom.

This was easily possible to do because there was very little monitoring of what was happening. If a teacher had convinced one of the Advisors that she could make a contribution to education by producing worksheets about pet armadillos in the classroom, then that was that - off she went. Some teachers really made the best of the opportunity that being away from day to day teaching offered them – but others didn't.

It was the same with job sharing. Plenty of colleagues took job sharing seriously and did it professionally, whilst others looked at the practice as a way of legalised work avoidance.

My attitude came directly from 20 years of working as a freelance journalist. Serious, professional freelancers – one of which I was proud to be – are true good news/bad news stories for magazines and editors. The good news is that a quality freelancer can produce outstanding results with no help, supervision or direction. We are the ultimate completer/finishers. The bad news is that we are very difficult to help, supervise or direct!

If an editor's needs coincide with what a freelancer wants to do, or can do, then it's happy days all round. If those needs don't dovetail then there will always be friction and, inevitably, a schism.

My situation was particularly interesting. The truth is that only I knew about Desk Top Publishing and understood its potential. My feeling is that my multiple managers, and there were many within Cheshire Education Service, had very little idea of what I was trying to achieve or of the technology behind the concepts.

For most teachers, this would have been an insuperable problem but I thought that I had won life's lucky lottery ticket.

I began work on the new magazine in September and, in some ways, the situation was beyond silly – it was frankly ridiculous. On the one side, I promised I would produce three, full colour magazines for the children of the Warrington Education District of Cheshire. This would be a total print run, over the year, of more than 100,000 copies. In simple terms, the task was publishing on a professional scale!

Better still, I would do this at zero cost to the Local Authority because I would fund the exercise entirely by sponsorship. As things transpired, I think that they did give me a nominal grant but it was only a trivial sum.

Further, I would produce the three magazines without any staff or infrastructure support.

One of the very senior managers at County Hall described my plan as: "The most public way of committing professional suicide I have ever seen."

I thought it was fantastic and I was happier than I had been for years.

The great joy, and there is no better word to describe the situation, was that you could have got 1,000:1 odds against me ever making a single magazine, let alone three. No experience. No support staff. No budget – no anything. The task was impossible – just about as impossible as my editor demanding a story about a bike which had just won a TT for my third ever article, or selling 5,400 Griffin motorcycle helmets from a two-bedroomed bungalow. Yes, impossible was home territory for me and I loved being there!

The fact that I was clearly going to fail led to everyone staying well away from me, for fear of being tainted by the disaster which was sure to ensue and this was just what I needed.

The new magazine was going to be called In Our Own Words to reflect that the content would be supplied entirely by the children. It was a big idea – huge even. The magazine would publish what the kids thought was worth seeing in print – the ultimate manifestation of the democratisation of literature. I was beside myself with excitement and, in absolute truth, I had not one molecule of doubt that I could make the project succeed both philosophically and, of equal importance, practically.

I wasn't interested in producing a discussion document or gathering together all the relevant research on children's magazines. Freelancers get paid when the editor receives the story and images – not before and never, ever if they don't deliver.

For me, anything less than the three magazines I had promised would have been failure. Second is first in the losers' race and I wasn't prepared to finish anywhere in this event except on the top step of the podium.

Like the good freelancer that I was, I had a very clear idea of what I wanted to do and how to achieve these aims. Getting there wasn't going to be a stroll in the park but the hard part of the problem was already solved: I knew what I was going to do. Working entirely on my own and trusting in my own ability to fail or succeed, I just could not believe how lucky I was or how much fun I was going to have. The flag had dropped and the bull***t had stopped. Now, I just had to win.

In fact, the job turned out to be much harder than I had expected – vastly more so.

The first job was to convince schools that they should contribute material to the project. Some were immediately supportive, others ambivalent and a few Head Teachers were out and out bullies who set out to make my life miserable.

It would be easy to say that I just laughed off the setbacks and that they didn't hurt. However, that would also be a lie because sometimes, after I had been verbally savaged or sneered at, I sat at home, stroked Bess with her head on my knee and truly did wonder if I had bitten off a lot more than I could chew.

What kept me going were those colleagues who saw, instantly, what a wonderful thing In Our Own Words would be for their kids. There are some inspirational, dedicated educationists in Britain and these wonderful teachers worked hard to make the project succeed. They believed in me – and I in them. As for the sneering non-believers, we simply left them where they were to rot in their own arrogance and insipid negativity. They were yesterday's news.

I was helped hugely by meeting Trevor Buckley, former Editor in Chief of the Warrington Guardian. Trevor had forgotten more about newspapers than the rest of us could ever learn in ten lifetimes and he had set up a company making large print newspapers for partially sighted readers.

I approached him, in all humility, for help with In Our Own Words and he taught me a vast amount – always with a smile, kindness and patience.

This book is naturally my view of history but, objectively, I can say two things about my relationship with Trevor. First, my work would have been hugely harder without him – maybe even impossibly so. Trevor gently fixed problems for me as they occurred and this gave me breathing space, to climb on top of the workload – which was immense.

In parallel, he improved In Our Own Words by removing some of the production pressures from me so that I was able to learn from him and then teach the kids.

Without Trevor, the magazine would probably still have happened but the service I provided to the children, and the finished product, would have been of a much lower quality.

The other big challenge was finding the money to fund In Our Own Words – but this wasn't nearly so great a problem as it would have been for most other teachers. I had been sponsored for most of my riding career and then I had owned, and managed, Tsubaki Racing - my own race team. Tsubaki Racing was a good team – highly professional and successful - which ran at a profit so making a sales pitch to sponsors for In Our Own Words was not a new experience. I had done the same sort of thing for many years with Tsubaki Racing.

The magazine's concept was sound, and I was confident in my own ability, so the money came in. By the end of the year we had made three, excellent magazines which had been distributed to schoolchildren in the Warrington area. 1,000:1 odds against succeeding? Not any more.

At this point I should say that I saw the immense potential of Desk Top Publishing, resigned my teaching post and went to Seattle or London to lead the digital revolution. Except that I didn't. The reason was simple. First and foremost, I was still in survival mode and this shouldn't be underestimated. It would be wrong for me to mis-represent the truth and say that after the divorce everything was fine and I was a fully repaired human being – because I wasn't.

A primary problem was girlfriends and, somewhat ironically, it wasn't a lack of them.

*****

Starting a new relationship aged 40 really is an odd experience – or at least it was for me. The situation is vastly different from teenage dating. For a young man, finding a girlfriend is easy. Is she pretty and fun to be with? Yes? Then the job's done.

But goodness me, the situation is very different for the middle-aged. The first problem is that everyone of this age carries with them a container load of baggage – including me!

Lots of ladies I met had been through rotten divorces, and/or long term relationships, and this sometimes led to humorous situations of the deepest black. For a fun night out try listening to a bloke and a girl, both of whom have gone through horrendous divorces and who want to spend the whole evening explaining how much they miss/hate/love/despise/admire/loathe their ex-partner. Talk about a rocking party!

Then there are the career girls who have spent their whole lives making professional progress and suddenly find themselves, at 32 years old, having never experienced anything but one night stands. As one of these lovely ladies said to me, less than an hour into our first date, "Are you always this boring or is this just a bad night?"

There were also some truly hilarious relationships. I had one girlfriend who became increasingly ambitious for my cooking and she would phone me every Thursday, with her order for Friday evening's dinner. She became ever more gastronomically demanding so I had to toil like a Master Chef contestant to get everything ready for eight o'clock when she arrived.

She was a very lively girl, but there were no fringe benefits for me after dinner – I was too exhausted after cooking for three hours!

Eventually, I met a really charming lady whom I liked a lot. She was lovely – smiling, intelligent and fun to be with. From our first meeting we got on very well. Her husband had died in tragic circumstances and, after several years of mourning, she wanted to start again. Critically, though I didn't know this at the time, she had a very clear child agenda.

I also didn't know that for three months I was undergoing a very thorough, albeit discreet and subtle, interview. We liked each other a lot and were one step away from being in love. I wanted to show her the France I knew from racing, not the tourist version, and so we had a romantic meal in a little restaurant on the banks of the Gironde River, upstream from Bordeaux. Everything went well and, as we held hands, she asked me if I wanted to marry her.

It was a bit of a shock but everything pointed in the right direction. She knew, and I knew, that she wasn't marrying me for money. On the contrary, she owned a large bungalow on the outskirts of Chester and had a good salary. Financially, it would be very much a marriage of equals.

We enjoyed the same things culturally and she loved me cooking for her. Walks together, along the River Dee and in Delamere Forest with Bess, were idyllic.

She also really tried to join in with everything I enjoyed – from my work with In Our Own Words to racing. In short, we were the perfect match – except for one thing.

My wife-to-be laid out the husband job specification and, as a professional person, it was as thorough as one would expect.

We would be married before Christmas and then have our first child the following year, followed by a second the year after. That was the deal. Two kids – and be quick about it too.

I tried to explain that I wasn't ready for kids. At one time, I had really wanted children but now I was 41 years old and I had a lot of doubts. I also didn't want a fixed, irrevocable timetable and could not handle the pressure of one. I was just getting my life back on to a sound basis and I needed to be completely calm in my own head before I could even consider the immense commitment of becoming a father – if I ever could.

Of course, none of this was of the slightest interest to her. Her female body clock was running flat out and the following morning I received my relationship P45.

"Dear Frank. You're fired. Don't you ring me and I won't phone you."

All I can say is that it's a long drive back from Bordeaux to Chester in total silence!

Back at home, I sat with Bess on my knee and we had a meeting. Bess and I were perfectly happy together, and the money was coming in nicely. We decided that we would simply give up girls once and for all - and forever! The Gironde baby ultimatum was the end of the line.

*****

The final part of what was now looking like a very happy jigsaw was that I met a motorcycle tuning genius called Fred Barlow and soon my Cheney was up to full works specification.

Fred was my age and had been an apprentice in the BSA Competition Department, where he had worked on all the Grand Prix machines. Although he had left BSA before I was involved with the factory, I knew of him – and his skill in preparing the single cylinder, BSA racing engines.

I went to his little workshop in Tamworth and we hit it off immediately, as if we were life-long friends. We rolled back the years, swapping BSA stories until it was far too late to be sensible – and we could probably have still been there in the morning.

Fred agreed to take the standard B50 engine in the Cheney and bring it up to works specification. In fact, this is not quite true because he wanted to lighten the flywheels and increase the compression ratio of the engine so that it made power approaching that of the best factory machines used by John Banks - but I had raced a bike in this trim once before and it was horrible. These fierce, highly tuned B50s were fine for superstars but not for me. I wasn't fit enough, or sufficiently brave, to master one of these fire breathing monsters so, after half an hour of trying to persuade me, Fred agreed that I was right and built a wonderful motor for me – fast, easy to ride and Muppet friendly, which is just what I needed.

Now I was solvent again and had a quick bike – two reasons for the sun to be shining.

In Our Own Words had been a success in Warrington and I had some seriously big ideas for its future.

Girls apart, everything was good but I was about to push my ideas right to the very edge of what was possible.

5

Big Dreams

RIGHT from my very first days in the classroom, as an unqualified teacher, I had dreamed of democratising literature. It was not an interest, or even a passion, but almost a religious fervour. Literacy had taken me from a Council House, and little prospect of achieving anything in life, to considerable success and a very pleasant life style: I was obsessed with the idea of literacy for everyone.

Literacy directly equates to knowledge – and knowledge leads to power.

That power might be deciding to live a modest life and work with Ebola victims in Africa - and what a highly admirable road this is to walk - or it could lead to status and financial security. The key thing is having the opportunity to choose your own life path.

The problem is that literacy is the province of the wealthy and well-educated. In the bluntest possible terms, not many kids leave school aged sixteen, start their working lives as a shelf painter and then go on to write fourteen books and 1200 feature articles. It's not impossible – but the odds are stacked against you.

I once had a blazing, eyes glaring, flared nostrils argument – and in public too – with a Senior Social Worker. She was expounding the virtues of Social Workers intervening ever more in the lives of struggling families. Her one answer to all the problems was more Social Workers; more support; more grants; more discussion groups and drop in centres – just hugely more intervention all round.

I rounded on her and said that the money should be spent on literacy. Make everyone literate so that they can solve their own problems, instead of being an underclass permanently in thrall to their supposed superiors in the support services.

I wasn't top of anyone's Christmas card list when that meeting concluded!

Now, I was on the brink of actually making my dreams a reality. Talk is cheap – action counts. It was another case of, "When the flag drops..."

Throughout my life, I have been blessed with some incredibly lucky breaks and, usually but not always, I have been bright enough to see the opportunities when they arrive. In this case, I did see what was on offer – and I couldn't sleep at night with excitement.

I was summoned to Cheshire's enormous County Hall – an immense five storey, sandstone monolith overlooking the old Dee Bridge across the river. My ultimate boss at the time was a wonderful educationist called Neil Fitton, who was Cheshire's Director of Education. He was a seriously galactic superbeing and very, very few classroom foot soldiers ever saw his inner office.

Despite his status, Mr. Fitton was quietly spoken, kind and courteous. He had copies of In Our Own Words on his table and made some very positive comments about them. I had been petitioning Mr. Fitton for most of the year with the idea of taking the project to the whole of Cheshire.

This was an immense leap, not merely a step, forward on every level. For a start, in 1987 Cheshire Education Authority was huge. The county stretched from the Welsh borders in the west, to the edge of Manchester in the east. The northern limit finished well into the Wirral Peninsula and in the south it was almost at the Shropshire town of Whitchurch. It took in major urban centres and tiny rural schools right up in the Pennine Hills.

In all, there were six Education districts and over 500 schools. My idea was very simple - and yet, viewed objectively, quite ridiculous. I would make a magazine every half term so that each Education District would have its own, individual publication. In all, the total circulation would be running very close to 200,000 copies. If you are going to have a dream, you might as well have a decent sized one!

I wouldn't have had Mr. Fitton's job for anything because it would have driven me bonkers in a single morning! Can you imagine the troubles which must have flown in through his window every minute of every day – constantly and endlessly?

A failing school closing - or new buildings at a successful one.

A silly teacher behaving inappropriately with a sixth former, or a distressed parent complaining that her child with Special Needs wasn't receiving the right level of care.

Politicians – local and national – the media and pressure groups endlessly wanting instant fixes: it would have been enough to break anyone.

Yet, in the midst of all this, Mr. Fitton found time to sit down and have coffee with a maverick teacher pitching an eccentric idea: that's the true sign of a great leader.

I understood the situation very clearly and I completely avoided doing what most teachers would have done – in fact, should have done. I didn't ask for staff, resources or any help at all. I simply promised Mr. Fitton that I would deliver the six magazines to the highest possible standard, and Cheshire's only contribution would be to pay my salary.

Why was I so confident? Well, for sure, it wasn't that I didn't understand that I was looking up from base camp at the bottom of an educational and logistical Mount Everest, with only a couple of sandwiches and the "Big Boys' Book of Climbing Enormous Mountains" in my briefcase to help me.

Rather, it was because the three strands that had been my life since leaving school were coming together in perfect synergy – each balanced with their siblings and none more, or less, important than the other.

First, I was a motorcycle racer – fiercely competitive and willing, quite literally, to put my life on the line: I wasn't frightened of pressure or failure.

Next I was a journalist and author – at home with words and books, and a fast and fluent writer. As a by-product, I also understood exactly how the media worked because I was a part of it.

Finally, I knew a lot about business and had made plenty of money during the last 25 years. Not only did I have entrepreneurial skill but I understood accounts, balance sheets, book keeping and all the administrative tasks which a commercial enterprise demands.

Time was rolling on and, as Mr. Fitton finished his coffee, he made me the most wonderful offer in the world. This was it, probably precisely verbatim, because the words were burned into my memory.

"Do a good job for me and try your best. I will support you here (at County Hall). If things go wrong, don't worry. I will find another post for you somewhere and on your current salary."

With that he stood up, smiled, shook my hand, and Sally, his ever present PA, appeared soundlessly from the background and, with her normal impeccable grace, showed me out. Yes, I was in the magazine business.

I like baking a lot and, that weekend, I decided to make a chicken and sweetcorn pie. Although there was only Bess and me eating the pie, I always took care to do the best possible job and, as I plaited the three strands of pastry to decorate the top, I saw the metaphor on the rolling board. Three individual and separate strands coming together to make something practical and beautiful. Racer, writer and businessman: I could do this.

*****

I have been trying to think of a straightforward way of explaining my time with In Our Own Words – and failing. It was like being sent on a mission to a new galaxy and then landing on a human tolerant planet - but where everything is different. I had to learn so much, so quickly, that the effort made me ill – yet it was unbelievably good fun, all day, every day. I'll try to give you a flavour of life at that time.

The immediate problem was how to actually produce the magazines. I had made the first three editions of the paper largely at home, clearly with the assistance of Bess, but the workload was shattering and my house looked like a permanent rubbish dump with kids' work and layout pages everywhere. It was obvious that I could never do six magazines like this.

With the blank sheet of paper and support which Mr. Fitton had given to me, the first job was to find an assistant. I put an ad in the local paper and was blessed to find a truly gifted lady who had been trained as a PA (Personal Assistant) by a huge American company. This was a real good news-bad news story.

Although I had been a very young Head of Department and then a Year Tutor, and was well-paid, I had never been given any secretarial or admin. support – none. Even Senior teachers within the school had to go down on bended knees for secretarial help. This meant that they wasted a lot of their time doing administrative jobs – and often poorly because they weren't secretaries. Teachers' skills are in teaching, not admin!

My school was no different from any other in the country. Good classroom teachers received promotion to management roles – but no training to go with the increased responsibility.

When I owned Tsubaki Racing, I had taught myself marketing by reading widely but I had never had a PA, and did not have the vaguest clue how to work with her. I was in for a real shock.

I started work with "J" bright and early at 8.45 on Monday morning. By 10am, we had our first eyeball to eyeball exchange. I spoke to a teacher who wanted to discuss her school's contribution to In Our Own Words, and I made an appointment to see her. How simple was that?

"J" waited for ten minutes and then demanded, not asked, to know why I had not entered the appointment into her master diary. From now on, she explained, everything went into the master diary and then she would update my diary, her diary and that of the project. No ifs, buts or maybes. This is how it was going to be done. I swallowed hard, looked embarrassed and got on with my work.

We got ready to break for lunch on Wednesday and "J" handed me her letter of resignation. I felt as if it had 24,000 volts running through it. My PA had only been with me two and a half days and she wanted to resign. This was hardly a good start to making the six magazines I had promised Mr. Fitton.

"J" explained that she simply could not work with me. My job was to run the project, and make magazines of the highest standard, and her job was to ensure that I was able to do my job properly and effectively. I wasn't doing my job and therefore she couldn't do hers and so there was no point in her staying.

I blushed and apologised and I asked her, in all humility, to explain what was wrong. She explained that I wasn't supposed to order stationery; stick stamps on envelopes; display work on walls or any of the numerous other things I was used to doing. My job was to manage and, although "J" was both softly spoken, and a complete lady in terms of her language, the message was clear. In translation it said, "Stop buggering about, grow up and do your bloody job properly – or else!"

I apologised, blushed again and promised to try harder – much harder.

"J" and I found an unused classroom in a lovely little Primary School and we started work. The system I designed was that children of all ages submitted work to the magazine through their teachers. We would then all meet at an "Editing Day" and jointly decide what was going to be in their magazine. It was the most democratic way of making a magazine I could devise - and it worked a treat.

After the Editing Day, other groups of kids would come into our office to design the magazine using Desk Top Publishing. "J" was every bit as good as she appeared to be and made everything behind the scenes run like a Rolls Royce turbine. Like all good PAs, she had charisma and when she spoke everyone listened – and no-one more intently than me!

We had some brilliant sponsors too and there was enough funding for me to appoint six, superb Area Co-Ordinators who worked with schools in their area to keep interest in the project high. As a racer, and team owner, I was comfortable with sponsors - but not of this quality and at this level.

Now, I was sitting in the Board Room of British Nuclear Fuels discussing children's literature with the Managing Director and those members of his senior staff who had been tasked with supporting key educational projects. This was grown ups' sponsorship.

The project's status also led to some hilarious moments. One of our key sponsors was Aldus, who made the iconic Pagemaker Desk Top Publishing Project. We were helped by a lovely bloke called Bob McLaughlin, who was the public face of Aldus in Britain and the key fixer of all their problems. Bob was a huge fan of In Our Own Words and wanted me to become an expert on using the programme in schools.

With this aim in mind, he sent me to an Aldus training day in Edinburgh, where Aldus had an important centre. I wasn't worried about sitting down alongside Aldus staff because I thought that I was pretty good with Pagemaker. I was about to discover the difference between a computer programmer and a programme user.

Aldus sorted out a nice hotel for me and I ambled round to their training base the following morning, relaxed, happy and in plenty of time for coffee. When I arrived, my colleagues for the day were all clustered in a corner, deep in intense discussion. They were programmers and they looked at me and the Sales Manager from one of Aldus' biggest re-sellers, who was the only other non-programmer present, with bemused contempt. I was about to find out why.

Our trainer opened up Pagemaker on the projector and asked us for comments. Thank goodness I had the common sense to keep my mouth shut before I saw which way that wind was blowing! The programmers launched into a heated debate – but about what I didn't have the vaguest idea. They thought in binary code; they worked in binary code and it seemed to me that they spoke in binary code too. I looked wanly at the Sales Manager lady – and then began drawing B50 race engines on my notepad.

I'd like to tell you how much I learnt from the day, and how it benefitted the kids, but I'm not quite sure that I gained any new knowledge – except that programmers are very, very, very clever and, it would seem, not quite human. Oh yes. Aldus served nice coffee and proper, heavy duty choccy biscuits.

★★★★★

From the outset I wanted In Our Own Words to have a high profile, not for my sake but so that other teachers throughout the country could see what we were doing and replicate it in their own areas. During the lifetime of the project we had wonderful patrons who helped us hugely in spreading the word.

It would be wrong to single out any one individual for praise, because they were all gracious and important to the project but, on a personal level, I was particularly fond of the MP for Warrington North, Doug Hoyle – now Baron Hoyle of Warrington. Doug was a super smart politician but he was also a genuinely nice, kind and warm hearted man. He was a Labour MP – and well left of centre too – but with an open heart, and mind, for the whole community. I respected him tremendously.

I will give you a tiny example of why he was, and is, a great man. In Our Own Words had reached such national importance that it was being debated in the House of Commons. Carol – you haven't heard about her yet but you soon will! – and I were invited down to London by Doug to listen to the debate.

The journey down was a difficult one and we arrived at the House of Commons late in the evening, tired and hungry. Doug's first act was to persuade one of the House of Commons catering staff to make us bacon butties and cups of tea. It only needed a smile and a wink from Doug to fix this.

Then, with another smile, he had us seated in the "Strangers" box – the only area on the floor of the House of Commons where anyone who isn't an MP is allowed to sit. For luck, we touched the statue of Winston Churchill, on the left-hand side as you walk into the Chamber, and then sat on the polished leather seats actually on the floor of the chamber whilst Doug extolled the virtues of In Our Own Words. It was an odd experience for a clubman motorcycle racer.

We also worked with His Grace, the Duke of Westminster, and this was another new experience. On one visit, his PA discreetly took me on one side whilst the Duke had a word with "J". Very quietly, he said: "Be careful what you say to His Grace today Frank, he's in a right mood over the price of tyres for the jet."

As it happened, the Duke was just as charming and professional as he was every time he joined us but it was an interesting window on a different life. We both had the same problems - but his had a lot more zeroes on the end!

The project grew exponentially and eventually, I tried to launch the magazine nationally, as a paid product. The actual launch was wonderful and our offices were packed with the great and the good including my new boss, David Cracknell - Director of Education for Cheshire and another keen supporter of In Our Own Words. I really was fortunate to have two strong advocates for the project.

The magazine didn't work as a commercial exercise because we lacked the capital, and staff, to take it to the next level. This is what is called the "Above the Line" reason. "Below the Line" was something else. I had a new idea.

*****

I had been brought up in area where crime was far from unknown. Except for my Mum drumming a strong moral code into me, I might have been a criminal myself.

Over the years, I had also become extremely proficient at writing Court Reports because a fair sprinkling of the kids I had taught were more than passingly familiar with being arrested.

There was even a euphemism for seeing a solicitor or being interviewed at Warrington Police Station. It was this: "Stephen's not in this morning Sir, he's got some private business." There was no need to ask what!

I didn't – and don't - agree with crime, or criminality, in any form but I could understand some of the root causes of it. If you don't have any prospects of a decent job, a nice house and all the other trappings of success in our capitalist society then crime can look like a viable option. It shouldn't, and no amount of disadvantage will justify criminal activity, but with no other viable option I could understand why kids went astray.

Changing the whole of society was a bit ambitious even for me but I did want to make some contribution and, as always, it had to be a practical one.

In principle, the idea was simple – but it would be far from easy to execute. I would go into Young Offenders Prisons throughout Britain and make magazines which the inmates would control. The new publication would be called "Inside Stories" and they would produce the words and drawings for the publication, decide which material would go into it and then design the layout.

At lunch-time, we would all sit down together – prisoners, officers and In Our Own Words staff – and have a civilised meal, as colleagues with equal status.

Inside Stories would be designed using Pagemaker, and printed on a commercial press so that the finished product was something which would engender a real sense of pride. Finally, the magazine would be distributed to prisons throughout Britain so that the young men, and women, who had made the paper would have a national voice.

In making this magazine, we would show these hard core criminals that good things could come from making an effort. The lunch would also open a window on how the rest of the world behaved – not junk food on your knee watching a soap on TV, but a polite, civilised meal with colleagues.

As I have noted, if you are going to have a dream, you might as well have the full fat, Grand Prix version, rather than some beginner's attempt!

There were a lot of challenges and they started with In Our Own Words. The project was so busy that I just couldn't disappear and run a second major enterprise on my own. My first duty was to Cheshire Education Authority, who were my employers, and the kids of Cheshire who were our customers. The saviour came through a wonderful new addition to the team.

Anne Goodier joined me straight from university for what was supposed to be a short, paid internship – and then she stayed. She was super bright, had boundless energy, a lot of physical courage and, most importantly of all, a truly manic sense of humour. All these traits were going to be essential if Inside Stories was ever going to work.

We also had another wonderful colleague, Marion Rotherham, who had been a buyer for a major retailer. Marion was rock steady, and every bit as good as me in terms of the day to day running of In Our Own Words, so Anne and I could take on this new project.

At this point I want to give some formal recognition to the Prison Service and to Prison Officers. The news tends to concentrate on mistakes made by the Prison Service or something that hasn't been done according to the regulations by an Officer. What the media forgets is that prisoners are invariably, but not always, dishonest and are sometimes difficult and even violent. Yes, mistakes are made but anyone who thinks that controlling the prison population is a walk in the park ought to have a go - because it isn't!

My experience was that the Prison Service was helpful and free thinking, in that they let us try to make the project work. Prison governors were just as supportive, as were 99% of the Officers. Finally, the prison education staff with whom we worked bent over backwards to help the prisoners.

Yes, there were some off the wall Officers who were hard work but they were vastly outnumbered by the hundreds who were helpful.

Then there were the prisoners…

First, let me end one myth once and for all – forever. Young men, and even more so young women, are not banged up for dropping crisp packets on the pavement or urinating in the street when they're blind drunk. In fact, you have to try really, really hard to get a custodial sentence because the whole system is designed to keep people out of prison, not incarcerate them.

This means that the prisoners who were inside, the ones we worked with, were at the serious end of the criminal spectrum.

We got to know the prisoner types quite well, as we made more magazines from Scotland to the Isle of Wight. For the avoidance of doubt, I have to be completely and totally clear that the next comments are made strictly within the confines of making a magazine within a prison. They are not in any way condoning or minimising the impact of crime. Rather, they reflect the practicalities of making a good magazine against a tight deadline – that's all.

So, my first choice as a prisoner representative for Inside Stories was always a wholesale drugs dealer. These young men were intelligent, lively and switched on and, as Benjy – who was one of my star students - once said to me: "Prison is an administrative inconvenience – just part of the business I'm in."

Drugs wholesalers were also open minded and fast learners. I always treated the prisoners with courtesy and explained not only the practice of making a magazine but also the theory behind it. I remember working in one prison and doing a little presentation on the best place to put an advert in a newspaper – the strongest location is always the top right-hand corner of a page – and one of my students was profuse in his thanks afterwards. It turned out that he used his local paper to send coded messages, and he wanted these to be seen effectively by his trade customers. Knowing the best location for the adverts was really helpful.

It's nice to know that you have made a positive contribution to society...

We usually, but not entirely, received very positive support from the prisoners. A few took part in the project to avoid work, being on lock down, or for a nice lunch but most really did try to be helpful and joined in with enthusiasm. Sometimes, it was particularly useful to have what might be called the overt support of key prisoners.

Category "A" prisons housed the most serious criminals and working in one had its advantages and disadvantages. In one Cat A establishment, things were not going well because one lad, in for multiple TWOC (Taking Without Consent or, as us civilians would know it, nicking cars) wouldn't work and was distracting the rest of the team.

These situations were always delicate. The easy fix, but one which I never once took, was to complain to the Officer who was always with us and the lad would have been back in his cell before the last word had left my lips. However, to do this would be to exclude the very people I most wanted to include and I would have felt an enormous sense of failure. The answer, ironically, was to demand more and faster work so that the young people almost ran from task to task. They were so busy that they didn't have the time to mess about. In this case, the strategy wasn't working and things were getting distinctly edgy.

I was getting on very well with one lad who had the physique of a Greek God but looked haggard and tired for a twenty year old. I have to reiterate that I am militantly against any form of crime, and acts of violence in particular, but sometimes I was moved to tears. This lad had been repeatedly knocked about throughout his childhood by a violent, alcoholic father whilst his mother did nothing to help him. He had then been passed from one foster home to another because he was quick to take offence with anything and everything, and was good with his fists and feet.

After some minor altercation in a pub, he hit his tormentor in the face with the business end of a pint glass and then set about him with his steel capped, working boots. The result was a seven year custodial sentence.

He went across to the TWOC lad and leaned across the table. The words were quietly spoken – but everyone listened. "Mr. Melling has told you to get on with your work so get on with your f***in' work now – or I'll see you after."

Young Master TWOC's pen arced across the paper like a laser and I didn't have a moment's trouble thereafter.

Although Anne and I worked with some very violent young men and women, and believe me some of the ladies were as seriously malevolent as any lad, I only once felt frightened. I was working in another Cat A prison and we were having lunch in the library. The prison had really got behind the project and the Governor had provided budget for the lads being taught catering skills to provide a spectacular lunch - the centre piece of which was a full salmon, prepared like a medieval banquet. It was an incredible effort, worthy of a Michelin starred restaurant.

I was sat next to a very pleasant Asian lad, who was serving time for armed robbery and was therefore hardly a big woossie, and we were both having a great time. The door to the library, where we were having lunch, opened and in came a prisoner - handcuffed to an Officer on each wrist and accompanied by three other Officers. He was in a particular unit within the prison, called "Special Cat A".

The room went silent as the lad entered and looked balefully at us. It was the face of an automaton – lacking any emotion at all, no sign of anger, frustration, greeting or even boredom. The face was utterly and completely without expression.

As one of the handcuffs was released, so that the prisoner could choose a book, the tension really ramped up. I made a point of never asking what crime a prisoner had committed, although I invariably found out whether I wanted the information or not, but in this case I was keen to know more about the manacled prisoner. The nice armed robber said: "Look Sir, you're not bad and you're trying to help us, so I'm going do you a big favour and not tell you what he's done. If you knew, you wouldn't sleep at night..." If a "Cat A" prisoner ever gives you this sort of advice, then accept it!

Prison life was an alternative universe to our world and sometimes I struggled to understand it. Here's a typical conversation as we were deciding what work to put into the magazine.

Prisoner: You know Sir, people like you have all the luck. If I was like you, Sir, I wouldn't be here.

Me: Well yes and no, but let's get on with sorting out this work...

Prisoner: Yes but it's true, it is, honest! I shouldn't be here. I should be like you, with a big car and a secretary and everything. (Actually, there was no big car, and Anne rolled her eyes at the thought of being anyone's "secretary")

Me: Yes, well, yes, but I do work very hard and…(my voice trails off because, with the certainty of the train hammering down the track towards me as I lay tied to the rails, I know the punch line is coming)

Prisoner: You know, I was just having a quiet drink with my mate and this lad started gobbing off and touched my mate's girlfriend. So I tapped him on the head with my baseball bat and he went and died. How's that for bad luck?

Me: But you had a baseball bat in the pub with you!!!! I don't go into a pub with a baseball bat…

Prisoner: You don't? (looks bemused, as do the rest of the group before they resume work). But if you had tapped him on the head he wouldn't have died and that's what I mean about people like you being lucky.

Me: Yes, yes. Come to think of it, you're probably right…

Truly, it's an alternative universe.

I have praised Prison Officers for their support of the project but, very occasionally, they were not absolutely on side and this led to a challenging time.

One particular magazine had the wrong runic signs on it right from the outset. When we worked a long way from our base, Anne always booked our accommodation. We arrived at a lovely, rural guesthouse and the charming lady showed us to our room. Note room – not rooms – the centre piece of which was a large double bed.

With a little smile, she said that she was very comfortable with gentlemen bringing their, errhmm, "Secretaries" (nudge, nudge, wink) for an evening in the countryside. Anne and I had fits – as did the lady when she realised that Anne was indeed a colleague not a "friend" - and we were hurriedly re-roomed!

Getting into a prison is almost as hard as getting out of one. On this occasion, the Officers on the gate really were not in a benign mood. First, they checked the letter of authorisation which the Governor had sent to us. This wasn't a difficult job because they had a photocopy of the same letter in front of them!

Then they went through our ID. Again, they already had this but you can't be too careful.

Next, there was a list of the equipment we were bringing – just to make sure that there were no files, drugs or weapons of mass destruction! Surprisingly, there weren't.

Usually, we were allowed – encouraged even – to bring my car into the prison to unload the equipment but in this case we weren't and so everything had to be carried. Anne and I staggered upstairs to the room we were using like two Nepalese Sherpas.

The lads with whom we were working were not the best students we had ever met and there was a bored, slightly sullen attitude dripping off the walls like malevolent condensation. In these situations, the answer is to crack on with the lesson and work the team hard. Flat out work is the cure for 99% of classroom problems.

I came to switch on the computer we had brought with us and, to my utter horror, found that I had left the security key in my car. Disaster!

I have praised Anne's courage and sense of humour already but never was this more needed than now. I was leaving her in the company of eight, hard core criminals – and an Officer who hadn't spoken to us more than twice!

Before I could leave, the gate staff signed me out on the visitors' list. I explained that I was just going across to my car, which they could see from their office, to get the key to the computer and that I would be back in a couple of minutes. They watched me cross the road, unlock my car, and then jog back to them.

The next bit was pure Monty Python.

"Name?"

"It's me, Frank Melling, I'm here to make the magazine with your lads. You've just signed me out."

"Have you any ID, Sirrrrrrrr...?"

(Keep calm Frank, keep very calm) "No, I'm sorry. All of my ID is with my colleague, in the room where we're making the magazine."

"I see Sir. No ID. Right then. Have you any letter of authority stating why I should let you in."

"No, that's with my equipment too."

"So, let me get this straight. You've no ID, and no letter, and you want me to let you in – to a prison?"

"Yes please..."

"I'll have to check this out."

And he did. Twenty minutes later, an Assistant Governor came down and walked me into the room where we were working. The scene was very interesting. It turned out that the Supervising Officer was a militant, evangelical Christian who believed that punishing criminals, as severely as possible, was the way to reform. He had Anne metaphorically, and almost physically, pinned into a corner trying to bring her to God.

Editing Days in prisons were always hard work physically, mentally and emotionally but we normally went back to the car with a smile and a sense of satisfaction. This time we didn't. We loaded up the car, drove round to a hill above the prison and just sat on the grass in silence for ten minutes: we were absolutely shattered!

Anne, inevitably, went on to great things. I spoke to her recently and she quoted this particular prison. "I always remember that trip very well. When someone comes to me and says they've got a problem or they're stressed I think, no you haven't – you should have been where I was that day!

"Once we were outside, the view was nice though."

And it really was.

Did Inside Stories change the world? The answer is clearly no. I think that projects like Inside Stories and In Our Own Words are close relations of literature, poetry, music or art. Looking at a Turner seascape doesn't alter anything in practical terms. The painting won't keep you warm or quell your hunger. Your headache won't go away and the traffic won't flow more smoothly on the motorway as you drive home.

What it can do however, is open your mind to possibilities. Art, literature, poetry and music all help by asking the key question for our progress as a species -"What if?"

For the kids making magazines, I wanted them to ask: "Could I be a journalist, or a manager, or express my deepest feelings in words or pictures? What if I really could?"

And for the young men and women locked up behind bars: "I enjoyed making that magazine and it made me feel good inside, without having to do anything illegal.

"I could eat at a table and talk without saying f**k, and that man and the girl listened to me without interrupting. I liked that feeling.

"What if there is a different way to live?"

For my part, I felt hugely privileged to make a sub-microscopic contribution towards encouraging young people to ask the "What if?" question. I had taken the opportunity which fate had put before me and done something with it. What I did was nothing very important but at least I did throw a grain of sand down to help smooth the road of humankind's progress.

I also learnt to identify the difference between a Colt Python and a Smith & Wesson 357 Magnum – and that's always a useful skill when you are proof-reading the caption under the lead image of a magazine's front page.

Now, I was about to learn a bit more about hand guns – but, this time, from looking at the business end of one being pointed at me.

6

What Gun Do You Carry in Your Purse?

I fell in love by accident. I didn't intend to fall in love and, in fact, after receiving my P45 for refusing to sign up to the "Fatherhood Programme" just a few months earlier, I was absolutely against the idea. But then I met a Primary School teacher whose husband had died two years previously.

She had flashing eyes, a permanent smile and a brain the size of a large planet. Her hands were strong and she was certain of her place in the multiverse.

We shared a huge number of beliefs and disagreed stormily over others. She snarled, bared her fangs and unsheathed her claws when she was angry and was my equal in every way. In short, she was 100% authentic woman. I loved her deeply and intensely, and still do today – all day and every day.

Best of all, when she came to my house, Bess put her head on my new love's knee – and she had refused to do this with every other female friend I had found!

My soulmate was Carol – and, by an immense margin, she was the best thing which had ever happened to me.

Carol was not from a motorcycling or racing background but took to bikes with enthusiasm and commitment. When I found out that she could warm up the B50 without stalling it – a very tricky thing to do – I knew I had to marry her. There's the limited range of a racer's brain for you!

The sun shone in every way that first summer. I rode at the Golden Oldies Mountain Grass Track at Bewdley, on the sort of day which makes you sure that England is the centre of God's beautiful universe. All the trophies were displayed on a table and Carol was very impressed. I promised I would win the 500cc class and that she could have the trophy.

After six very tough laps, I did win and on our way home, Carol put the seat down in my car, cradled the little plastic cup on her lap and fell asleep. I drove home in silence, continually sneaking glances across to check that she was still there - frightened that she would evaporate like some lovely dream as the morning sun streams through the window, because truly I had never been so happy in my life. I wanted nothing and needed nothing except to see Carol sleeping next to me, with a £4.99 trophy in her hands.

Everything was good in every way with In Our Own Words, Inside Stories, writing, racing and of course being with Carol every day. We had two salaries, plus my income from writing, so things had come a long way since the days when I had to budget carefully for even a single packet of Batchelor's Savoury Rice. Even so, I was getting the same itch that I have always had from being a child. I wanted to do something different – something a bit edgy, with a lot of risk but the chance of high rewards.

*****

I was very well aware that the classic motorcycling scene had not taken off in America, in the same way that it had done in Britain, and that the pound sterling was strong against the dollar. These two parts of the equation needed to be in place before anything else could happen.

The internet was still very much in its infancy and so personal contacts were still solid gold – and I knew a lot of people in America.

In the corners of home garages and motorcycle shops all over America were old bikes gathering dust – unwanted and neglected. In the USA, these were close relatives of scrap whilst in Britain they were highly desirable collectors' items.

The final part of the equation was that, in order to make the best use of my contacts, I needed a British dealer with a sound infrastructure - who could deal with the logistics associated with importing a lot of bikes in bulk. I was fortunate to find Cyril Chell, the owner of CG Chell Motorcycles in Stafford. Cyril was an old time, wheeler-dealer-entrepreneur with a wicked sense of humour and a finely honed business brain.

Our agreement was simple. I would find the bikes and we would jointly finance them. Cyril would clear the bikes through customs and then sell them on, mainly to the trade. I am not keen on partnerships but I did enjoy working with Cyril. We were both scrupulously fair and honest with each other, not only in the strict financial sense but morally too and this made me very happy.

The next part of the story is particularly interesting. When I formed a relationship with Carol, I was told on many occasions to protect my house. I had come within a whisker of losing it in the divorce and "friends" said that I shouldn't take the same chance twice.

I couldn't live like this. I was in love and was going to spend the rest of my life with Carol so I wanted, and needed, to be totally committed to her: not 99.999% but utterly and unequivocally giving. So, I gave her complete access to everything I owned and did so with a happy heart.

Wyrd bid ful aread...

By the same token, Carol sold her house and said that if I thought that buying bikes from America was a good thing then it was and we would do it together. She laid every single penny of her money on the table. No caveats, questions or "Plan B": go for it!

So we did – and, other than ma faithful hoss and ma six gun by ma side, I was back in the Wild West.

Initially, the pace was quite gentle. The difference in time zones meant that we were always ahead of the US so I could work all day at my "real job" – and then work at night on the American business.

I phoned and faxed – pre-internet remember – my contacts and they found enough bikes to fill a container. Cyril was as good as his word and we got our money back – and with a profit too.

This was great so I upped the pace. Now, we had a container a month and there was a lot of money sloshing around. I had, a long time since, reached the limit of all Carol's money, and mine, but the Midland Bank – now my best mate again – was dead keen on expansion and so they funded a large, very large, overdraft.

In those happy days, things were different and I actually had a relationship with my Business Manager. He knew that I was careful about risk assessment and management, and so supported me wholeheartedly. Sometimes this was very necessary. On one occasion there was an enormous storm in the Atlantic – a full-on hurricane – and when this happens even the huge container ships slow right down, almost to a stop.

The system I had with Cyril was predicated on containers arriving regularly, the bikes being sold, and the money churned round for the next container load which was being purchased. Now, in the height of the storm, containers were not arriving and were not being unloaded - or sold. However, bikes were still being bought and needed to be paid for.

The answer was incredibly simple. I phoned my Bank Manager, told him about the storm and said I needed to borrow another £45,000 – and that was that: job done! No credit scoring, application forms or anything else – simply a Bank Manager with authority who knew his customer. If Managers had been able to think about their decisions, rather than chasing sales targets, the world would have never faced the banking crisis of 2008.

The biggest problem we faced was sourcing sufficient bikes quickly enough, and so came one of the most interesting periods of my life – and that says something!

I was put into contact with a genuine, 101% authentic "Good 'Ole Boy" from Missouri who was interested in selling bikes to us in bulk. I need to digress slightly here to explain that the best US bikes were not from sunny California, as is often thought. The problem with California's bikes is that they are used all year and they also suffer from ultra-violet degradation of the rubber and plastics. Yes, they are rust free but they are usually tired too.

The real gems came from the Mid-West. Here, bikes are used only in the summer. Fall (Autumn) and Spring are very short – maybe only six weeks, maximum, in length and then the winters are savage. So once the Fall starts, bikes are put away in heated garages and don't come out again until the weather is warm and dry.

MG, our new buyer, knew this as well as I did and so set out on epic buying journeys right into the heart of America.

At first, everything was great and MG turned up some stunning finds, many of which I wish I had bought from Cyril and kept myself. How about a pair of zero miles, six cylinder Honda CBXs or a brand-new 1966 250 Suzuki?

I didn't keep them because I wasn't a collector, and the bike buying was a business. I do look back with some pangs of regret – but not very often.

From MG's point of view, he had won the Rollover Lottery ticket. From scratching a living, he now had an English client who paid promptly and never haggled over the price. The money rolled into Missouri in a way he could never have imagined.

There were two ways of dealing with this windfall. The smart thing was to protect the Golden Goose which was busily laying the eggs, and make sure that it stayed very happy. The other was to take a quick hit and pocket the money.

MG used to send us a fax with a description of the bikes he had bought, along with the cost of each motorcycle. We then paid him, plus a generous commission. He loaded 44 bikes into a container and sent them off to us.

The system was based on trust and common sense.

It worked very well until MG thought of a better way. What happened if he mis-described the bikes and still got paid? How smart would that be?

Clearly, the answer was not very clever at all because neither Cyril nor I were stupid. The first batch of "mistakes" we overlooked. The second raised our hackles and by the third set of errors and omissions, we were seriously hacked off. Cyril and I had a meeting and it was decided that I would go across to America, sort out MG personally and get the job back on the road.

This seemed to be the perfect solution because Carol and I were now married and I wanted to show her the real America – away from Disneyland and Florida. Our marriage ceremony had been both a very lovely and moving experience - but also sad. At the time, we were both committed Anglicans but the Church of England would not allow me to re-marry in Church because I was divorced and had therefore sinned. It was an interesting view of someone who had been abandoned by his wife but, regardless, that was the Church's judgement.

A kind, gentle and overtly Christian Methodist Minister agreed to marry us in the tiny chapel at the end of the lane. My Mum came and Bess was a bridesmaid. Carol made a pretty lace collar for Bess and she sat between us, taking a close interest in proceedings. Afterwards, the Minister's wife gave her a Bridesmaid's present – a beautifully wrapped Bonio, in a handwritten envelope.

We took our wedding vows literally and very seriously, and afterwards I cooked for us all: it was perfect in every way.

Carol took this picture just after we had returned from our epic American trip. Here's Bess, as always within touching distance of me, supervising the job. Not a dog but a wonderful furry person who I still miss most days.

The sun started shining when Carol came into my life – wife, best friend, business partner and a very good race mechanic!

The "Baby With the Pointy Head" soon became a very good friend. Here she is collecting her trophy after I won the 250cc class in the first Cambrian Rally, on Martin Crooks' incredible little DR200 Suzuki.

It has been such a pleasure, and an honour, to be associated with Crooks Suzuki for over forty years. This is the T500 Production Racer which Martin, Les and Roy built for me. It flattered the rider tremendously and I won a lot of hill climbs on it. This picture is from the Saltburn Hill Climb which was one of my favourite events.

Finding the Cheney JBR was an incredible piece of luck and the bike brought me more pleasure than even the works BSA I rode. We still have the Cheney – it's one bike we could never sell – and the good news is that it has just come back from a fantastic restoration job by Roger Taylor, of RTS Racing, and now looks as good as it ever did in its prime.

Winning the Vintage Grass Track Championship in 1994 was both the best, and worst, season's racing I have ever had. Here are Carol, Elizabeth and me, all melting in the blazing Kent sun and then a picture of me "riding the pegs" – the only way a motocross machine can beat a thoroughbred grasser.

In Our Own Words

Written and produced by children for children

65p

ISSUE 21

Written and produced by Children for Children

"In Our Own Words" is a very special magazine. It is the only publication on national sale which is controlled entirely by young people just like you.

Everything you see in this issue is written or drawn by children. You can send in any sort of story or poem or picture and I will guarantee that it will be looked at carefully by a team of editors and considered for publication in the next issue. You can send in your contributions directly to our office yourself or you could ask your teacher to help you collect a number of pieces of work together. What you choose is entirely up to you. It could be a long article on the environment, or a poem describing your feelings when your pet died, or a silly joke. Everything is welcome - provided it is your work and it pleases you.

You can also join us as an editor. It doesn't matter where you live, just write and tell us why you want to be an editor and we will do our best to get to get you to one of our Editing Days.

Finally, you can design the magazine using our computers. We have the very latest ICL computers with Aldus Pagemaker - which is the same system as many newspapers use to produce their pages. You can use this equipment too.

This is your magazine - join us in the fun now –

"In Our Own Words", Lindfield Close, Moore, Near Warrington, Cheshire, WA4 6UG. Or 'phone us on 0925 740799.

Best wishes
Frank Melling
Project Director

ISSN 0956-2851

I was more proud of "In Our Own Words" than anything else I did in education. The magazine was a phenomenal success and we, the "we" being almost entirely the children with some help from their teachers, regularly produced 200,000 copies of the publication each year. Best of all, the kids really did control the magazine. Of course the experts and consultants just couldn't handle this idea either intellectually or emotionally. Freedom had to be rationed and only naughty Hippies like me believed that it could, and should, be available to everyone.

Inside Stories

Volume 1
Issue 1

Eagle by D J A

WORDS

**WORDS ARE SO
INADEQUATE TO
EXPRESS THE
OVERWHELMING
SENSE OF FEELINGS
I HAVE FOR YOU
I FEEL EXCITED
AND ELATED
I FEEL STRONG
AND CONFIDENT
I FEEL STABLE
AND WARM
THOUGH I CAN'T REALLY
EXPLAIN HOW
I FEEL
I DO KNOW THAT
I AM VERY HAPPY
INSIDE
THANK YOU**

What is Freedom?

People have their own ideas about freedom. I am at the moment in custody so I have the right to tell you, who are free, about freedom because I've lost mine! At least I can try to help you retain yours. But it is up to you in the end. People who have never lost their freedom abuse it and take it for granted. They never realise it is the greatest gift we have.

They don't know that when you lose your freedom, you lose your mind and the things you have built up. The ones who break away from the chains of prison life then they are the ones who have truly realised how much freedom means to them and they are the lucky ones.

Freedom is a part of life which so many people take for granted and they think that anyone inside is just criminal. "Scum only belong where they are - behind bars!"

But being behind bars does change the way you look at everything. You really appreciate what freedom means. When you come out of prison you really long for the simple things. When I came out the last time my eyes were drinking everything in. Just seeing simple things like kids playing in the street. An everyday thing to people on the out but to someone who has been away, it's great to see with your own eyes.

ON THE OUTSIDE

It's not just your loss of freedom which goes when you are inside. It's not being able to pick your own food and how much you eat. And also the loss of freedom to do very simple things which are part of your everyday life on the out. All this loss of freedom, if it builds up in you, can really get to you. You feel really helpless, and in my case I normally end up fighting back the only way I know how - with my fists!

And all this causes is a loss of privileges and more frustration. Simple problems can cause a lot of trouble inside!

by M. Hughes

Written, designed and edited by young offenders for young offenders and supported by British Nuclear Fuels Plc

"Inside Stories" was very important to me for a whole host of reasons. I suppose that the key one was that I could have easily been one of the young men serving a jail sentence, except for having strong moral guidance from my Mum as a kid. I don't know what, if any, good the magazine did in real terms but perhaps working with the project ignited a tiny spark of hope in some of the young people and showed them that there was another way to live other than criminality. Interestingly this way of thinking has now, in the last few weeks, become government policy.

Frank the Hippy at Montlhéry on Sammy Miller's incredible Norton Kneeler — the bike which almost got me death threats from the French marshals.

I have ridden many more of Sammy's fabulous bikes over the years and my favourite of all is the absolutely magical, 1957 Gilera "Four" — and I actually got paid for riding this!

Thunder at the Tower and a crowd which filled the venue. We learned a lot from this event!

Here are Carol and Mike Hunt hustling at the Manchester Bike Show. Mike was a master flyer distributor and, along with Ian Jackson, Chloe Dickinson and a legion of other volunteers, really brought in the crowds.

Martin Crook and his team did a fantastic job with Thundersprint Technical Control, processing 220 bikes in 90 minutes – and treated every rider with courtesy and respect.

Riders' briefings were at 7.45am and were a key part of the Thundersprint running well. I liked doing them and everyone attended - without exception. That's Giacomo Agostini in the brown jacket, looking thoughtful, right at the front where everyone could see him. He was a true star.

We were married on 4 July – an auspicious day for someone who had worked for Americans all his life. Being more than rather bad with dates and names, it was also useful for me in terms of remembering our wedding anniversary!

Carol was teaching and I was working at In Our Own Words so it was an easy decision to postpone our Honeymoon – particularly so because I had a plan and quite a big one too! The first part was that I would visit MG, sort him out and recover the money we were owed.

We would then drive up the spine of America, visit the legendary Sturgis Rally in South Dakota, and then head down the western edge of the Rockies before returning home. We would drive around 5,000 miles and be together 24 hours a day for three weeks. It was one way of confirming that we were right for each other!

We flew into Dallas Fort Worth and then caught a little propeller driven commuter plane to Missouri. MG met us at the tiny airport but there was a distinct sense of unease. I had strong feelings that this was not going to be the most straightforward meeting I had ever undertaken.

MG looked exactly what he was: a 19th century backwoodsman who had blundered into the 20th century through some secret portal deep in the woods. He was probably six and a half feet tall – perhaps even bigger than this – and must have weighed 22 stones.

The stitching on his jeans and shirt was stretched to breaking point wherever the cloth passed over bunched muscles. However, the most interesting things were his hands. I have big, strong hands from a life-time of racing but my hand simply disappeared inside the huge cave formed by his enormous, scarred fingers. I got the feeling that if he used about 1% of the strength available to him, then my hand would be turned into a soggy cabbage pulp.

MG smiled but the expression lacked warmth and welcome. More interestingly, his eyes darted about – first to us, then to the airport concourse and then the road outside. I really expected to see a sniper about to open fire on us from across the road.

By contrast, MG's wife fussed over us in a near swoon. She had never met a "foreign" person and, better than merely foreign, we were English. She didn't quite ask how often the Queen came to stay with us but you could see what she was thinking. After all, how many English people do you know who don't live in castles?

We set off in MG's little Chrysler with the front, left-hand side taking a distinct downward angle with the weight of MG in the driver's seat. In the back, Carol charmed MG's wife as we took in rural America. The roads gradually went from dual carriageway, to the cross-state main routes, then the County Highways and, eventually, a compacted dirt road which led to MG's house, bordering some seriously untamed woodland. The house was a neat, white painted clapboard building bordered by two enormous barns. As we pulled up, a giant Doberman – with a puzzled expression – ambled across the yard to greet us. The pony sized dog was called Conan and he did look an awful lot like his human Dad – or perhaps vice versa.

Mrs. MG was solicitous in the extreme and showed us to a small bedroom which was where we would stay for the night. The room was neat and spotlessly clean but she explained that they rarely used it because it was primarily for storage. And she was being completely accurate. On three walls was a veritable arsenal of hunting weapons, ranging from traditional, heavy calibre rifles to more modern, high velocity guns and a whole rack full of shotguns. The centre piece was a huge bear trap made of two immense, serrated arms which snapped shut over whatever happened to step inside it – and it wasn't capable of trapping only bears!

Mrs MG had placed a vase of freshly cut flowers beside the bed, for Carol, because her sister in New York had said she should always do that for English visitors.

When we had "freshened up", as Mrs. MG invited us to do, we went through to the kitchen and Carol gave the lady of the house a lovely English, lead crystal bowl which we had bought as a gift. Mrs. MG all but fell on the floor with delight but MG was only marginally more than totally unmoved.

We drank coffee for a few more minutes and then MG spoke. "You 'bin sendin' me faxes 'bout money I supposed t' owe you. We need t' talk 'bout this."

Suddenly, the temperature fell by about 20 degrees as it began to snow in the kitchen!

MG explained that he had faced many expenses which he hadn't even mentioned and that clerical mistakes were easy to make.

I wasn't fazed by tough negotiations and so I put my coffee down on the table and looked MG straight in his small, dark eyes. The key thing at times like this is to separate the problem from the person. You may, or may not, like who you are dealing with but it is important to separate the deal out and to stay calm, quiet and objective. MG had stitched us up royally. He knew it. I knew it and that's all there was to it. Equally, there was no point in becoming personally upset because this wasn't going to get us a single penny more.

MG remained calm too. On the table was a Colt Army automatic pistol. I knew this weapon well from when I used to shoot one in England in the 1970s. It is a formidable piece of equipment and fires a huge, .45 calibre bullet which is designed to stop any attacker with one shot.

MG picked up the pistol, cocked it and I saw the hammer come back into the firing position. I have a very, very clear understanding of weapons and of how dangerous they are: the Colt was now ready to do nasty things. In real life no-one ever gets slightly wounded and cries "Ouch" from a close range pistol strike, like you see in films. In the case of a Colt .45, the best which could happen was that someone was going to lose a limb – and that would be the optimum outcome: much worse was likely!

Everything went very quiet as MG picked up the Colt and delivered his next line: "You know Frank, a stranger could die out here and it would be 50 years before anyone would find the body..."

As I looked at the pistol, with the dark blue colouring worn away from the barrel's edges through heavy use, and the chipped, brown, sweat stained wooden grips, I forced myself to stay very calm. Pointing directly at me was the cavernous, 1/2" wide hole at the business end of the gun. I made an instant decision.

"Hey. It's no problem MG. These things happen when you are sending faxes backwards and forwards. Mis-understandings are easy to make. I'm sure we just got things wrong at our end. Lovely coffee though and it's a great place you've got here."

It was a smart decision. The pressure escaped like a safety valve flicking open, and the sun streamed through the kitchen windows again. The birds began singing outside, Conan came to have his ears tickled and suddenly the world was a better place.

Would MG really have shot me, or me and Carol? I very much doubt it. Everyone was calm and only trained, professional assassins kill in cold blood.

However, I knew from my time with Inside Stories that the vast amount of murders happen by accident and this was my real worry – and it was a valid one. My concern was that if I stood up and raised my voice - MG would do the same. If he then picked up the Colt to make a point and I objected - the next thing we know, a round has been discharged by accident. At this point, everyone is taking an immense bet that the Gods are in a benign mood - but sometimes they aren't.

So I smiled, remained seated and very quickly moved the topic away from mis-described bikes, monies owing and any other contentious subject. MG eased the hammer down on the Colt, put it back on the table and we were all best mates again.

Throughout, Carol had remained completely calm and I had yet another reminder of why it had been a seriously smart decision to marry her.

We had a delicious southern dinner with lots of fried chicken, fried onions, fried peppers, mashed potatoes and cornbread. No wonder MG was on the chunky side of huge!

That night, as the rain lashed down outside, Carol and I cuddled up very close – and, as the wooden walls vibrated in the wind, we hoped that MG hadn't left any of the armoury hanging on the walls loaded!

The following morning everyone was friends and we had another, highly slimming breakfast of eggs, bacon, pancakes (loaded with syrup of course), toast and jelly – jam as we know it. I looked at Carol and her eyes said what I was thinking: "That's us fed for the next three weeks!"

MG and his lovely wife took us into town, to collect the hire car we were using for our trip and it was a fascinating experience. Just as we were pulling out of the yard, Mrs MG squealed in horror. "Heavens above, I've come out without my gun!"

MG tutted, as all understanding husbands do, and his wife scurried back a few minutes later with a neat little Beretta .25 automatic in her hand.

Mrs MG was all woofles and blushes at her over-sight and turned to Carol for support. "I'll bet you never forget your gun, do you Carol? What gun do you carry in your purse (handbag) honey?"

Carol explained that she didn't carry a gun in her handbag – not now, not ever and nor did she have any desire to do so.

The MGs were utterly bemused, and confused. No gun? Goodness, this was the equivalent of Carol going out shopping stark naked. What strange folks these English people were…

MG explained how he protected our bikes. The first line of defence was a sprinkling of concealed bear traps, hidden just at ground level. At first this took some understanding. We were truly horrified. They were next to the barns in the yard. What happened if someone stood on them?

MG smiled: "That's what they're there for…"

Inside the barns was Psycho. He was a deliberately in-bred, American Pit Bull. I had taken a glance at him through the barn window earlier in the morning. I had never seen a dog less like the domestic animals I knew and loved so much. This creature quite literally foamed at the mouth and threw himself, repeatedly and violently, at the steel mesh where he was contained. Even from outside the barn, the dog looked psychopathically dangerous – and he was!

MG was full of praise for Psycho. "I let him out last thing at night and if'n he gets hold of someone in the night the only way he's goin' a' let go is by me stickin' a brush up his ass. Man, he's a 100 per cent pure, reliable killer."

On the way into town, our American hosts gave us a candid run through of race relations in their area and, to be honest, even now I see no point in reporting the detail because we didn't like what we heard and the comments made us feel intensely uncomfortable.

We weren't offended for any politically correct reasons but simply because one part of humanity shouldn't speak about another section of human kind in this way. It wasn't right, it wasn't fair and it wasn't reasonable: we wanted no part of it.

When you see "The Dukes of Hazzard", and the Good Ole Boys living free from government constraint in the woods, of course it's great. Down with Big Government and let us all get on with our lives. It had been my mantra all my life.

However, the reality was different. I didn't want Carol to feel that she had to carry a lethal weapon in her handbag and I didn't want to protect my bikes with man traps which maimed, or with psychopathic dogs. In the final analysis,

I was English to my core and I just wanted everyone to be reasonable, well-mannered and not kill anyone – please.

*****

However, like all coins there are two sides and the final part of our induction to life in the rural deep south came just three weeks later.

We had a fabulous trip and arrived back at MG's house late one evening to be told that, the following day, there was a treat for us. We were going for a Southern night out to see the legendary Box Car Willie - a hard core Country and Western singer who adopted the style of a Hobo on the road – complete with oil stained overalls, torn hat and soot smudged face.

Before the trip, we had another cultural experience. "Little Mikey", who was MG's assistant, arrived in MG's battered Chevvy pick-up. Little Mikey had darting, suspicious eyes and a bad stutter. When Mikey went to batter Harley back into his cage – and that's a job I wouldn't have volunteered for – MG explained that Mikey suffered from severe epilepsy and had problems paying for his medication. He was also very unsure of us, having never met anyone from outside the USA.

We had a coffee together and Mikey explained that he wasn't pro-gun because he didn't trust them. He preferred an alternative method of self-protection.

With a flourish, he eased back his denim waistcoat and there, underneath his left armpit, was a huge – as in absolutely enormous – Bowie knife.

Mikey withdrew his knife from its leather sheath and it quite literally made a whooshing noise. He laid it on the table and both he and MG beamed at the gleaming blade like proud parents. "You can always trust a knife in a fight…" opined Mikey - and MG agreed.

Mikey was so pleased to meet us that he wanted to show us off to his Dad – Mikey Senior. They lived in a trailer park, adjacent to one of the main roads running into town. The experience was fascinating - and very moving.

The word often used about trailer park people in America is "White Trailer Trash" and I find this as offensive as any other social or racial stereotype. However, it struck a particular chord with me because I was the English equivalent of White Trailer Trash – social housing, alcoholic Dad, left school at sixteen et al.

Little Mikey's Dad invited us into what was, quite frankly, a squalid trailer and shifted dirty clothes from one of the bench seats so that Carol could sit down. He treated us as royalty and was lost for words or conversation.

The centre piece of the trailer was a huge Confederate flag and when, out of courtesy to him, I made an admiring comment about its size and quality he beamed. "Yes," he said, "we should never have lost the war except for them sly Yankees."

Mikey Senior and Little Mikey were another window on an America I didn't know. All my American friends and business associates were well educated and lived in nice houses, with freezers bursting with food. Down in the trailer park, few people had even completed High School and they existed on a hand to mouth basis. Was it any wonder that they felt abandoned by the American system and the American Dream? What sort of dream is it that leaves a significant slice of its population living in squalid conditions, without proper education or health care?

We could see why they clung to the myth of the Confederacy and the psychological, as well as physical, protection which came from being heavily armed.

It gave us a lot to think about.

MG had hired a mini-bus and the whole extended family was very well lubricated with their home produced moonshine by the time we were piled in. In this situation, where killing and maiming people were (probably) off the menu for the evening, they were lovely people and were both incredibly kind and almost solicitously courteous to us.

We were taught all three verses of "Dixie" and, for fear of causing offence and discovering that someone was still carrying their personal protection aid, we joined in lustily with "The South Shall Rise Again" at the end of verse three. In view of the mood, I felt that this was no time to begin debates about Confederate philosophies.

The whole group was wonderful company and you had to admire their independent spirit, and revulsion with the professional Washington politicians whom they abhorred with enthusiasm. We had a great time and blew our train whistles on cue along with our hosts and the rest of the audience.

Equally the fact remains that MG was dishonest, violent and racist – and there was no amount of singing and smiles could hide this.

By the time we had been dropped off at the tiny airport the following day, I had lost all interest in doing any further business with him.

But now to return to the three weeks in between, where we saw the many other faces of America and I learned to admire Dale B. Klingingford III.

7

A Fortuitous Meeting With Dale B. Klingingford III Leads to a Complimentary Hotel Stay

WE ate a huge breakfast and thanked Mrs MG for her hospitality. Carol politely refused her generous offer of the loan of lady friendly handgun but expressed her thanks at the kind thought.

We reversed our Ford hire car out of MG's yard, headed west for 50 miles and then turned north. It would be a shade over 900 miles to the Sturgis Motorcycle Rally in South Dakota, which was our final destination on this leg of the trip. The journey would be straightforward compared with those epic adventures you read about in the travel books. There would be no arid deserts or bivouacs next to campfires, sharing unspeakable bits of stewed animal with wandering nomads. Probably, although not absolutely certainly, no-one would shoot us either. Regardless of its simplicity, the journey would be important to us both in many ways.

Critically, we had to find ourselves. We were no longer Mrs. Young and Mr. Melling but Frank and Carol wearing bands of gold which tied us together on every level – emotionally, spiritually, intellectually and physically. We would not be out of each other's sight or touch for three weeks, and this would test the honesty of our relationship. For sure, anyone can be smartly dressed and control their mouth for an evening – even me - but 22 days in each other's company was going to reveal any cracks.

I sang Simon and Garfunkel's "America" silently to myself. We were going to find America and, hopefully, ourselves on the way

We drove north on Route 13, one of the oldest arterial highways in Missouri. I knew a lot of America from my numerous visits but Carol was amazed at the huge distances we covered without any apparent change in the scenery. It was 170 miles to Kansas City yet her finger hardly changed position on the map as we ticked off the miles. She was learning, at first hand, what a huge country this was.

After crossing the Missouri River we stopped for a late lunch at a Wendy's Restaurant. Wendy's showed the overwhelming power of America in a way which no nuclear missile or invasion of a foreign state ever could. We ate from the same menu, served by identically smiling staff providing a perfectly reliable meal, just as we would at any Wendy's outlet spread over 5,000 miles. To put this distance into perspective that's the same distance as Chester to Kabul, in Afghanistan, or Chester to Moscow – and back! Yet, the Americans had cracked the commercial logistics of this vast, internal empire in an awe-inspiringly efficient way.

The food was fairly priced, tasty, safe to eat and the rest rooms (toilets) were immaculate. No wonder America looked pityingly at the amateurish way the rest of the world did business.

We drove on through the vast Kansas fields and looked on in awe. A complete British farm would fit comfortably inside a single field of rolling, golden Kansas wheat. Stretching out in every direction was an ocean of wheat, produced with an efficiency which the rest of world can only envy. This was the true might of America.

We also learned that we could enjoy the silence of neither saying anything nor needing to speak. Carol rested her hand on my thigh and this was all that I needed. Her hand told me that I had nothing to fear and that she was there forever.

In the evening, we pulled off the Interstate. We went to look for a motel in one of the small towns which exist symbiotically, like remora fish alongside the great white sharks which are every Interstate in America. We had driven almost 600 miles but, looking at the motel, there was no way of separating it from any other budget priced motel anywhere in America. Nothing was better or worse – nothing was more or less challenging. It was a room for the night for travellers journeying north and south. That was its purpose - and its sole aspiration.

On the way to the motel we had passed a small, and clearly privately owned, diner and I wanted to eat there to show Carol another side of America. We had ridiculously large portions of ham, eggs, sausage, hash browns and peas washed down with immense cups of coffee.

The service was excellent, as it invariably is in these diners, but as we ate we noticed that we were being given extra special care with a rota of different waitresses coming across to check that we were happy with our meal and offers to re-fill our coffee cups. Eventually, one of the older waitresses spoke:

"Say, s'cuse me, but, but you're not from 'round here are you?" The moment she spoke she stepped back from the table, for fear that I would rip the rubber mask from my face and appear as my true self – a psychopathic warrior from some distant galaxy.

I smiled re-assuringly. "No, we're here from England – on vacation."

The reaction was almost the same as it would have been if I actually had been a warrior from the far reaches of the universe. The lady was only one step away from shrieking.

She said: "Eng-a-land. Ohhhhh, that's so cool."

It was fortunate for the owner's takings that the diner was quiet, because we were soon surrounded by the rest of the waiting staff and one of the short order cooks.

The questions were fascinating. Where did we live? Okay, forget Chester but the idea of being only 200 miles from London meant that we were almost in our capital city's suburbs. What did we eat? What were our houses like? Did we have TV?

I am sure that now, in the age of the Global Village powered by the internet, the world is much smaller but only 25 years ago England was a strange and distant place to small town America.

The most moving question came from the youngest waitress, who hadn't spoken at all up to this point. She was extremely nervous but I smiled encouragingly and eventually, in a soft voice, she asked. "Have you ever seen the ocean?"

The word ocean is used for what we in Britain called the sea but the question moved me to tears. For this young lady who had probably not travelled far from her home town, and for certain hadn't been outside the State of Kansas, the question was highly pertinent. She was 1200 miles from the Atlantic seaboard and 1800 miles from the Pacific pounding the Californian coastline.

Her questions were very touching and brought me almost to tears. What does the ocean look like? Is it very big? What does it smell like? Is it safe to walk in it?

For us English, never further than 70 miles from the seaside, the questions might seem naïve or even silly. But they weren't. The young lady had looked at pictures of the ocean in magazines, and in the movies, just as we have seen endless images of the Moon and Mars but have no concept of what the surface of another planet really feels like. So it was for her.

I hope that I was suitably respectful and kind because she and her colleagues were the warm soul of America's heartland and Carol and I were both very moved by, and grateful for, the interest shown in us.

*****

We had left without eating breakfast in the morning and this was not a smart thing to do. It was only just over 300 miles to Sturgis but suddenly the full weight of international travelling hit me. We had been a whole day getting to MG's house. Then there had been the thought of being shot, or fed to Harley, and this had kept me wide awake. Day three had been a solid, six hundred miles of driving and now I felt that I had been smacked on the back of the head with a baseball bat.

Not only was being able to relax becoming an issue but the ruler straight I-90 Interstate cut through the South Dakota Badlands for hundreds of identical, empty miles and these had a truly narcotic effect on me.

Eventually, I found myself wandering across lanes and Carol called a halt to the journey. We found another remora hotel which provided cheap, clean, almost government regulated, standard Motel accommodation and I fell asleep without even getting undressed.

I woke up to find that Carol had taken off my shoes and jeans without disturbing me, loosened all my other clothing and covered me with a sheet. Being married was nice.

We had survived on some Coke and Nacho chips all day and I was ravenous. Outside our room, there was a large, black Ford pickup carrying three equally large, black Harleys. The owner was just opening the truck's door. Although I am not a Harley fan, I was in America so I wanted to bond with the locals. I made some vaguely complimentary remarks – vague is always good when you don't really know what you are talking about – and the pickup driver introduced himself as Steve. He had just arrived from upstate New York with his pal Scott, having driven nearly 1000 miles in a day. Gas, restroom, Nachos, drive – over and over and over again. One driving and the other napping, until eventually they decided that they needed a break. This was long distance driving, American style.

Like us, they were heading for Sturgis but with the intention of selling the third Harley at a profit which would pay for their whole trip.

It was not only exhaustion which caused them to buy a motel room but also the fact that the little town housed a legendary self-service restaurant.

We followed the New Yorkers through the little town and there, on a small hill, was a garish red neon sign proudly advertising "All You Can Eat Farmers Buffet". The car park was huge for such a relatively small diner and was packed solid with cars, pickups and trucks.

We rolled our Ford next to Steve's pickup and got out. "See the parking lot?" Steve waved an arm at the hundred or so vehicles. "That'll tell you all you need to know about the food. Full parking lot's a guarantee of good food."

The restaurant was an odd experience because it was much more a school or military canteen than even the utilitarian diners of the Mid-West. By the front door sat a cashier. We paid our entry fee and then away we went along the long line of dishes – truly eat all you can or could ever imagine eating.

Steve gave us his professional advice. "The ribs here are great. Get some ribs." There was a hint of anxiety in his voice for fear of some other, more savvy customers nipping in front of us and clearing the mountain of pork ribs which would have fed the whole of our local village fete in one sitting.

We obediently piled pork ribs on to our enormous plates, then brisket, followed by a hamburger, and pieces of steak, mashed potatoes, hash browns and sweetcorn. And…

The vast array of food just went on and on until, with Steve momentarily distracted, we sneaked back to the table where Scott was seated.

I whispered to Carol that we had to show willing and attack the feast with some degree of commitment and so we did. Then came the hammer blow. Steve arrived with four gigantic plates of desserts. It was just too much. One of the pieces of pie shared between the four of us would have been too much but one each! We saw death by bursting bellies as imminent.

We needn't have worried. All four desserts were for Steve and, he beamed proudly as he explained the rules of the game. We needn't be anxious about making the wrong choice because, "You can go round as many times as you want…"

So this was truly America. The land of plenty; of supremely skilled business people; of immense excess walking hand in hand with abject poverty; of gentle – almost touchingly naïve – kindness alongside a violent gun culture. We had not come to America to judge but only to observe, and try to understand this wonderful country of immense contradictions.

We left Steve and Scott re-filling their plates and explained that we were exhausted - hence we had lost our appetites. They were polite and wished us a good night's sleep. They hoped that they would see us again in Sturgis.

On the way back to the Motel, we were to see yet another face of America. On the edge of town, we were recklessly passed by a battered pick-up truck with three young men in the back. I braked sharply to avoid a collision and then held up my hands in despair – not an obscene gesture but simply "Why on earth did you do that?"

One of the young men put down his bottle and fired three rounds from a handgun into the air. He was quickly followed by his pal, who let loose with his rifle. The shots were not aimed at us but they were an indicator of just how quickly things can change in America, which is truly a land of extreme contrasts. One moment, we were being treated like minor royalty and given tips on getting the best food on to our plates and, an hour later, someone was standing in the back of a pickup shooting a gun to give us a warning.

Our journey was not across the empty deserts or through snow covered mountain passes – but it did require us to keep our eyes, ears and minds open – and our mouths closed – if we were to make the best of the boundless opportunities there were to learn from the experience.

*****

The Sturgis Motorcycle Rally is now a much slicker and more commercially focussed event than it was in 1991 when we arrived but, even so, it was jaw droppingly impressive. It's a rather odd event and in a strange place but, nonetheless, it's one I would recommend that anyone with an interest in motorcycles should attend.

The heart of the event is still the tiny town of Sturgis. The town – no more than a few streets - was originally a "Scoop Town". This lovely expression stems from the fact that it was built adjacent to Fort Meade in 1878. The off duty troopers came into town where residents scooped the pay out of their wallets for all the sorts of goods, and services, young men demanded.

Sturgis was named after the commander of the Seventh Cavalry, Colonel Samuel D. Sturgis, who later became Fort Meade's Commanding Officer. The fort was a key strategic point in terms of suppressing the Lakota Sioux who were, understandably, more than a little bit hacked off at having their land stolen by incoming white miners prospecting for Black Hills gold.

By 1938, Fort Meade was in its final stages of usefulness so the good residents of Sturgis needed "Scoop Town" MkII – and the Sturgis Motorcycle Rally was born.

Maybe this analysis is a little cynical because when Clarence "Pappy" Hoel purchased an Indian Motorcycle franchise and launched the Rally, it was hardly a huge money spinner. There were just nine participants in what was then called the Black Hills Classic. The Jackpine Gypsies Motorcycle Club was formed at the same time and the club, an interesting blend of the amateur and professional, continues to run the event today.

At first sight, there wouldn't seem to be much attraction for me at Sturgis. The main street, cunningly labelled Main Street, is closed off and about 59 zillion custom and cruiser motorcycles park on either side. We left our hire car a few hundred yards away – an unimaginably huge distance to walk by American standards – and then ambled up and down the street looking at the big, fat motorcycles glistening in the hot, South Dakota sun.

Draped over, round and on the bikes were Norse warriors, complete with horned helmets, Nazi Storm Troopers and gimlet eyed, patch wearing club members with keep-away-from-me stares.

There were also lots and lots of buxom ladies with their ample bottoms hanging out of leather jeans which were clearly five sizes too small, and their top halves squeezed into leather bikinis, the quality of whose stitching was really tested to the outer limit. In short, it was great.

In the evening we sipped Dr. Peppers and ate buffalo burgers, accompanied by a giant helping of fries, and let the experience wash over us.

Perhaps the most surprising thing about the Rally was its good nature. Yes, there was very occasional gunfire in the distance and some raised voices on the darkened streets at night. It's also true that motorcycles are stolen and that theft levels are raised. However, all this needs to be put into perspective. The Sturgis Rally effectively doubles the 500,000 population of South Dakota for week, with an additional half a million visitors. Imagine what would happen if an English county had twice its normal residents for seven days. It would be like World War III.

There is no empirically accurately figure for the amount of money which the Rally brings into South Dakota but it is truly immense. In 2012, Rod Woodruff, President and CEO of The Sturgis Buffalo Chips Campground – an immense site of almost 600 acres – said: "When you get right down to it, the positive economic impact of this thing (the Rally) has to be between a half billion and a billion dollars. And that's in a state that has a $3.9 billion budget."

We played our part by buying a t-shirt for Carol and a fine, American made penknife for me. After all, it was expected. There was also a rather poignant purchase. As things turned out, there never was much gold in the Black Hills and the Lakota could have been left undisturbed. However, one of the shops on Main Street was selling little bits of Black Hills gold in hand-made jewellery. It was grossly over-priced but I took one look at Carol and knew that we needed something a bit better than a t-shirt to remember this trip. There was a tiny piece of Black Hills gold, a bit bigger than a large grain of rice, and it had been encapsulated in an elegant glass bead to make a pendant. We both loved it. Carol wore the necklace all day – and I sneaked admiring glances at the necklace, and her, when she wasn't looking.

Some years later, our house was burgled and the necklace was stolen. I am sure that the thieves must have only got about 50p in the pub for it - which is very sad because the necklace meant so much to us.

The final insult was that they were really third rate villains who tripped over the patio step as they made their escape, dropped the TV they were stealing and broke the big ceramic pot housing Carol's favourite Gardenia plant. If we had to lose our precious memento of Sturgis, we would have at least liked it to be stolen by a decent class of thief!

Away from Main Street, there were rock concerts and ride outs. I don't want to sound like some Health and Safety Commissar because with my obsession for racing motorcycles alone, even without the rest of the "dangerous activities" portfolio thrown in, it would be hypocritical. However, I have to say that the idea of riding without a helmet really stressed me. It's one thing to have lumps of your body torn off because you are riding in jeans or shorts but there is something vastly different about having even a minor knock on the head. Yet, tens of thousands streamed out on to the beautiful South Dakota roads and very few wore any head protection. What was almost as bad was that those who did wear helmets favoured what, to my racer's eye, looked like cooking colanders or fake Nazi helmets. Why would you ride a £20,000 bike and then spend a tenner on a bit of cheap plastic to protect your head? It was, and is, an unfathomable mystery to me.

It was also strange because there is a very eclectic mix of riders at Sturgis. Some had travelled vast distances, riding their Harleys the length of America. A good number had trailered or trucked them in, as our friends from the Farmers' Buffet had done.

However there was a white collar elite too. We met a dentist from Los

Angeles who, with four friends, had their Harleys sent from California to Sturgis whilst they flew across in a hired Lear jet. This chap, with gleaming Hollywood teeth as one might expect, was witty, sophisticated, extremely well-educated and clearly very wealthy yet, it seemed to me, he must have had very little imagination. How else could you ride round in dense traffic with nothing on your head except a pair of designer, Ray Ban sunglasses and a Harley bandana?

*****

However, there was – and is – more to Sturgis than just Main Street, rock 'n' roll and ride-outs. The Jackpine Gypsies have always been a sporting club and key features of the Rally, in the year we were there, were their short track and half mile races - cousins of our speedway – and a fabulous hill climb.

British hill climbs tend to be rather like twisty sprints but held up hills, on roads with a tarmac surface. American hill climbs are simply an enormous hill with the idea being just to reach the top. I was a bit wary of the short track races – and, in view of the number of big crashes we saw the night we spectated, I was right – but having ridden thousands of miles of enduros I couldn't see much of a problem with riding up a hill. In this respect, I was guilty of serious mis-judgement.

The Jackpine Gypsies were truly lovely. They assured me that they would find a nice, safe bike which would give me an idea of American hill climbing. This was all that I wanted because I had a contract to write a story about taking part in an American hill climb and this did not involve me doing well nor, more importantly, getting killed in the attempt.

We were introduced to a wonderful American racer who had a Yamaha XS650 hill climber which he was willing to let me ride. The bike had been bored out to 900cc and was now running on a mixture of methanol – the alcohol fuel which speedway and drag bikes use – with a dash of nitromethane for a hefty power boost. Nitromethane is used widely by drag racers because it roughly doubles the power an engine makes but it is a seriously dodgy liquid and burns poorly – hence the big flames belching out of drag bikes' exhausts.

FR, the Yamaha's owner, was all smiles and pleased that he was going to have a British rider on his bike – but he was disconcertingly vague about the machine itself. The one bit of information I did glean was that the frame was broken - but that was no problem, because he was a whizz with the welding torch.

In fact, FR was a multi-talented man. He did a lot of fence repairs for ranchers, organised funerals and mended agricultural machinery. This might seem like an odd mix of skills but South Dakota was still very much a rural community, where people sorted out their own problems. In an area like this, fixing things was as much a philosophy as a way of life.

We went to bed that night tired – but I couldn't sleep. Years of racing and testing bikes had given me hyper sensitive antennae which were very finely tuned to bad auras in the multiverse, and my sensors were vibrating like crazy.

I tossed and turned and kept Carol awake until sometime in the early hours of the morning - and then I fell into a tortured sleep. About 13 seconds later, the bedside phone rang. I prised my eyes open and through the mist saw the red numbers on the LED clock: 03.47. Who could be phoning us at quarter to four in the morning?

The voice was cheery – and it belonged to FR. "Great news Frank. I've just finished welding the frame and all that I've got to do is put everything back together and we're ready to go racing." I mumbled some words of thanks – and then fell back into the bed for another period of duvet wrestling.

Inevitably, the alarm went off a couple of milli-seconds after I dozed off and it was time to head into Sturgis. We arrived at the hill climb, on the outskirts of town, and it really was an impressive piece of mountain. The slope stretched up from the dirt paddock at a solid 45 degree angle but the tricky bit was a sharp lip which ran across the hill about 50 yards from the start. If this had been a National Enduro in Britain, the hill would have been covered in clubman riders stuck and struggling but I wasn't over-awed because I had always been good on steep climbs.

We worked our way to the end of the paddock and found FR – and the Yamaha. One look at the bike told me all I wanted to know about the machine. I had spent a lifetime riding, and testing, motorcycles and I had a finely tuned eye for what I was about to ride. In this case, I didn't need any skill or experience to recognise that FR's Yamaha was a total heap of bison poo. There simply wasn't anything right on the bike, from the arc welded repairs, to the frame, to the bent handlebars - and everything in between.

Carol was new to the bike racing scene but she had been with my machines often enough to know what looked right and what didn't – and her anxious look at me just fuelled the desire to find the nearest toilet.

However, the situation was tricky on many fronts. First, FR was a genuinely nice person who had worked all through the night to prepare the bike for me to ride. Carol and I place a lot of store on good manners and it seemed to be the height of discourtesy not to ride the bike, after all the efforts which FR had made on my behalf.

The twin sister of upsetting FR was that the Jackpine Gypsies had gone to a lot of trouble to find a bike for me and I had promised them an article about riding in their hillclimb. I couldn't let them down either.

I looked at Carol, shrugged my shoulders and got changed into my riding gear. This job had to be done so there was no sense in worrying about it.

FR beamed and cracked up the Yamaha. Or at least this is what he tried to do. The big twin coughed and banged but refused to fire on two cylinders. I babbled silent prayers to every available Moto God in the Multiverse that the blessed thing wouldn't ever run.

My prayers went unanswered because, after another prolonged fit of coughing and sneezing, both cylinders chimed in – and the thing ran flat out. FR fussed around trying to stop the motor but the big Yam was having none of it. Both cylinders were on a mission!

Eventually FR found a cut-out button, hit it and great flames poured out of the exhaust as unburnt fuel ignited in the red hot pipes.

At this point, I reached a decision. Not for anyone, or anything, was I going to ride a monster like this up a 45 degree hill where it seemed an absolute certainty that it would rear up and either seriously injure or kill me. All racing is dangerous – but only the truly stupid start an event confident that they are going to get hurt. Although I have manifold flaws and weaknesses, being thick isn't one of them!

I gave the bad news to FR and he was genuinely apologetic and upset. Just five minutes more and everything would be good – except that it wouldn't be. I knew it. He knew it – and so did the group of spectators who had gathered round to see the action.

I was really fed up – utterly broken hearted. I had let everyone down and also here I was in the middle of America, in my riding gear, and I wasn't going to get the chance to attack that magnificent hill. How bad was that? I sat down in the shade next to our car, about as disappointed as it was possible to be.

A head came round the car's front wing. It belonged to Dale B. Klingingford III. Dale spoke so softly, he was almost inaudible. Would I consider riding his Honda?

I could have hugged him – except that we didn't even hug girls when I was growing up in Warrington in the 1960s, let alone blokes – but I leapt up and followed him to his truck. Parked next to it was a very strange motorcycle.

Dale was from Utah – the heart of American hill climbing – and he was a serious competitor with his Honda. A long time ago the Honda had been a motocross machine but now it had a 50% longer wheelbase than a standard bike. This was so that full power could be applied up cliff-steep hills without the bike flipping over backwards.

The 450cc, two-stroke engine had been tuned for brute power and the whole bike had been lowered for more stability. In short, it was a serious piece of kit.

But the star attraction was on the rear rim. Instead of a normal, motocross knobbly tyre there was a huge paddle tyre. These have great bands of rubber running at 90 degrees across the tyre and provide ridiculous amounts of grip as they dig into the earth.

Best of all, the whole bike looked neat, tidy and serious. I flicked the throttle open a couple of times, as racers have done since the start of motorcycle sport, and the throttle slide clonked smoothly closed in a most reassuring manner.

This machine was a million miles away from FR's fractious and life-threatening Yamaha.

I have always tried to be honest in telling these stories and the absolute honest truth is that I am no star racer. Yes, I can ride competently but put me up against a quality rider and it will become pellucidly clear how little ability I have.

However, what I do have is a God given talent to be able to ride any motorcycle instantly and without practice or preparation. Being able to do this is not so much down to ability but rather it's more of a knack – like being able to rub your tummy and pat your head at the same time. The genesis of the skill came as I rode hundreds of different bikes as a teenager – left-hand gear change, right-hand change, two-strokes and four-strokes of every genre from road racing bikes to mo-peds – and everything in between.

The knack, and I want to use that word again, is more mental than physical and I have been with vastly more talented riders who don't have it. The key thing is to be able to tightly compartmentalise each bike. So, if I am riding a cruiser I put the "Cruiser Riding" chip in my brain and I'm not distracted by thinking about race or dirt bikes. It works the same for a flat tank vintage bike with fully manually controlled ignition and throttle. I play with all the levers, fully relaxed and without ever thinking how crude are the systems.

So it was with Dale's bike. It had a clutch and a throttle like any other motorcycle and given these constants, I could find out about the rest of the bike during the 100 yard ride from the truck to the start line.

The final part of my lack of concern was that I love riding in front of audiences and the bigger the better. Other than having almost zero ability as a rider, Grands Prix would have been my natural home. The flags, the cheering, the PA don't stress me as they do most other clubman riders. Rather, all the flim flam lifts my spirits and I get carried along on the excitement: Frank Melling GP rider. You can see why I have never taken mind altering substances with an imagination like mine!

The competition was simplicity itself. We would have two runs at the hill and the person who got furthest up would be the winner. Looking at the slope reaching for the blue South Dakota sky, I could see that getting to the top wasn't going to be straightforward.

In the collecting box, there were dozens of serious hill climbing bikes ranging from converted motocross machines, like Dale's bike, to giant Harley engined monsters running on all sorts of exotic fuel and belching flames like penned up dragons.

The Harleys really were intimidating – for many reasons. The v-twin engines were started via a chain saw motor applied to the front engine sprocket - and then another chain saw was used by the pit crew to shave their stubble. The first part is completely true but I was too frightened to make eye contact with the Harley High Priests to see what they used to trim their beards!

All up the hill, and along the base, were thousands of spectators eating and drinking and whooping and cheering: it was great.

The more time I spent with Carol the more I liked her. Yes, there was all the soppy love, and I fancied her to a ridiculous degree, but I was just as much in love with her courage and intelligence. Both of these traits were about to lead to tension – and a real 5* row.

As things transpired, Carol was a natural sports photographer. I taught her camera settings but she had the photographer's eye for what made a good pic – and you can't ever teach this.

We agreed that she would climb up the hill and photograph me just after the artificial jump which was 50m from the start. This was going to be a banker picture because I would either leap gracefully over the berm – or fall in a big heap with the bike on top of me. Either way, it would make a good, strong image.

She set off with two cameras as I mounted up on Dale's bike. Now, I had the length of a football pitch to master the bike. Things did not get off to a good start. In fact, the consequences could have been very serious. I gave the Honda a handful of throttle and let out the clutch, to feel where it was going to bite. Remember, I hadn't even ridden the bike a single inch so far.

The result was an enormous "rooster tail" of debris which spewed out from the rear tyre – and all over the paddock. Three or four of the other racers came across to express their displeasure with my actions and I felt very lucky that I wasn't looking down the wrong end of any of their personal protection equipment! Thank goodness MG and Little Mikey hadn't been in the paddock…

I carefully trickled up to the collecting box and waited my turn to be called forward to a huge log, chained to the floor, against which bikes rested as a start line.

As soon as I went through the entry gate, everything became calm. I wasn't thinking about how near I had just been to getting shot or knifed, Carol on the hill or even the bike. On a good racing day, everything just slows right down and becomes a very peaceful bubble. Now, it was just me and the hill.

Mastering big hills on a dirt bike is as much psychological as it is riding ability. The best way I can think of explaining the technique is that it is a relative of those rugby players you see, looking through the goal posts before they take a kick. You will see them almost climb inside the ball as they look down at it and then lift their eyes, slowly and meticulously tracing a path through the centre point of the goal posts before they boot it.

Hill climbing is a bit like this. I looked at the hill and saw myself at the top. All that I had to do was to ride to the other me, who was already there waiting and the job was done.

Even in my inner bubble of calm, I heard the commentator screaming. "And hereeeeee's FrankaaaMelllllllingggga all the way from Engaaaland. Go Fraaaaaannnnkkkkkk!"

And the crowd dutifully whooped and cheered, as well brought up Americans are trained to do from birth.

I had a last look at the projected me waiting patiently on top of the hill, revved the Honda flat out and banged in the clutch. This was no time for subtlety. The acceleration was truly startling and I had never ridden any bike, off-road or on, which provided traction like that paddle tyre.

I knew that there was only going to be one way to get to the top and that was to hit the berm hard and then deal with the inevitable wheelie – whilst hoping that the Honda's enormous wheelbase would keep it stable.

The jump arrived with the Honda still accelerating like a ground to air missile and it took off beautifully. At this point, a normal dirt bike, under this much power and up such a steep slope, would have wheelied and looped – but Dale's Honda didn't. On the contrary, the front wheel lifted and the bike wriggled about but it settled down in an instant. Now, I knew that I could do this because it was just a matter of keeping the throttle pinned and hanging on.

Fifteen seconds later, I was at the top. I turned the bike at 90 degrees to the hill and waved to the crowd like some World Champion on the top step of a Grand Prix podium. Clubman racers really are easily pleased! The tiny figures waved back and I soaked up the ecstasy of success. Motorcycle racing is a hard, dangerous pastime even for muppets like me but at moments like this it was worth every penny I had spent, and every minute I had been in hospitals up and down the country.

I rode down the return path and back to the paddock with a smile which nearly split my face in half. Now, all that I needed was a congratulatory kiss from Carol and the world would be a perfect place. Except that there was no sign of Carol.

I set out on a hunt for her. It seemed to me that the paddock and spectator areas now contained nothing but back patch wearing bad asses and I was out of my mind with worry. Had she been robbed, assaulted or something far worse?

Out of a sense of duty to Dale, I rode the Honda for the second run but this time my bubble was well and truly burst because I couldn't stop worrying about Carol. I made a mess of the start and crashed before the jump but I didn't care.

When I got back to the car, Carol was there waiting for me with a huge smile and open arms. I was furious and almost tearful. Suddenly there was a large, empty space around us as my new fans stood well back. I explained, and that's being very generous to how I spoke, how worried I had been. Carol responded with Zen Buddhist calm. The reason that she hadn't come down between the two runs was that it was just too much of a trek to go up and down the hill twice: it was as simple as that.

It was a valuable lesson for me. I had married a physically brave, and very tough, woman with a fine brain and she would, and does, make her own decisions in her own way. I admire and respect this but with my hyper active imagination, and all the fun we'd had with MG, it was tough to accept at the time. As I said earlier, we were learning about each other as much as we were discovering America.

Carol smoothed my ruffled feathers and everything was good after five minutes – and the fans returned.

Prize giving was spectacular. No other rider in my class had got anywhere near the top of the hill so I won a truly enormous trophy. Afterwards, I was interviewed by the local newspapers and talked to a couple of radio stations for what seemed like hours. Certainly, they weren't going to let the double novelty of having an English visitor, who had just won at Sturgis, slip through their fingers.

Later, we drove back to our hotel with Carol's hand in its normal place on my thigh whilst the two and a half feet high trophy, a masterpiece of genuine plastic gold, authentic fake rubies and real marble rested on her knee.

When we walked through the lobby, the proprietor was working at the check-in desk: he was very impressed with the trophy!

At this point, I need to digress a little bit. Sometimes, after too much red wine, I have a vision of Judgement Day where, clearly, I will be in the naughty boys' line. All the decent quality bad people – the politicians, religious leaders, Civil Servants who concoct egregious and petty laws, corrupt bankers and people who won't answer the phone when your new computer programme won't work – they will all be judged by proper, fully trained, professional Angels.

Meanwhile, down at my end will be a spotty, Work Experience Angel with greasy, uncombed wings, who is doing a couple of weeks judging fifth rate miscreants like me before returning to Sixth Form Angel College.

He will look down at my list of misdemeanours and what happened next will be high on the list.

Our hotel owner was really excited: "Say, that's a great trophy you've got there. And you're from England. Are you, like, an English World Champion?"

I smile and nod the nod of the truly modest world superstar. "Well, it's not something I discuss – it's not the English way…"

The Work Experience Angel noted that one down.

"It'd be great if I could have some pictures for the lobby, you know me and you – a World Champion – and the trophy. That'd be great."

"Well, of course, but normally my agent handles all my photographs…"

Another one glowing red on the Work Experience Angel's list.

"Say, how about I comp you (give the rooms free of charge) for your stay and you do the pictures."

There's a little, modest sigh that only a truly generous World Champion could manage – followed by a quite savage kick delivered to my right ankle by Carol. Ouch, that hurt!

"Yes, of course. It would be a pleasure."

So, there I am - a newly crowned World Champion, with an enormous trophy and a free hotel room. Believe me, life doesn't get any better at my end of the racing spectrum.

It was the perfect way to end our Sturgis trip.

8

My Baby's Got a Pointy Head

WE arrived back in England in a very happy frame of mind. The trip had confirmed lots of things which we thought were true – but now we knew for sure. First, we loved each other – and in every way.

Then we were confident working together and in pressured situations. Our strengths and weaknesses didn't have to be explained, discussed or defended. We knew how to work with each other almost instinctively.

Finally, and perhaps most importantly of all, we liked each other's company. Excited, and in wonder at America, or bored with the endless Interstate, freshly showered or smelly and grubby, we got on well with only a healthy smattering of bared fangs and unsheathed claws. We were a lucky couple.

We were still living at my house and this wasn't good. You will note the pronoun "my". I had bought the house in the divorce settlement and it was my name on the mortgage. This was not good because it should have been "our" house – legally, emotionally and spiritually.

Things were made worse by the fact that you can never, ever erase every single trace of the previous occupant of a house unless you completely rip it apart. Carol was endlessly patient, and solid as a rock emotionally, but she would find a pack of kitchen gloves that had been at the back of a cupboard for three years – I wasn't much interested in wearing gloves for housework – and this would be the brand that my first wife had preferred. Then, she would come across a book with my first wife's maiden name written in it, dating from our time together at St Katharine's College. It was the little things like this which irritated me, even though the niggles never once caused any waning of Carol's permanently blue aura.

So we went house hunting. This was a much harder job than you might think because Carol, urban girl that she was, had fallen in love with the Cheshire countryside. There was every reason to do this. Cheshire is picture book pretty with lush green fields and woodlands dotted everywhere. The countryside is also archetypally English with no vast vistas stretching out like America, or even Europe. Rather, Cheshire is on a human scale – almost like an enormous garden. The manicured look isn't too surprising since Cheshire has had human occupation for the last 400,000 years and so, by now, the natives have had a bit of practice at perfecting the landscape!

I had been brought up in a Council House, where you could hear next door's cat yawn, and Carol had lived in her parents' much more upmarket, suburban semi. Over the years, we had both done well but now we didn't so much want a posher house, and there were plenty of those about in Cheshire, but a different way of living.

Maybe it was America, and all the space, but we decided to go rural. That was the easy bit. The next part was distinctly more challenging. After the divorce, my house was mortgaged to the hilt so we were really buying a property on what we had made from importing the American bikes and selling Carol's house in Derbyshire. Borrowing money was easy – but not in the quantities we needed for our dream home.

Like all aspirant country dwellers in Cheshire, we turned first to the uber upmarket "Cheshire Life" magazine as our first call. When I looked at the property pages I thought that they were connected directly to a decent, 35,000 volt electronic ignition system - the shock was so great. We needed triple what we could afford to get anything like our dream home.

So, we put the dreams away and became more pragmatic. There was a really nice, completely detached house next to a redundant ICI chemical works at Winsford so we would have complete peace and quiet. And yes of course the glistening, iridescent green water in the puddles is completely natural, explained the gleaming toothed, highly polished Estate Agent.

Another good one was the immaculate house with an immense garden, next to an almost deserted train line:

"ALMOST NO TRAINS USE T-H-I-S L-I-N-E!!!"

Screamed the lovely lady – as the London express roared past at 120mph.

Then there was the gentleman who had been caught in a compromising position with his secretary and was fighting his wife for custody of their house - whilst trying to sell it without her knowledge. At the same time as her husband had been facing challenges in the trouser department, she had been seeking entertainment in the arms of his business partner who, additionally, had been enjoying the delights of yet another secretary and was going through his own divorce. Or something like that…

Carol and I looked at each other wanly and held hands. Monogamy and fidelity looked like easy options.

We threw our net ever wider – into Wales and the most inaccessible parts of Cheshire which would have meant a long drive for both of us to reach our places of work every day. Then, precisely at house 134 – and I actually did keep a record of how many houses we viewed – I hit gold in the local free paper.

Not too far away from us, down a tiny country lane, was a shabby farm worker's cottage. It ticked almost every box on our list. First, and of critical importance, we could afford it – or more accurately, the Midland Bank thought we could afford it!

There were plenty of reasons for the modest price. Cheshire is a very mixed county in terms of house prices. The eastern edge of the county is where every other house has a football superstar as an occupant. In Wilmslow and Knutsford, the average house price is three times that of our rural, farming area and all this was good news for us.

Things got even better. We weren't even in the desirable area of our already cheap location: that was a couple of miles away at the top of the hill. Down where the peasants dwelt, or did at the time, our nearest Post Office would be four miles away and the doctors' surgery nearly eight. Local amenities were easy to count because there weren't any.

Next door neighbours were scarce too, with a solid ¼ mile to the next house on either side of the property.

The house itself was an ex-farm worker's tied cottage and so it was hardly a Cheshire Set des. res. In fact, it was plain almost to the point of being very nearly a dump. In terms of just being somewhere to live, it was a heck of a step down from either my very posh bungalow or Carol's lovely detached house in Derbyshire.

Finally, the vendor had really ruined what little charm the cottage had, with some horrendous DIY "improvements."

There had to be some major attraction for anyone to want to buy the house – and there was, but only if you wanted to go hard core rural. The rear of the cottage faced one degree off compass south and the sun flooded into the back garden from dawn until dusk. And what a garden! There was a scruffy lawn surrounding the house and then half an acre – that's half a football pitch – of rough grass paddock.

In every way, it was genuine rural living and the possibilities to make this house into our home were infinite. I haggled with the bad mannered vendor, we paid up and moved in.

It's only when you're actually living in the house that you start to find out the truth, the real truth, about what you have bought. So, there we are, surrounded by boxes, with nowhere to cook and nothing to sleep on. Still, Carol is smiling and we're both really excited. She goes up to the horrible flock wall paper in the tiny main room and gives a gentle tug at a piece which has been half torn off the wall. Underneath, everything is in such a delicate state that a huge area of plaster crashes to the floor exposing the brickwork. Welcome to Restoration Central.

Getting this property sorted out was not going to be a ten minute job or fixable with a quick trip to the DIY store!

Carol did a wonderful job in making the cottage immediately inhabitable and I began spending what little spare capital we had on improving it. Having been educated in Warrington, where engineering was not so much a job but a compulsory way of life, I had been taught how to produce technical drawings at school. I was impossibly cack handed at this but Mr. Norris had shouted down my right ear sufficiently often to terrify some basic skills into me.

Whilst Carol cleaned and scrubbed, and made sure that at least we didn't die of inhaling some sort of germ which had been untouched for the last 20 years, I first measured the house and then made a scale drawing of what was going to be our new, south facing lounge. The tricky thing was to make sure that the new room would be as big as possible but without dominating the existing house. On our searches, we had come across many rural properties which looked ugly because they had enormous extensions tacked on to small, older properties. I kept on re-drawing the isometric projection until the proportions looked right – and then measured the scale and produced a plan, end elevation and side elevation drawings. The quality was appalling but the drawings were to scale and could be followed by a builder – which they were.

Finally, I made scale models of all our furniture from plasticine and laid them inside the plan to make sure that everything would fit.

I ought to write another book entitled: "How Not to Go About Restoring a Cottage" because we made every error it was possible to commit – and then invented some new ones. On the journey we met a lot of dodgy characters who seem to exist just to exploit underfunded beginners like us. Managing a restoration project is difficult at best and only one step away from impossible for novices like us. But, we stayed – just about – afloat and eventually we had somewhere decent to live.

It was going to take many years, and a lot of money, to get the cottage just how we wanted it to be but we had made a good start in just 12 months and this was great. It was also important, because Carol had something on her mind.

*****

Inevitably, it was the 32 year old's milestone. Carol not only wanted a baby – she needed one, and badly too. For my part, I didn't. I was perfectly, completely happy with her, Bess and our new house. There was nothing else I could, or would, want.

Although I am not a woman, and don't have the biological clock ticking furiously away, I did understand how Carol felt. When I was at the same age, I was as broody as any woman and used to beg my first wife for a child. Eventually I accepted that she didn't want children, in the hope that she would be happy with me forever. It just shows how wrong you can be!

Very much on my mind was the disaster on the banks of the Gironde, three years earlier, where my wife designate had given me my P45 for failing to sign up to the baby programme. Following this debacle, I was literally catatonic with fear at the thought of losing Carol if I refused to be a Dad.

My final problem was concern for the baby. I was 42 years old and terrified of getting parenting wrong. If I had a child, I wanted it to have every experience a kid with a Mum and Dad in their 20s would enjoy. I wanted the little one to climb trees, swim in big waves, fall off a swing in the garden and have lovely birthday parties where everyone became silly - and I feared that my age would hold me back and prevent me from giving the baby its birth right.

So, we made a baby - which was a lot of fun. I promised the unborn child that I would do my best to stay fit and that it would have every opportunity that would have been there if I was 20 years younger – and I hope that I kept my word.

Anyone who says that seeing a birth is the most wonderful thing in the world must be inhabiting an alternative universe from the one where I saw Carol heave, sweat and struggle until our new daughter popped out. The whole process was time consuming, messy and painful. There has never been a truer adage that if men were the ones giving birth we would have got everything sorted out millennia ago.

Not only that, but the hospital wouldn't even give me a cup of tea or a sandwich, so I was parched and starving by the time Elizabeth arrived.

All new babies are stunningly ugly. They don't look much like real humans at all and have absolutely nothing to commend them. Elizabeth actually wasn't too bad, except that she had a very pointy head. I mentioned this to the mid-wife who said that I should be grateful that everything else seemed to be okay and I should stop complaining. It was fair comment. All the key bits were there – plus a bonus.

I actually held Elizabeth before Carol, who was getting herself sorted out after the delivery. The new baby, just a second or two old, had darting eyes. She sat in my arms and her eyes roamed all round the darkened room. There was clearly someone at home inside her pointy little head. As far as babies went, I actually quite liked her.

For the first few weeks I was only a bit player in the infant business. I passed the baby spanners, polished the cot and cleaned up, but I couldn't do what came to Carol automatically. When I saw Elizabeth cuddled up to Carol and feeding peacefully, it was staringly obvious that this was how things should be: a mother and baby in harmony.

I tried my best to control the traffic wanting to see the new baby and, to a lesser extent, her Mother but the truth is that I was only the car parking attendant and caterer. This first six weeks are the unique time for mother and baby and so blokes should do their best to accept the status quo, do what they can to help and just wait for it to be over.

It was a long six weeks but I came home from work one evening and the baby had stopped being a baby and had become a human. It was odd. At 8am it had been all soggy, useless and baby like and at 6pm it was a tiny human who recognised its Dad. How strange was that?

The new human liked me - and I liked her. We got on very well together and enjoyed each other's company. We had named the baby Elizabeth, in honour of Bess. Secretly, I hoped that she would be as good a human being as Bess was a Collie.

From the start, Elizabeth and I did a lot together. I changed her nappy, told her stories and played with her constantly. We had a lot of fun.

I could claim that I was trying to be modern man, or attempting to shoulder my share of the parenting responsibility, but this would be untrue. I did everything with Elizabeth for purely selfish reasons just because I enjoyed myself so much.

Elizabeth had a great time too. Carol could change a nappy in the blink of an eye and Elizabeth was always quiet and co-operative. When I changed a nappy, Elizabeth was in hysterics laughing and was thoroughly naughty, kicking her tiny legs in the air and generally turning what should have been a 90 second job into a 15 minute playtime. Very often, nappies went on the wrong way round but Carol always quietly sorted everything out because she saw how close we were becoming: what a wise woman is my wife!

However, the highlight of the day was a rather odd one – especially so because it was important to Elizabeth as much as to me. Once I had arrived home from work and settled down, I would always try to read for fifteen or twenty minutes. It might be a broadsheet newspaper, a book or an academic work – but never anything child centred or baby friendly because this was my time to relax. I used to cradle Elizabeth in my right arm and explain to her, in completely adult language, what I was reading and the material's content.

Clearly she had no language yet, or much body movement, but she was always intensely involved in the process. She never cried, or asked to move, but instead her eyes followed either my finger, as I pointed at words or phrases, or turned to my face as I gave an explanation.

I wasn't consciously teaching her to read but words had dominated my life and had rescued me from what was certain to be a pretty miserable future. Now I was letting her swim in language, both written and spoken, just as a baby dolphin is completely at home in the sea in which it lives. More than anything else, I hoped that she too would come to love literature.

*****

Racing, quite rightly, had taken a back seat during "Operation Baby" but Carol was keen that we should continue racing for a number of reasons. Most importantly, she wanted our life to carry on as normal and not become something different because of Elizabeth's arrival. She knew how much racing meant to me and that being on a bike would keep my head in a stable place.

She also liked racing herself. The paddock is a very warm, intimate place – like a tiny village – and it was a good place to be with our new baby.

I must kill one politically correct myth. Baby "experts" said that Elizabeth would be stressed by the noise of race bikes and would howl or probably end up deaf and blind. What a load of complete bison poo! From a very early age, she loved being in race paddocks and, before she could even speak, was excited when she saw the race gear being packed.

Her first race was a vintage grass track meeting. She was passed around from family to family and everyone cooed and oooohhed, and aaaahhhhed and said what a lovely baby we had - and we were all very happy.

Bess came with us and she was happy too because Carol had managed the situation of introducing a very bright furry person, disguised as a dog, to a new baby very well indeed. Bess had been at the epicentre of my life for five years and, in all seriousness, Carol was the only girlfriend I had of whom Bess approved. If this sounds ridiculous, there is nothing I can do to change the facts – because it is absolutely true.

So, the family unit became Bess, Carol and me. Then the baby arrived and Bess could have been marginalised. Except that Carol is much wiser than to make such an obvious, and potentially disastrous, mistake and so Bess was closely involved in everything to do with Elizabeth right from the moment she arrived home. She became a doggy version of a big sister / Auntie – or something along those lines. Certainly, it was fascinating to watch the care Bess took with Elizabeth and the infinite patience she showed.

At the time, I was hovering between racing in vintage grass track meetings and classic motocross. The Cheney was very competitive in both disciplines and I got some good results. As I have noted, I have always liked big events and so I entered the Pre-65 Grand Prix at the famous Farleigh Castle track, near Bath in Wiltshire.

It was a fabulous meeting, just like a real Grand Prix but for classic motocross machines. I was riding well and was holding a solid, upper mid-field place – maybe 7th or 8th or something like that. Heading downhill, another rider clipped the Cheney's clutch cable and this flicked the handlebars sharply to the left. It wasn't dangerous, or even reckless, riding but just one of those non-incidents which happen in racing all the time. 999 times out of 1000, in a slow-speed accident like this, the rider is back on his bike in seconds and it's just a trivial embuggerance. This time it wasn't.

In simple terms, my shoulder hit the ground at ninety degrees instead of taking just a glancing blow and I immediately knew that I was hurt – and badly too.

I got a push start from a couple of marshals and rode the bike back to our car. The half mile trip back was very painful and I knew that this wasn't good.

Carol helped me load the bike onto the trailer, got me changed and we headed off to Bath's Royal United Hospital. Here's a tip you won't find on many websites: don't visit any A&E department at the beginning of August, because this is when all the Junior Doctors start their new contracts – or it was in 1993!

I was seen by a brand-new, freshly unwrapped doctor who had just started in A&E and he was clearly heading for future stardom – but not in the medical profession! He wiggled my left arm about and declared it free of all problems. I felt the bones quite literally crunching in the space where my collarbone used to be and which now wanted to burst out through my skin. In view of the high quality treatment Bess received on the rare occasions she was ill, I wondered if there were any vets open in Bath on Sunday evening!

The following morning, I was feeling quite ill so I took myself off to the hospital in Chester. I knew that things were not good when the nurse spoke to me with her very best calm face, and in one of those, "You really don't want to know this..." quiet, gentle voices.

I have infinite sympathy for doctors and nurses and have received some outstanding treatment from them over years – but not this time! I had badly broken the clavicle in three places and so I asked, begged even, that the bone was re-constructed so that it would heal straight. I was treated with utter contempt by the Specialist, who regarded accidents caused by motorcycle racing as siblings of injecting heroin or getting hurt whilst conducting a bank robbery.

He said that the collar bone would heal of its own accord and tough on me. Now, 25 years on, I would have screamed and shouted and threatened to sue for negligence, or simply have used the internet to find someone who would do the operation privately.

The problem was that we had a new baby, a new house and were short of money. So, I allowed myself to be bullied into submission and, even after a subsequent corrective operation, I am typing now with my shoulder aching. The moral: insist on your rights as a patient because it's your body and the doctor treating you is going home at the end of the shift – and they're not taking your problem with them!

*****

I didn't race again that season and when I did some serious trail riding on my road legal dirt bike, my shoulder hurt like heck so I was beginning to think that motocross was going to be too much for me. I had smashed the clavicle to pieces – and on the same shoulder that I had already broken once before – so it was clear that a whole range of Gods were giving me a lot of hints. Maybe one was that I should hang up my riding gear permanently.

I have praised Carol's wisdom constantly in this story and it is starting to look like some sort of artificially wonderful, imaginary relationship where we walk hand in hand making doe eyes at each other. Nothing could be further from the truth. We have some spectacular, all-singing-all-dancing downs as well as wonderful ups because, like everything else we do, we like to give arguments our very best shot - with no holds barred.

Even so, the absolute truth is that Carol is very wise when it comes to personal relationships and she sees things I don't.

That winter, I sat in the lounge, completely fed up because my shoulder was really hurting – and I do mean genuine pain – and I was beginning to feel that the sum total of racing, having a baby, paying for the house, running In Our Own Words, writing and everything else was just too much for me. I needed to become settled again, climb on top of my world, and I was going to use Elizabeth as an excuse to stop racing.

This was wrong – and Carol told me so.

She explained that racing was hard wired into my psyche. It was a spin on René Descartes famous: "I think therefore I am."

In my case, it was: "I race therefore I am."

Carol was blunt. First, if I was going to give up racing then do it honestly. Don't blame the injury - she's a hard girl, is my wife – pressure of work, paying for the house and particularly, do not - under any circumstances - attribute retirement to Elizabeth. Stand up straight and just admit that you don't want to race ever again and then shut up.

It was tough love. Whoooooaaa there... Never, ever race again? Now that was dry lip time. Never is a long, long, long time and I was just signing up to being permanently absent from the track.

But there was gentle love too. Carol held my hand and said that she would help me with the injury, get the bike ready for the next season and that I should remember Elizabeth's smile when she saw the race gear being loaded in the car.

It was a very moving time and, of course, she was right.

We decided that I would give up motocross and ride grass tracks instead. I had ridden with the Vintage Motorcycle Club and I really liked the people there. We were especially fond of two of the key players in the Grass Track Section, Mike Coombes and his lovely wife Barbara, because it was they who had introduced me to Vintage grass tracking.

I entered the first event of the year – I seem to remember it was at Spalding, in Lincolnshire - and I won all the 500cc races against some good riders on Jawa and JAP grass machines. Although only nominally a club race, the VMCC events attracted some fine riders from all over Britain and I was really pleased to have won.

On the way back, Elizabeth was sleeping peacefully in the back of the car. Carol squeezed my hand and said: "You're leading the VMCC championship now. Why don't you try to win it this year?"

I was completely taken aback. Throughout my riding career, I had never competed in a national championship because racing had always been made to fit in between work commitments. Now, Carol was suggesting that we devote a whole racing season to chasing a championship.

I waffled and prevaricated and gave all the reasons why I couldn't/shouldn't do a season of championship races and then Carol, wise again, hit me with the killer blow – and right in the man bits too!

"If you won the championship, think how proud Elizabeth would be of her Dad – and you could show her the trophy…"

Ouch! That one hurt – and good style too.

So we set off on what, in some ways, was the worst season's racing I have ever had.

As I mentioned, the VMCC was a national club so individual championship rounds were scattered all over the country. Instead of rocking up somewhere we specifically wanted to race, we turned up at every event where we had to race – and I hated it.

Carol became obsessed with points. Nothing else counted. Points mean championships and so she kept a tally on not only what I was scoring but the performance of my rivals too.

We rode at one meeting in deepest Kent – so far south that I am surprised the locals didn't speak French! It was a horrible track, tight, with thick clouds of dense red dust, and blisteringly hot weather too.

I barely practised, it was so hot, and poor Elizabeth just lay on a blanket in the shade of the trailer, wearing nothing but her nappy, whist Carol fanned her constantly. She was a good baby and drank gallons of weak juice otherwise I think that she would have melted.

I got second place in the Championship race, had the bike back on the trailer and was driving home before prize giving. If this was Championship racing, give me my casual, amateur approach any day of the season!

The penultimate race was near to Banbury and it just shows what a mess my head was in. I have always been a lightning fast starter and this particular track was uphill with a tight top corner. In fact, it couldn't have been better for someone riding a motocross machine against grassers.

The elastic flew back – and I made a total and utter mess of the start and came within one cough of stalling the bike. Now I was in 12th place out of 12 riders. Carol's calculations, which I knew by heart, said that if I won or finished second I would take the championship because there weren't enough points left for me to be overtaken.

A secondary benefit was that I wouldn't have to go all the way to the south coast, 300 miles from home in Chester, the following week to clinch the title.

I slammed the Cheney through the corners in a manner which would have been considered to be reckless when I was a teenage racer and had no brain. There was no thought about my injured shoulder then.

On the final corner, I committed a not very sporting kamikaze pass on one of my best grass tracking friends. He ended up almost in the ropes – and I was champion.

I was more than extremely pleased, and very proud, but that was me done forever with Championship racing. Now, when I look at some sulky MotoGP star I can empathise with how they feel.

The VMCC championship was also the perfect end to serious dirt riding. For a Muppet rider I had done well and won lots of trophies in every form of dirt bike sport. Now, I had even won a national club championship – how cool was that?

But, tarmac racing was beginning to tempt me and this was going to open a vast new vista of exciting experiences. Perhaps I would have something else to show to Elizabeth.

9

Bonjour. Je Suis Pilote

THE injury to my clavicle and shoulder really shook me up. I didn't lose any time from work, and Anne and Marion were both great, but the constant pain was wearing me down. The NHS is a wonderful thing, and the concept of open access to health care for everyone ought to be a basic human right, but I did struggle dreadfully to convince anyone that I was hurting – and a lot too.

Eventually, more out of a sense of desperation to stop me pestering them, one of my GPs referred me to Professor Simon Frostick – if I would pay to see him. So much for free health care! Professor Frostick worked from the Royal Liverpool Hospital and had an international reputation in the treatment of shoulder injuries.

The doctors I saw were blunt regarding why I was allowed to see Professor Frostick: they were fed up of me complaining. Professor Frostick would see me, tell me directly that there was nothing wrong and that I was a whinging hypochondriac who should shut up, go home and let everyone get on with treating genuinely sick people.

The plan was simple and foolproof – except for one minor problem. I saw Professor Frostick, was slightly taken aback by his sharp intake of breath and then relaxed immediately - because I was about to be treated for what was a very real injury.

The pain was coming not from my clavicle but my shoulder. The accident had been bigger than I had imagined – and I knew that it was a biggy! I had dislocated the shoulder and the muscles were in a mess. Things weren't helped by my collar bone poking into my neck, and I was adding to the problem by twisting my shoulder in a vain attempt to stop this happening.

Professor Frostick could not have been kinder or more encouraging. The fix, he said, was to take a chisel and re-work the collar bone so it lay more or less flat. This would not mend the muscles, and I would always have problems, but it would help.

So I went into the Royal Liverpool as a private day patient at 7am and Carol had me back in the car, heading home, by 2pm. There was no overnight stay, post-operative care or anything else because we were doing the job on an ultra-tight budget.

We could only afford the bare necessities – the key thing being Professor

Frostick's woodworking skills. Once the bone was re-modelled, and I had been sewn up again, it was time to get up out of bed and away from hospital bills the second I could.

Carol was waiting in the hospital car park for me to come round after the anaesthetic. I phoned her the moment I could see the contacts' list on the phone and she was up on the ward a few minutes later, easing me into my clothes. That's a racing wife in perfect action! Cut out all the peripheries and concentrate on the job. When the flag drops again...

Carol thanked one of the nurses for their help, explained that we were leaving - and off we went. An hour later I was enjoying excellent post-operative care with a cup of milky coffee, two rounds of toast and Bess lying on my lap having a nap.

My keenness to get home led to a quite amusing situation. After the operation I had been left unattended in a small cubicle, off the main ward, and - it seemed - out of everyone's mind. This next bit is 100% true.

At about 4pm, the phone rang. It was one of the ward staff asking Carol if she had visited me that day and did she know how I was feeling. They were slightly concerned that my bed was empty and didn't look as if it had been occupied for some time. Clearly, no-one had taken Carol's thanks and explanation that we were leaving seriously. Even so, six hours to work out that a patient was missing was an interesting form of management.

It was a wonderful relief not to have a bone sticking into my neck and, sure enough, my shoulder did, very slowly, get better.

The injury also generated some interesting conversations between Carol and me. There were lots of bits of my body which weren't in the best condition and the damage had all come from racing accidents.

So, here's the big question. If I had sat at the feet of some celestial super-being just before my first ever race and been told that in 36 years of racing I would break numerous bones, come within a few minutes of dying from a punctured lung and generally suffer a lot of pain but I could prevent all this simply by never going on the track, what would I have chosen? The answer would have come in a flash: let me race.

Nothing compares with the purity and honesty of racing. Truly, when the flag drops the bull***t stops! I would rather come last in every race in which I have ever competed, than never have known the utter joy which comes from being on the race track.

Ideally, I would like to do a bit better than finish last and, doubly ideally, I could have done without the injuries too but life isn't perfect so the injuries, the money, the time, the manic joy at winning and the inconsolable depression of not, were a worthwhile and fair exchange.

However there was still one little episode left in my clubman racer's off-road saga: I rode for my old sponsor, Crooks-Suzuki, one last time.

After the operation, my shoulder was getting better every day. I exercised it – incompetently because I sometimes did more harm than good – but it was drifting slowly back towards being useable again.

Even so, my shoulder wasn't fit for purpose when it came to motocross so it was time to seek pastures new and move on.

I read about a brand-new event called the Cambrian Rally in the weekly Trials and Motocross News magazine and it seemed like something I could manage, even with a beaten up body. The idea for the Cambrian Rally came from Bob Perrin and Bob Jefferies of the Welsh Trail Riders Association – one of the leading enduro clubs in Britain. There was a hint of irony in WTRA organising the Cambrian because the same group was also responsible for the savagely difficult Beacons Enduro but their heart was in the right place because the club genuinely wanted to cater for the whole off-road community.

Enduros were becoming ever tougher – the expression is "technical" – and so the two Bobs aimed their new off-road rally at road going trail bikes, which were not designed for the super demanding sections now becoming standard in every enduro.

The Cambrian would be run almost entirely on the shale forestry roads and would be much faster than a conventional enduro because the route would be easier. This suited me, and my damaged shoulder, perfectly. It also played to what modest skill I had as a rider because I was always quite good on the fast, shale roads.

Not only would the course be easier but pure enduro bikes were banned and riders were restricted to road biased trail bikes. Like all regulations, this one was severely tested in reality because the boundary between a highly modified trail bike and a full on enduro bike was very, very thin indeed. Regardless, the idea was a good one in that it made the Cambrian more accessible to riders who would not normally compete in a tough enduro. The problem was that I didn't have a dirt bike which I could race.

I had always kept in touch with Crooks-Suzuki - not only Eddie but also his son Martin, who now ran the original Crellin Street premises. It is difficult to articulate just what a thoroughly nice person Martin is. He said he had a second-hand Suzuki trail bike in stock which might just fit the bill - the lovely little DR200.

The DR was a genuine trail bike with a single cylinder, 200cc, four-stroke engine. It was aimed at gentle off-roading and also as a student bike, for teaching beginners the basics of dirt bike riding. The engine produced only 21hp, a very modest amount of power, and was way behind anything else in the 250cc class but it was light and, like all off-road Suzukis, I was sure that the handling would be impeccable. In fact, it was going to be perfect for a still wounded rider to take for a wander round the Crychan Forest.

Martin was incredibly kind and generous, as always, so he took the DR into the workshop to check that nothing would fall off and put a pair of proper dirt tyres on the bike. That was the machine preparation done.

I took my side even less seriously. I was flat out with In Our Own Words, and Inside Stories, so my pre-event training was limited to riding the DR up and down the lane outside our cottage twice and adjusting the clutch lever. To say that expectations weren't too high is something of an understatement. Nonetheless, I was very grateful to Martin for allowing me exorcise the daemon which had haunted me since the accident at Farleigh Castle.

The Crychan is one of the areas in which the SAS trains its elite Special Forces' soldiers - and with good reason. Even in the height of summer it can snow in the Crychan, and the joke is that if it isn't actually raining at the moment, then the deluge has either just stopped - or is about to start.

When I rolled the DR up to the start line, the weather was atrocious. Clouds of wet sleet were blowing across Llandovery Rugby Club's car park and the sky was so black that it looked as if an energy conscious angel had dimmed all the lights. In conditions like this, I was glad to be riding such a friendly, undemanding little bike as the DR.

The first off-road section was only a few miles out of town and confirmed what I already thought I knew. The DR got left for dead in terms of speed but equally, it was as sure-footed as a mountain goat.

The bike was humming along but, about an hour into the event, I was beginning to get properly concerned about the conditions which were really bad. First, the sleet turned into snow as we climbed into the Crychan and then it switched to torrential rain.

In weather like this, it is really important to stay very clear headed and focussed. The better riders were still intent on racing hard but, for me, the key thing was to keep my goggles down in order to protect my vision and to make no mistakes – not even a single, minor error. Truly, it was a case of make haste slowly.

So, the miles ticked off and the hours went by. I was soaked through to the skin and becoming increasingly cold. The danger signs began when I started to feel drowsy but the race adrenaline kept me focussed. Eventually I brought the DR, which had been faultless all day, back to Race Control in Llandovery.

By the end of the Rally, I was in a pretty bad way and a kind Irish rider asked if I needed help to get undressed. I did - so we peeled off my clothes and he helped me into the showers. Fifteen minutes of hot water later, I was better again. Racers have very little brain to damage!

The real shock came when we looked at the results. Through simply sticking at the job, and plodding round the course which had caused so many retirements, I had won the 250cc class. I was delighted as much for Martin as for me.

The best was yet to come. I carried my beautiful little girl onto the stage, still wrapped up in her heavy duty baby clothes, and she grasped hold of the trophy on my behalf. Things couldn't get any better.

I did ride in some more dirt bike events but they were now very physically challenging for me. The whole idea of freezing almost to death whilst riding round a forest had lost its appeal. Now, my interest had been caught by other forms of motorcycle sport.

*****

The 1960s was a wonderful time to be riding a motorcycle – particularly if you were a hard core biking addict, as I was. The period was on the very cusp between the end of traditional motorcycling, where bikes were the exclusive domain of hard core riders who needed skill, mechanical aptitude and sensitivity to coax the mainly British machines into life, and the Japanese way of doing things which required the owner just to put petrol into his bike and press the starter button!

For my part, I could do both – and with natural flair. In fact, there was no bike which I couldn't instantly master and no form of motorcycle sport which I hadn't tried. That was the good news. The bad news was that I was never really any good so I had no delusions of grandeur about my position in the motorcycling world.

As well as riding in competitions, I always had road bikes and I was competent on the tarmac too – not exactly GP fast but no slouch either.

Through the grapevine, I heard about a tarmac hill climb being held in a country estate called Loton Park, near Shrewsbury. The estate had a track in the grounds which was built for racing. It was almost a mile long and about as wide as a shale forestry road. When I was riding enduros seriously, my tuned, PE250 Suzuki would often run up to 70mph on dirt tracks so I was already in a comfortable position in terms of the likely top speed at Loton.

The problem was a bike. I didn't have a tarmac race machine and I certainly wasn't going to buy one for what might well be a single outing. The fix was simple. Since the hill climb was the sister of a forestry enduro section, but with tarmac instead of dirt, I would ride the Cheney. I borrowed a rear road tyre, to replace the fierce knobbly rubber which the Cheney normally carried for motocross, and put a second-hand, 21" trail bike tyre on the front and that was that. I left the bike on motocross gearing and set off for Shropshire with Carol beside me, Elizabeth behind me in her baby seat, and Bess keeping an eye on proceedings from the back of the car.

In hill climbs competitors run individually against the clock and, with my shoulder still in a mess, the idea of not battling for track position suited me perfectly. The atmosphere was very laid back and this was ideal because it left time for me to be with Carol and play with Elizabeth and Bess. In short, it was a very recreational form of competition. Although I didn't know it at the time, I was also absorbing a lot of information which would be useful later – very useful indeed.

I rolled up to the start line, very relaxed. The starter smiled, I launched the Cheney through the first timing beam and off I went. I didn't find the course particularly challenging, although the Cheney was more than a bit wayward on corners, but it was good fun and a very pleasant way to spend a Sunday.

I didn't take home a trophy but everyone in our team had enjoyed themselves so this looked like something we should do a bit more seriously.

Sometimes, I have to change the order of events to keep the thread of the story. In subsequent years I took to hill climbing quite seriously. With Martin Crooks sourcing all the bits, two more members of the extended Crooks racing family, Manx Grand Prix winner Les Trotter and his mechanic Roy Dixon, built two really nice Suzuki T500 race bikes for me and I won lots of 500cc class awards and even set the occasional hill climb record on these.

This was great but what was more important was that Carol and I really grew to love the hill climbers and their attitude to life. They were seriously quick and determined racers, on tracks which were narrow, bumpy and sometimes quite terrifying but they were also overwhelmingly friendly people, not to say kind.

If we ever had a mechanical problem, there was always help on hand and we were constantly swapping children with the other hill climb families so it was a wonderful place for Elizabeth to grow up.

However during the winter after my first hillclimb, my mind started to wander – hardly a new experience – as I read about a classic revival festival at the legendary Autodrome de Linas-Montlhéry, near Paris.

This circuit was something of an odd place, comprising of a concrete speed bowl like a very poor and ancient version of Daytona but with a bit of a twisty circuit added to it. At one time, it had been the premier racing circuit in France and had hosted pre-war motorcycle Grand Prix races, as well as the Bol d'Or 24 hour marathon. However, it was a desperately dangerous place to race. Three marshals had been tragically killed in a single accident in 1964 and top flight events had abandoned the venue.

The revival festival was organised and promoted by the French Classic Magazine "Moto Legende" and the first event was run in 1993 so, just a year afterwards, I was in the right place at the right time.

I am very fond of the racing expression, "When the flag drops the bull***t stops" and you will have read it on a number of occasions in this book. However, these classic revival events were the obverse side of the coin. At a festival, when the flag drops the bull***t STARTS – and goodness me, the bovine excrement really does fly around in industrial quantities! In fact, it could be strongly argued that the greater the amount of airborne manure, the better the event.

The problem was, once again, that I didn't have a suitable bike. With an entry of galactic superstar racers from the Golden Age of GPs and their equally important bikes, I could hardly rock up with a Cheney motocrosser fitted with trail bike tyres.

Inevitably I had to turn to Martin Crooks because he had re-purchased the Crooks-Suzuki T500 production racer which had won the 1970 TT and, as a very useful by product, had kick-started my career as a journalist. In an utterly outrageous bit of advertising, if you haven't read the story please do buy "A Penguin in a Sparrow's Nest" because it's a good tale of how, sometimes, taking an enormous risk can lead to equally gigantic benefits.

Martin agreed to lend the bike to me but with the wholly understandable caveat that I must ride it ultra-gently and not, under any circumstances, fall off what was an important piece of two-wheeled motorcycling history. I could be treated by the NHS – the bike couldn't!

Obviously I agreed – not only verbally but with my heart too. I would rather have chopped off both legs than put even a scratch on Martin's machine.

Carol loaded the car with all the riding gear, fuel, tools – and baby of course – and off we set for Paris.

The trip was a steep and very interesting learning curve. For a start, the Audi estate car we had at the time was on the way to getting sacked before we even left home. It looked nice, and drove well, but for a week long trip with a baby, we needed space not style. Regardless, Carol squashed everything in and we headed south.

Our first stop was at Compiegne. Money was still tight so we stopped at a Formule Une hotel – one of a vast chain of over 230 budget hotels stretching across France and now, even further afield.

The manager was a bike fan and when he saw the Suzuki in the trailer, and I explained that it had won a TT, he virtually dropped on his knees in worship. Clearly, a motorcycle of this legendary status was far too important to be left outside all night so, as all true race acolytes would do, he opened up one of his spare rooms so that the Suzuki could have a peaceful sleep in air-conditioned comfort. Thank goodness it was well-behaved and didn't hit the mini bar during its stay!

The following day, we arrived at Montlhéry and I was about to face a major shock. Entry to the paddock was via a dowdy tunnel which goes beneath the actual track. We drove through it – and popped out into what was classic road racing heaven. There were literally hundreds of bikes parked everywhere, over a huge area, and the party was well and truly in full swing – and this was midday before the event was due to start. The wine was out, the barbecues were fired up and the music was loud. It didn't take long for me to get a good idea of which way this job was going...

Everyone was very friendly but it soon became apparent that my "O" level French was woefully inadequate. Don't believe anyone who says that it's only the English who can't speak foreign languages – the French are right up there with us!

Still, I battled on, got Martin's T500 scrutineered and all the paper work signed off and completed. It was time for a walk around the paddock with Carol and Elizabeth and an attempt at coming to terms with this new world.

I was writing a story for a British magazine but, to be quite honest, I felt completely out of my depth. Look, that's John Surtees - seven times motorcycling World Champion and the only man to win the Formula One car as well as bike titles – and he's sat on the back on his van. What's he going to say if a Muppet likes me asks to speak with him?

In fact, John was the complete gentleman. He was courteous, professional, patient and smiled. It was a perfect introduction to the classic revival scene. Later on, I had the honour of working with John again on a number of occasions and he remained, I know it sounds almost 19th century to say this, the perfect gentleman. In view of the wastrels who are made Knights of the Realm in every single New Year's Honours' List, why John is not a knight is one of the great mysteries, and injustices, of the British system of allegedly recognising greatness and achievement.

Just a couple of vans down from John was Nobby Clark, personal mechanic to Mike Hailwood and Giacomo Agostini, and - once again - an utter gentleman. This is the difference between great achievers and those who merely think they are good or worthy of recognition.

What could I, or anyone else, say to Nobby Clark - the only non-Japanese mechanic in the world who Honda permitted to work on the legendary six cylinder RC166 race bikes - except to thank him for finding the time to speak to me?

Nobby is a motorcycling deity and yet, from his quiet voice and unassuming demeanor, no-one would ever think he was even a helper for a club racer. In his presence, I felt very humble and extremely conscious of my true status in the motorcycling world.

Maybe this is why the next bit of the paddock tour didn't quite work out as I had intended. In simple terms, I was becoming star struck and more than a bit overawed with the job of interviewing so many legendary riders. This is probably the logical reason. However, there may be another.

As every year passes, I am becoming increasingly convinced that there is some form of fate governing our lives. If you are religious, fate might be packaged in a God. Those with a fondness for astrology will look to the alignment of the planets. I don't really have much idea about the reason except to say that, for me at least, things happen in strange, unexpected and even odd, at times, ways. Equally, they don't happen too!

Crouching over a bike, intent as ever, was Sammy Miller, a rider I knew well. I had worked with Sammy when he was head of Honda's trials programme and I was always slightly unsure about how to approach him. There were a number of reasons for my reticence. First, Sam is a perfectionist in everything he does.

99.999999% of perfection is abject and total failure in Sammy's eyes. With this endless search to be the best at everything he does comes a certain, let's say, irascibility and impatience.

I never see these traits as being anything other than positive. Sam was the greatest trials rider of his generation – not merely the best, but utterly dominant. He was also the finest development rider and a brilliant, visionary businessman so you can hardly blame him for being intolerant of anyone who doesn't give of their best.

But there are many sides to Sammy and I wish they were better known. He has a fantastic sense of humour, is utterly reliable and the complete professional. If NASA wanted a classic bike delivering to Mars, the best bet in the world to get the machine there on time, and to specification, would be Sammy.

My problem was three-fold. First, I was out of my depth. Second, I didn't know what to say to Sammy and third, he was working on a very odd looking Norton and was wearing his: "Disturb me at your peril!" face.

So the planets weren't quite aligned, or the Gods were on their tea break or whatever, but instead of doing my job and interviewing Sam, I ambled off and bought a cone of frites so delicious I am surprised that they weren't banned under some culinary form of the legal highs law.

That night we had a nice meal in our hotel and, ever so slowly, my brain swept the dust and cobwebs away from the bits of French vocabulary I knew and the words spluttered and clanged about. Goodness me, did I wish that I had paid more attention in Miss Pilar's French lessons!

The following day the weather was foul and I was back, panting up the knowledge mountain. I was tempted to make some joke about total immersion learning because the rain hammered down in stair rods and poured down the steep, concrete banking in glacial torrents. This looked like a re-run of the Cambrian Rally – but on concrete.

Not that it stopped the wannabee boys - who had been psyching themselves up with the assistance of French vin ordinaire all night - from showing their form. Their performance can be summed up no better than in Casey Stoner's immortal words regarding Valentino Rossi, after Vale t-boned him at Jerez in 2011. I dream of being able to say something as good as this just once in my life: "Obviously your ambition outweighed your talent."

So it was with the Montlhéry boys. One hyper enthusiast dropped his tricked out XS650 Yamaha café racer into the soaking wet left-hander where I was watching, at a speed which would have frightened Casey Stoner himself. In the next few seconds I knew that I was going to be impressed – either with the Frenchman's riding ability - which was of a standard guaranteeing automatic World Championship status - or the resultant crash.

Unfortunately for the history books, it was the latter. The front end of the Yam let go and the rider pirouetted elegantly through the air – which gave him plenty of time to observe his naughty bike bringing another three riders off. Although this wasn't racing, clearly the job did need a lot of thought and care – particularly so because I was riding Martin's bike.

I was much better off because I was riding with some experienced ex-racers who were well aware that concrete is hard. What they thought of my riding I can't imagine because I went round every corner with the bike almost vertical, for fear of sliding off.

After the second session, I breathed a huge sigh of relief at making it back to the paddock with not a scratch on the T500. I could see Carol standing by the trailer and I raised my visor and relaxed – two fatal mistakes.

A ten year old came hurtling across the paddock on a little Honda Monkey bike and I had the option of mowing him down or trying an emergency stop. The bottom line is that you can't instantly stop a road racer on a wet concrete road and so down I went. The bike wasn't badly damaged but the tank had a dent in it and I seem to remember that the fairing was scratched too. I was so upset that I almost burst into tears.

We didn't talk much over dinner that night. I always liked feeding Elizabeth at meal times but on this occasion I was so maudlin that Carol took her from me whilst I sat there, pushing the food around my plate with a 50/50 mixture of feeling sorry for myself whist being utterly mortified at what I had done to Martin's bike.

Things were no better in the morning and I was ready for loading up and going home but Carol, wise woman that she is, told me to stand up straight, stop feeling sorry for myself and get back in the paddock with a notebook and camera. It was tough love of the best possible kind.

And what a change had happened overnight. The sun had come out and, although I didn't know it as we drove under the track, the Gods had finished their tea break and wanted some amusement.

Sammy was by his van and was all smiles. Clearly, the sun was pleasing him too. We fell into easy conversation and I explained how fed up I was – doubly so because I had nothing to ride and the track looked great. I didn't mention the fact that I had fallen off the T500 because no-one looks admiringly at a journalist who damages borrowed motorcycles – they really don't!

Then I took a leap into the dark. Would it be possible to ride Sammy's Norton and write an article about it?

Sammy thought about the prospect for some milli-seconds and then, with a huge smile, agreed along with the caveat: "And don't drop the bloody thing!"

Me? Fall off a bike? As if!

At this point in the story, I need to explain something about the Norton I was about to ride because it was one of the most fascinating motorcycles ever to come out of the Birmingham factory. At the heart of the bike was the fact that, unlike a conventional motorcycle, it had no saddle. Instead, the rider knelt in two aluminium trays - one either side of the engine.

The Norton Kneeler was built to attack two problems simultaneously. First the bike was the most aerodynamically efficient motorcycle of its day, being far lower than its contemporaries and much more slippery through the air.

Not only did the Kneeler prove to be faster than its contemporaries in terms of top speed but, despite its ungainly appearance, everyone who rode it had nothing but praise for its handling. And, it must be remembered, this was from team riders who were competing on the famed "Featherbed" Nortons, at the time acknowledged to be the best handling bikes in racing.

The key to the Kneeler's success was its low centre of gravity. The motor hung between the duplex top tubes in a manner extremely reminiscent of a modern Superbike, whilst the fuel and oil were actually below the line of the cylinder head. This meant that the great mass of the bike's weight was concentrated low and along the centre line of the bike.

The early bikes had two problems. The first was fuel supply, so Norton engineer Ernie Walsh hit on the idea of driving a fuel pump from the left-hand side of the inlet camshaft to a header tank which fed the Amal G.P. carburettor. Excess fuel then returned to the pannier tanks. In practice, the system worked beautifully.

Less successful was the streamlining which, initially, was too efficient and starved the motor of cool air, causing over-heating problems.

The riding position on the "Kneeler" was unique and quite disconcerting because no-one ever kneels on, or in, a bike. It might seem odd but this didn't bother me in the slightest. I have a very clear idea about my riding ability, or lack of it, but I never doubt that I can ride any motorcycle instantly. I had been testing motorcycles professionally all of my life and the "Kneeler Norton" was just another bike with a throttle, engine and two wheels like all the rest. In this case, lots of things were in slightly unusual places but this didn't put me off even a little bit.

Not that everything was completely straightforward. This is how I reported the words of Sammy's mechanic, Graham Head, at the time. "As far as we can tell, Ray Amm (Norton's works rider) was about 5' 4". You're 6" taller. Come off and they'll have to cut you out - if you don't die in the fire first."

Graham's judgement was absolutely right. In order to get me on, or more accurately in, to the bike Sammy and Graham had to hold it upright whilst I literally squeezed my body into a space never designed to take it. Once inside, I couldn't move to the front, back or sideways. Fifteen minutes later, this was to have some interesting repercussions.

Managing a wan smile, I nodded to Sammy and off we went. Sammy and Graham pushed enthusiastically, I dropped the clutch and, fortunately, the Norton wheezed once and the motor caught. I dipped the clutch and instantly fed in the power before it fell over and crushed me. Above ten miles an hour, everything became very stable and, incredibly, it was easy to forget that I was lying down over the engine with my knees supported in two aluminium trays.

In fact, forgetting that the bike was a kneeler was the secret. With a shallow steering head angle, the self-centring effect was marked and the "Kneeler" held its line effortlessly. Cornering was merely a matter of peeling into a bend with the slightest shifts in body weight - truly elegant and effortless motorcycling.

Changing gear was more of a problem, simply because my foot was jammed so tight in the rear fairing. Even so, with patience, the four speed Manx gearbox was as sweet as a conventional gearbox - although slower.

If you ride bikes for a living you tend to get hardened about ghosts and legends but as I tucked in behind the fairing of the fabulous 1953 Norton "Kneeler", I must confess to having a few prickles on the back of my neck.

On a dull, overcast November day in 1953 Ray Amm, Norton's genial Rhodesian genius, covered 133.71 miles in a single hour on the same Montlhéry concrete saucer I was riding now. That would be hugely impressive on a current race bike running on a modern, high grip speed bowl. In the damp and danger of Montlhéry in early winter, and with only 36bhp - less than the power of many scooters - the achievement was incredible.

As the DOHC Norton motor beat harshly beneath my chest, and the bike bounced over the expansion joints in the concrete speed bowl, it was impossible not to feel that this was more than just another ride, on just another bike. Nudging up towards 100mph on Montlhery's precipitously steep banking, the Norton held its line wonderfully - raising the question of what the bike could have done if internal factory politics had not killed it off.

There's no denying that the penalty for making a mistake was weighing very heavily on my mind so I rode the Kneeler very circumspectly indeed.

Jammed tight in behind the fairing as the off-white tarmac went by in a blur just ten inches from my knee, I was filled with admiration for Ray Amm, who battled the rain and rough concrete of Montlhéry.

The chequered flag came out in a theatrical wave of Gallic exuberance and I was pointed towards the paddock entrance. It had been a wonderful experience, I hadn't crashed Sammy's half a million pound bike and the sun was shining but then...

Of course, life couldn't be that simple.

I couldn't stop. I was trapped in the Norton with no way of getting my legs out - so off I set for another lap of the track, dutifully waving to the spectators because I was now entirely on my own.

As I dropped down off the banking, the chequered flag was waved much more stridently – and the smiles had gone. I pointed down at the bike and the marshals gesticulated back at me – as I set off again.

By the next lap, the black flag – waved only at riders who must stop immediately – was being held vertically in my face and a whole group of officials were taking notes. Come on Gods, we all like a laugh but sooner or later the bike is going to run out of fuel and then I am really in line for a serious problem!

My saviour came in the form of Carol's sharp thinking. She worked out what was happening and on the next lap, four fit French marshals were tensed up, like 100m runners in the Olympics. I eased the Norton down on to the start straight and they launched themselves at the bike like fag smoking Usain Bolts, in overalls of course, as I cut the engine and coasted towards them.

I needn't have worried though. They caught the bike in plenty of time and Sammy and Graham prised me out and into safety. Everyone exchanged man hugs and all my sins were forgiven – but I certainly needed the mayonnaise and salt fix which was built into my lunch time frites.

There are two addenda to this story. First, Martin was seriously cross with me for dropping the T500. It didn't matter about the wayward child on the Monkey bike – I was responsible for the damage and that was all there was to it. I agreed with him.

Fortunately, Martin forgave me and we remained friends which makes me very happy.

Second, riding Sammy's Kneeler Norton was the start of a quite wonderful relationship which has seen me have the great, the very great, honour of riding some of the Sammy Miller Motorcycle Museum's most exotic motorcycles. I still can't quite work out why I have been accorded this privilege but, since Montlhéry, I have ridden many of Sammy's machines – including his Moto Guzzi V8 and that's one bike which everyone would like to have on their motorcycling CV.

I will conclude this story with more observation. I learn in a very unstructured way. I struggle with exams because the idea that "a" follows "b" which is the precursor of "c" is always cloying.

Not through any deliberate attempt, I think in a very disjointed and unorganised way. For me, it is perfectly reasonable to count 1, 2, hedgehog, banana, Beowulf, 6, nuclear reactor, 8 and so on because my ideas don't live in neat and tidy compartments. Rather, everything is thrown into a huge cognitive skip where concepts rub shoulders with other ideas which they wouldn't normally meet.

Also, information is never discarded. Instead, it's simply chucked into the skip on the grounds that I might need it at some time in the future. I sometimes struggle to remember faces and names but I can describe the precise colour of the sand in the Lucerne Valley where I rode in a desert race forty years ago, or the smell of the Corsican maquis which I haven't visited for two decades.

Although I didn't realise it at the time, there was a veritable avalanche of ideas piling into my memory skip and these were going to be very useful in the future.

10

Good Times

PERHAPS one day I will write a book just about In Our Own Words but in "The Flying Penguin" I want to give some postcards of what was a truly wonderful time in my life – and in many ways too.

Things were so good it is difficult to know where to start. I know that some people are tough enough – mentally, emotionally and physically – to perform at their best regardless of their personal circumstances but I'm not one of them.

I can manage intellectual and physical pressures easily, and thrive on them, but the emotional side is always challenging for me. So it was vitally important that Carol and I laughed and argued, loved and snarled, drew non-negotiable lines in the sand and then immediately crossed them for a hug, for me to do my best at In Our Own Words.

The baby with the pointy head was growing up to be a lovely little girl who came out with her Dad to look at bikes and buy tools, and then returned home with her anorak covered in the pie gravy which her Mum had specifically said that she couldn't have.

The cottage was making good but slow progress, and Bess kept a managerial eye on everything and everybody. In short, things were great.

I was very proud of In Our Own Words and remain so today. I had been influenced by some of the ideas of the Hippy movement when I was growing up in the 1960s, and so I took the peripheries of these counter culture concepts and wove them into the philosophies of In Our Own Words. There is a certain irony in this statement, in that I was vehemently opposed to the Vietnam War but equally strongly supportive of the British nuclear deterrent. In the same way I was a passionate advocate of free speech, and of breaking conventional rules and practices, but militantly against mind bending drugs. Perhaps I was a skinny latte Hippy – or Counter Culture Lite!

At the heart, the very epicentre, of the soul of In Our Own Words was the belief that the students could, and should, have the right to control the content of the magazine. I believed in this central tenet of the project with a religious fervour.

I am now going to sound all luvvy and arty as I write this section but I still want to tell you how I am feeling. The palms of my hands are damp and my hands are shaking as I remember working with these young people. The students ranged in age from six or seven years old to Sixth form and, together, they were chatting and discussing work and debating; co-operating and smiling; hurling pens on to the table with frustration; giggling at a funny story they had just read and sighing, and rushing round the room filled with the joy of making their own magazine. Nothing I have ever done in my professional life provided more satisfaction or greater pride because it was learning at its most pure and involving - free of tests, reports, assessments and league tables. This was kids learning and doing, solely for the love of gaining new experience and, as a teacher, I could do no better.

I was learning too – and growing up. I worked with many cutting edge companies like Aldus, Nestle, British Nuclear Fuels, the computer chip manufacturer Intel, and petroleum giant Shell. I gained ever more confidence and ability to make sponsorship pitches but I also learned how utterly disposable I was. This knowledge was to prove very useful to me in the future.

Cheshire Education Authority's attitude towards the project, and Frank Melling, was very ambivalent but it suited me perfectly. I was never a political player in the education game. I didn't socialise with senior Cheshire staff and In Our Own Words was based in Runcorn, an unfashionable part of Cheshire and a long way from Chester where a smart, ambitious teacher, running a prestigious project, would have demanded to be located.

I was intelligent but I didn't have any conventional ambition. Rather than promotion, I had bigger things on my mind.

I received very little overt support from Cheshire but the Authority – under the direction of Neil Fitton and David Cracknell, the two wonderful Directors of Education for whom I worked – did give me the one thing I needed more than anything else: this was freedom. Being on the far edge of the educational galaxy, and unconstrained by steering committees or planning groups, meant that I was free to develop new ideas at a frenetic rate

These two superb leaders protected my back from interference by the next level down of management and I was very conscious of, and grateful for, the trust they showed in me. With their blessing, I was able to push the project in to brand new areas.

Not that I was completely immune from dabbling by managers who thought that they should show their power, and sometimes this had hilarious consequences – if you like black humour.

I think that my managers in Chester struggled to work out why I was not always petitioning for funds and, like so many things with In Our Own Words, this had a lovely outcome.

It was decided that the Project would be audited to find out where our funding was coming from and to make sure that it was not being mis-used or, worse still, going into my back pocket.

The chap doing the job was a Cheshire County Council "A" list celebrity in that he was the newly retired ex-Chief Auditor for the whole County – and a top grade forensic accountant as well. If there was anything dodgy, he would find it and there would be a gallows erected outside County Hall before the end of the day.

For my part, I couldn't have cared less. Everything was run with scrupulous honesty and as for there being a lot of money coming into and out of our accounts, so what? Handling hundreds of thousands of pounds was hardly a new experience for me. We earned a lot of money, made a lot of money and spent a lot of money – and thousands of kids benefitted as a result.

I asked Anne and Marion to be as a pleasant, open and co-operative as possible but not to let the audit interfere with our real work.

The first morning was seriously tense as the girls provided bank account details and receipts. For my part, I just got on with my job and played no part in the proceedings because I had other, more important, things to do.

By the end of the day, everyone had relaxed. The auditor could tell that we were squeaky clean and if we couldn't find ten or fifteen pens we had bought for an Editing Day, he was quite happy to accept that the kids had chewed them and so we had thrown them away.

By day three, the Auditor had become a huge fan of the Project and started to tell us of the scams he had uncovered over the years. Wow! Don't believe that all of Local Government is purer than the driven snow!

Best of all, he came to the next Editing Day and worked alongside the kids choosing the work for the magazine and, for me, this was supreme vindication of what we were trying to do.

As In Our Own Words became ever more widely known throughout the country, teachers from other Authorities used to visit us for help setting up their own magazine. One particular switched on Advisor had secured a serious lump of money from his LEA (Local Education Authority) to make a clone of In Our Own Words in his area. He also had six staff seconded to him, full-time, which was double the number we had working on our magazine.

He spent a day with us in September when we showed him what we did, the planning required and the logistics of the operation and then bought him lunch – from our budget! I thought that this was very kind.

I saw him the following July and asked him how things had gone. He was really pleased. During the year, he had conducted a series of detailed analyses which led to three reports and a discussion document – but not a single magazine. In the same period, we had made just shy of 200,000 copies of In Our Own Words – and distributed them to schools.

As well as making six magazines each year, and producing six editions of Inside Stories, we provided lots of other services to teachers and schools. One of these was another element of the project which gives me intense pride: it was work experience for a very special sub-set of Cheshire pupils.

I have a very clear idea of my own intellectual ability. I know how intelligent I am without the need for any bovine excrement - and I also know how far I am behind the cleverest people. Like my riding ability, I am sort of good clubman bright!

Because I am relaxed about being me, I love working with people who are really, stupendously intelligent. Not all teachers, or employers, share this attitude and I have seen – with my own eyes – really clever kids treated very badly by teachers who are frightened of being shown up by their students' intelligence.

All British kids take part in work experience either at fifteen years of age or seventeen – sometimes both. This can be valuable experience, and the young people can learn a lot, or it can be a complete waste of time, with the kids doing nothing but brushing up or making the tea for a couple of weeks.

There was one sub-set of kids who were particularly difficult to place for work experience and who often had a miserable time as a consequence. These were the super-bright – of whom there was a fair sprinkling in Cheshire.

Let me give you a flavour of these young people and why they could be hard work. A slightly shy, and somewhat diffident, young lady approached me at an Editing Day and asked if she could do her Work Experience at In Our Own Words. She was a very nervous and fidgety fifteen year old, but she crackled with energy and enthusiasm so I knew that she would have a good time with us. I tentatively agreed that she could come to the project but she lived south of Nantwich, and I was worried about her parents having to drive her 30 plus miles, each way, to our office every day.

She explained that her family was not very well off and didn't have a car. I looked suitably disappointed but she was all smiles. Out came a folder and there, in meticulous detail, was the plan for her to catch a bus at 6am to Nantwich, then another to Crewe, followed by a train to Runcorn and a final bus to our office. All this would be funded by working as a cleaner in a garden centre at weekends, and by doing extra baby-sitting.

She had a great time with us and is probably now a boss spy with MI6 or has some other, equally high flying job.

Another girl was gossiping away over lunch and, apropos almost nothing, mentioned that she was keen to do modern languages at Cambridge. She was studying French and German at school but had fancied learning Spanish too and so was teaching herself at home in the evenings. Her school rated her so highly that they had provided a free entry for GCSE! Moments like this reminded me of what a thickie I was with my paddock French!

The key to making work experience a happy and rewarding experience for these kids was two fold. First was to recognise that they had an incredible work rate – and one which could be sustained for hour after hour, at peak perform-ance. From the moment they walked through the door, we stacked them with more work than they could handle – but they often proved us wrong by completing it. All day, every day, we worked them relentlessly and they thrived.

The second part of the equation was to give the kids a lot of genuine responsibility. You can't fake anything with these mega-brains so we would give them genuine responsibility to undertake tasks which would cause us a lot of trouble to sort out if they went wrong. For example, booking schools into Editing Days, designing pages of the magazine with children visiting the Project or administrative tasks such as calculating how much food we would need for refreshments at public events.

Sometimes things did go off the rails but this was never due to lack of effort or thought – merely that the kid had not been in that particular position before. I saw these mistakes, although I never viewed them in this pejorative way, as a vital part of the work experience the young person did with us in that I wanted them to learn from things not going precisely to plan.

I need to conclude by saying that I had a great time with these astonishing young people and it was really good to be reminded of where I sat on the intellectual ladder. You only have to hear a fifteen year old recite most of Shakespeare's Henry V, and then give a critique of the respective performances of Laurence Olivier and Kenneth Branagh, to know that you belong in the non-winner's end of the brain paddock!

Our Work Experience students were invariably meticulously well-mannered and wrote beautiful letters of thanks for their time with us. I've still got one from a brilliant English scholar who, as an aside, was also a Michelangelo standard artist. Clearly, the writing was a magnificent piece of prose but around the edge of the letter was a flock of cartoon sheep, grazing the margins in the style of a medieval manuscript. I can't imagine what it must be like to be so talented.

However, the greatest indication that we were serving these young people's needs was the number who came back to us and worked, for free and without expenses, when they were not at school. I remain deeply moved by the affection and loyalty they showed to us.

*****

Away from making magazines I was having an equally good time writing for a range of British and American motorcycling magazines. The only thing missing was that I didn't really have a home. Freelancers are strange creatures in many ways. We are very difficult to employ, in the sense that we refuse to sit still in meetings and won't be told what to do. However, we do like to be loved and stroked and all the other things which keep self-employed paranoia at bay.

At the time, I was a regular reader of the Daily Telegraph – one of the giants of the British mainstream media. Every Saturday, they carried a huge motoring supplement which covered every possible sector in the four-wheeled world plus some bike material too.

I rang the newspaper and, after the normal chasing around and fobbing off, I got to speak to the Editor of the Motoring Section, Peter Hall. We got on immediately. Peter was quietly spoken, erudite, confident and enthusiastic. He also knew exactly what he wanted and how a piece should be delivered and when. For a freelancer, these are invaluable traits because there is nothing more disconcerting than working for an editor who doesn't know what he is talking about and therefore can't commission the work he needs. Peter was simply a joy.

I sent him some classic bike material, he published it and the reader reaction was good. The final part of the equation was that the Telegraph paid well, and on time, and this was the cherry on top of what was a lovely cake.

Working for the Telegraph was also a serious eye opener – and in many ways. Motorcycles are always second best to cars but when I phoned somewhere and said, "This story will go into the Daily Telegraph" if the red Axminster carpet wasn't rolled out then the very posh, acrylic pink appeared.

It was a lovely position to be in as a freelancer and I tried very hard not to abuse the privilege I was given. It's important to keep your eyes firmly fixed on reality in situations like this. No-one thought that Frank Melling had any power, status or even value - except by association with the Daily Telegraph. Once you think that you are the story, instead of the messenger, then you really are jogging enthusiastically along the road to perdition.

Equally, there were some occasions when I was allowed to enter a different world of privilege which simply doesn't exist in the motorcycling universe.

When you read the stories about the latest bikes in magazines it might seem very glamorous for the journalist to be out in Spain, riding around on a brand-new motorcycle whilst getting paid. It is incredible fun – but it's not nearly as exotic as it seems from the outside.

A key factor is the brutally tight schedule because the bike is being introduced to journalists from all over the world in just one week. Typically, you will fly in – budget airline of course – and go straight into a press conference that same evening, followed by a meal. The following day, breakfast will be served at 07.30 and followed by riders' briefing 45 minutes later.

Then it's out to ride the bike, two photo sessions and back for a post event meal with the manufacturer's staff.

Throughout, the bike journalists will, to put things at their kindest, be casually dressed and laid back but equally they will be super knowledgeable. No-one gets invited to a bike launch who is not at the top of their game.

Finally, there might be a launch gift to say thanks for coming. This could be a pen, a notepad, t-shirt - or nothing. You will, however, definitely get the memory stick containing the press packs and the images the photographer took of you in action because the manufacturer needs you to have the pics for the story you are going to write.

As you are leaving that evening, or if you are lucky the following morning, the next lot of journalists will already be occupying your bedroom.

Occasionally, when all the Daily Telegraph staff journalists were busy, and the regular car freelancers couldn't find the time, I would be invited to attend a car launch – and it was like walking into a different world.

The best one for me was an invitation to drive the, then new, Skoda Octavia on a frozen lake in Norway. Now this might seem like a silly, frivolous thing to do but Skoda were frantically re-branding themselves in the 1990s and wanted lively, positive coverage in the mainstream media. None was more mainstream, or more prestigious, than the Daily Telegraph.

The first shock – and for a biking freelancer it really was a big one – was how Skoda intended getting us journos to Norway. I drove down to Stansted and was met by an immaculate young lady who took me across to the Business Aviation area and – surprise, surprise – not some knackered old charter airline with seats designed for gerbils who had been dieting hard, but a gleaming, three engined Dassault Falcon business jet.

There were a couple of other hacks from the national press already there and we weren't kept waiting long – remember, this was pre 9/11 and security was vastly more easy going. Moments later, another Hollywood smile equipped young lady eased us on to the plane. I can't really provide an in depth appraisal of business jets, only ever having flown in two, but if you do happen to win the rollover lottery, I would highly recommend even a second-hand Falcon because it is a seriously lovely way to travel. Equip it with a couple of delightfully attentive cabin staff – "Would Sir care for champagne and canapes now or a little later?" – and you could get me interested in flying again. For sure this beats "Grottair", with your knees around your ears in some new Yoga position, every time.

When we arrived, there was Miss Gleaming Teeth Mk.III waiting for us. I wonder, is there is a special agency just supplying these Vogue replica ladies?

Off we went to our hotel which someone said jokingly – or at least I think they were joking – had once been a Royal Palace. I was escorted to my huge room by, yes, the Mk IV Tooth Fairy. On my bed was a beautifully arranged package of Skoda goodies, the like of which no bike journalist like me had ever seen. It's a good job that we had our own private jet to get home – I did like writing that phrase – otherwise I would have gone bankrupt with the excess baggage charges.

Naturally, the dinner was spectacular – no self-service buffet here - and the ratio of Skoda staff to journalists was awesome.

The following day we played about on a track laid out over a frozen lake, which I thought was great but not exactly challenging work.

In the afternoon, there was the chance for a ride on a dog sled but I was the only journalist who took up the offer. I found it odd that my colleagues from the other nationals seemed quite unimpressed by the efforts Skoda had made but I guess such things are taken for granted when you come to expect, or demand, such high levels of hospitality.

★★★★★

The best job I did for Peter and the Telegraph also involved cars but this time, it was at the basic end of the scale. Peter phoned me and asked did I have any quirky ideas for a Christmas Special story – but it had to be something really different.

There was an ad in the travel section of the Telegraph for flights to Ouarzazate - the Gateway to the Western Sahara - and they were quite expensive. To take a family of three was going to cost £1500. This got me thinking about a satirical article. At the time, the papers were full of those suntanned iron men who were chucked out of the Marines for being too tough, and who struck out across the Sahara in a tricked out Range Rover, living on a diet of dried goats' testicles and green slime harvested from long forgotten, Bedouin wells.

To poke fun at these serious adventurers, we were going to have a Christmas lunch in the Sahara Desert – having driven there in the most basic, bog standard, non-adventure car imaginable.

The further away the car was from a Landrover, with a high-level air intake and sand ladders, the better the story would be.

Elizabeth was ten years old and could, only just, be persuaded not to have Christmas at home playing with her mates but out in the Sahara Desert with Mum and Dad. However, she did impose one condition. From babyhood, she had a favourite teddy bear who rejoiced in the name of "Flat Brian". This wonderful creature had travelled all over Britain, Europe and America, and had very quickly become flat through a mixture of extreme affection and being used as a pillow. If Elizabeth made any trip, then Flat Brian had to be on board too and, as things turned out, he played a vital part in getting us home in one piece.

For the idea to work I needed the help of someone with second-hand cars in stock and I was very fortunate to know Brian Phillips, the owner of TWG Hyundai in Northwich. Brian represents all that is good about humanity. He is a brilliant businessman but is also full of fun, with a manic sense of humour, and a kind streak a mile wide.

TWG Hyundai in Northwich had a V registered 1.3 Accent for sale, right on the button for our budget. The Accent was reviled by journalists for being dull, lifeless and the most evil thing on four wheels. Worse still, this particular vehicle had suffered the depredations of being a loan car - hammered and abused for all of its 29,000 miles. Still, it was a five door model, had a big boot - and TWG agreed to service the car as part of the deal. Basic as the car was, the baby Hyundai was far from being a banger - as we would find out during the next three weeks.

The trip made a cracking piece in the Telegraph and was a lot of fun to write. It met Peter's brief and so everyone was happy. However, it many ways it was what didn't go into the official story which was more interesting.

I had spent over three years in Libya as a teenager and was very happy. There were no religious tensions and Christians, Muslims and Jews all rubbed together, alongside each other, happily. These memories make me particularly sad when I see the present, multiple conflicts. No God wants to see suffering in his, or her, name and if you asked 999 out of 1000 people in those countries where war is now rampant they would tell you that all they want is to be left alone to live in peace. It's the lunatic fringe who want, and need, culling for the good of the rest of humanity.

At the time, the Moroccans we met were the epitome of kindness. Let me give you an example. We stayed right in the centre of the old town in Marrakesh. I wanted to get the full on Moroccan experience so we chose an ancient Riad – a traditional Moroccan town house.

On the way back from the market, the taxi driver couldn't find our Riad so dropped us somewhere in the general area – along with an apologetic smile. We weren't mugged, or threatened or scammed but, instead, a shopkeeper called a mass meeting in the street and teased out the clues to where we staying and then arranged an escort. Try getting that degree of help in a British city!

On another day, the excellent restaurant where we had been eating was closed because it had been booked for an enormous wedding reception. We were told to wait a moment and then the owner came back and said that the Bride and Groom insisted that we eat and had arranged a personal first floor cubicle for us to share their meal. Again, imagine gate crashing a British wedding reception!

There were other cultural differences too. We arrived at a major lorry crash which closed the four lane road entirely – and the Moroccan Emergency Services were in full swing. The truck had been carrying 44 tonnes of tomatoes and these were being cleared up at lightning speed by a posse of locals with wheelbarrows, donkeys and shopping bags. No-one was bothered about the lorry – but those tomatoes really were worth having for families with very little income.

Every day, we learned something new as we pressed on further and further south towards the Sahara. The trip also showed us how thin the veneer of civilisation actually is. We might think of showers, deodorant and central heating as being essential but they are soon relegated if there are more pressing issues.

On Christmas Eve we decided to stay in a Berber Kasbah, on top of a hill and looking south towards the desert. The roof was made of reeds and we could see lots of stars through them, which was very romantic. Less than idyllic was the arctic wind howling through gaps in the walls! The three of us cuddled up together in one bed under a camel hair blanket which, ordinarily, we wouldn't have offered to our sheep as bedding but which kept the wind out. Luxury!

We didn't quite manage Christmas Dinner in the desert, but on the 27th we drove the little Hyundai out into the Western Sahara until we could see no trace of mankind and had a picnic with our Christmas tree and mince pies.

We were 2,400 miles from Cheshire, genuinely in the desert and felt quite proud. Then, a nice Berber gentleman appeared from nowhere on his Peugeot mo-ped to sell us fossils. It wasn't a perfect result but we were well satisfied.

All that remained was to get back home safely. On the way back through the Atlas Mountains, it began to snow – and properly too. We ended up in a hotel in the centre of the mountain range and things looked grim. The hotel manager could not have been more helpful and he told us, politely but bluntly, that we were lucky to be safe and warm because the roads, both behind and in front of us, were now closed. If everything went according to plan, we could expect to be free in five days.

This was bad news. The ferry from Santander to Plymouth was booked for four days hence and I had both to get back to work and to return the little Accent to Brian. This was not good. A five day wait could not happen.

We gently pressed the hotel manager to see if there was any way out of the mess. The interrogation had to be done really sensitively, because we didn't have the precise French vocabulary.

He shrugged his shoulders and said that it might be possible to make it out of the mountains if we drove east and north along a part tarmac and part dirt track which would, eventually, bring us out at the coast.

There were two problems – and major ones too. The first was that if we wandered off the road, we really would get lost. It's frustrating not to find the industrial unit you are looking for on an estate but that degree of lost is a lot different from trying to work out which bit of mountain you are looking at. Being confused in Morocco really can be a bit more than a nuisance.

The second issue was that if everything went perfectly we would end up on the eastern side of the Rif Mountain range. These are much smaller than the Atlas Mountains but they do have some very special challenges of their own because they are one of the world's greatest centres for growing marijuana – or Kif as it is known locally.

We had heard a number of stories about supposedly hip Westerners who had travelled through the Rif on dope buying expeditions, only to get well and truly spanked either by the Moroccan Police as they left the Rif or the Spanish Authorities as they tried to enter Spain. There are areas in the Rif which are tourist friendly but in order to make the ferry back home, we would have to take the direct route right through the Central Rif.

I'm not much of a fan of stereotypical generalisations because they are as often wrong as they are right. One which particularly irritates me is that women can't read maps. In Carol's case, it couldn't be more inaccurate. Not only can she read maps but the lines and squiggles make sense to her in a way which they never do to me. For Carol, bunched lines translate directly into real mountains and scales become actual miles. I can write a story about the journey – but Carol will get you there every time.

So we filled the little Accent to the very brim from the single petrol pump next to the hotel, opened up the utterly invaluable Michelin map of Morocco and set off with big, fat flakes of snow falling from a deep grey and purple sky: there wasn't a lot of conversation...

As things turned out, the drive was easier than we first thought. The dirt parts of the road were well compacted and the tarmac was easy to follow because there was only one road. After four hours, we stopped at the base of some magnificent mountains and ate our emergency rations of pot noodles – not exactly gourmet dining but hot and filling.

That evening, we were welcomed – and the Moroccans really are lovely people – into a small hotel with clean sheets and a toilet which sort of worked: that was good enough for us.

The Michelin map showed a clear route through the mountains which would eventually bring us to Ceuta and the ferry for Spain. I have to smile when I hear the Spanish getting all hot and bothered about the British presence in Gibraltar because they have two, much bigger enclaves which are officially and legally parts of Spain on the Moroccan coast. Pots and kettles spring to mind!

Ceuta is the smaller of the two and is just 18 miles from Spain, across the Straits of Gibraltar. Once we made it to Ceuta we were virtually in England – except for the 700 mile drive to Santander and the ferry home!

Elizabeth is an inveterate gossip and we used to talk for hours in the car, particularly on the way back from race meetings, whilst Carol napped. Equally, she was, and is, also a sensitive girl so she cuddled Flat Brian and looked out of the window in silence whilst I concentrated on driving and Carol chanted out the directions like a rally navigator on a special test. This was not playtime.

Was the journey dangerous? Yes and no – but not for the reasons you might think. Once we got into the mountains, dope was for sale everywhere. If you have driven through Spain or Portugal then roadside fruit vendors will be a familiar sight. Take out the melons and apricots and substitute tables of cannabis resin and that's the Rif. Best of all, if this is the correct adverb, there was a Rif version of a car boot sale. In a large clearing were dozens of vans and cars, all with cannabis laden tables – piles of the stuff!

Every time we slowed down, a smiling Moroccan would leap out with his packet of dope just to make sure that we didn't leave the Rif without a souvenir.

We didn't fancy getting out for a walk round and a coffee but, equally, we didn't feel in any real danger – just out of our comfort zone.

By contrast, the road conditions were full on suicidal. Moroccan driving standards are generally low and often worse than this! Drivers like to make extended eye contact with their passengers and signalling one's intentions is considered a bit of a waste of effort. In the Rif, these traits reached new lows and the last thing I wanted was to ding Brian's Hyundai in the middle of an area which had virtually declared independence from the rest of Morocco.

The danger wasn't big woossie English paranoia either. We passed a line of bodies, respectfully covered up, following an accident where a bus had left the road and plunged down into the ravine below. Injured passengers milled around but, at the time we went by, there was no sign of any emergency services. Clearly, the golden rule was don't crash!

The problem was that miles of the roads were sheet ice and very challenging. For us, this reached a real bottom clenching moment of truth as we came out of the forest and started to drop down from the mountains.

Half a mile ahead I could see a sharp right-hander – obviously free of any safety barriers because this was the Rif - and, in between, the ice was glistening as it began to melt in the midday sun. Racers are good people to have on your side in situations like this because, in moments of real pressure, everything conveniently slows down and there is no panic.

Ahead of me was a couple of hundred metres of hard, wet ice followed by 50m of bone dry road, where the sun had burnt off the moisture, and then another 100m of ice before the corner.

It took a lot of self-discipline not to touch the brakes – no ABS remember – on the first icy section but to simply let the Hyundai just ease down the road in second gear.

The nano-second we reached the dry bit of tarmac, I did the ultimate emergency stop and then immediately released the brakes and let the car coast again.

When we reached the corner, which thank goodness was in the dry, we scrabbled round untidily with the tyres screaming. On Carol's left was a two mile drop to the valley floor below – which was littered with burnt out debris from drivers who had not been quite as lucky as us.

Carol gave my knee a re-assuring squeeze and we both exhaled. This was all the adventure driving we wanted to do!

However, there was one final amusing postscript to the Rif adventure. For the final ten miles, we were pursued and frequently passed – not aggressively but closely – by a big, yellow Mercedes carrying three young men. Every time they went by, the chap in the back waved and held up packets of what was either dope or perhaps liquorice – who knows?

The night before, we had been warned by the Moroccan hotel owner that the police had a rather naughty scam which they worked on silly foreigners. Towards the end of the Rif, a couple of apparently friendly locals would sell the visitor a small amount of dope at a bargain price. Half an hour later, where the Rif finished and mainstream Morocco began, there would be a police road block. The tourist would be stopped, asked if he had any drugs, which he clearly did because the team had just sold them to him. The tourist would then be heavily fined and the drugs confiscated to be re-sold to the next Muppet who thought he was on to a good thing. Greed and naivety are dangerous friends to have as travelling companions in the Rif.

The nearer we got to the end of the Rif, the more insistent became the gentlemen in the Mercedes - so I came up with a game changer. I got Elizabeth to sit up straight in the back of the car and every time they passed us, Flat Brian waved his paw.

Flat Brian was a real show stopper. At first they looked utterly bemused and then smiled and waved back at the majestic bear. What a star!

Fifteen minutes later, we arrived at a full on road block and the Police Officers there were all smiles – and looking forward to waving Brian goodbye.

The drugs saga was not quite over. The rest of the journey down to Ceuta was dull. No drugs. No crashes. No tomatoes blocking the road. Yawn.

We gave the obligatory 5 Euros to the fixer at the gate to the port and he had us into the ferry queue in a flash. Carol found a battered box of Pringles and we munched the time away until the ferry was ready to load.

Three very heavily armed Spanish Policemen, along with an equally tough looking German Shepherd, were making their way down to the line of parked vehicles. There was none of this, "Good morning Sir and Madam. May we have a quick look in your car please?"

The dog simply leapt into the vehicle and started sniffing.

The gentleman three cars behind us saw what was happening, abandoned his car and was away in a flash, leaping the security fence like an Olympic athlete. Perhaps he didn't want to share his liquorice with the dog.

Now, it's time to get back to the main story because In Our Own Words had reached its peak – and I had another idea.

11

Goodbye to All That

THE Moroccan story has put things somewhat out of chronological order so I now need to jump back to In Our Own Words.

My ambitions grew with the Project and I wanted the magazine to have a national distribution. Cheshire Education Authority was willing to let me do this – as long as I didn't ask for any funding. Viewed objectively, I made the wrong decision. I didn't have the staff, the budget or the infrastructure to take the magazine nationally but, of course, if anyone had said that I wouldn't have listened for a single second because I was somewhat more than self-confident. Every other part of making In Our Own Words had been a runaway success, so why not a commercial publication?

The truth is that making the magazine is only a tiny part of being a successful publisher. Just as important is the distribution, striking deals with printers, arranging delivery and the myriad of other vitally important logistical activities which need to happen before you walk into WH Smiths and buy your favourite publication.

Not only did we not have this vital infrastructure, I wasn't much interested in creating it either. I was passionate about seeing the kids choose work, and make wonderful publications which made them smile with pride, and I loved having gifted young people working with us. By contrast, talking to distributors about getting In Our Own Words into newsagents' boxes (the trade term for their daily deliveries) bored me.

The highlight of this period, or maybe the lowlight, was making a pitch to the distributor's sales agents. This took place in one of the large chain hotels, just off the M1 motorway in Derbyshire, and was a truly bizarre experience.

The young man speaking before me produced a series of computer games' magazines. Something like, "Sniper Killer and Death Dealer Enthusiasts Weekly" was the lead title. He had a whole man-bag full of similar magazines too. The presentation had flashing lights and sound and was so slick that I am surprised that there wasn't an explosion at the end, covering everyone with sparkly bits, like you see at the Challenge Cup Final. Everyone cheered and the sales reps were salivating at the thought of their commission on sales.

Then I came on stage, with my single publication, and explained what a wonderful magazine In Our Own Words was, and how much the kids loved making it. I'm not a bad public speaker but on this occasion I prayed for a large hole to open up and a gang of helpful devils to pitch-fork me down into a pit of molten lava, never to be seen again.

I completed my four minutes, received six seconds of dutiful applause and then invited questions: there weren't any.

I felt a bit of a pariah at the buffet lunch. Whilst the spotty youth with the games magazines had the reps hanging on to his every word, I was left in a corner with a cold chicken drum stick and a single sausage on a stick.

Eventually, a bloke about my age ambled across. He was clearly an old hand at this job because he had a glass of white(ish) wine in one hand a pint of beer in the other: the hallmark of a real professional. He smiled and said: "Can I be straight with you?" I encouraged him to be so. "Look, it's like this. We've only got a tiny amount of time to pitch our magazines and we're not going to waste it on one mag when we can get a whole batch in and on to the shelves – it's not going to happen.

"It's a wonderful thing you have done but it's just not commercial. It's a smashing thing though – any chance of some for my kids?"

I gave him half a dozen different copies and with that, he smiled and slid across the nibbles encrusted carpet tiles to the bar.

*****

I suppose that, viewed objectively, the highlight of In Our Own Words must have been the National Launch. This was a wonderful two days and it remains a memorable moment from my career in education.

The Launch also showed how easy it would be to get distracted from reality if you started believing your own PR.

We had two absolutely outstanding 12 year olds working with us on the run up to the launch and the next story illustrates how much trust was given to teachers 20 years ago. At about 2pm, Anne took a phone call: it was from the Frank Bough Show in London.

At the time, this was a major chat show and they wanted me, and some children, on the programme that evening. This was a real manic job because we badly needed the publicity but the only kids whom I could trust on national TV, and were instantly accessible, were the two girls working with us.

It was full on panic stations but we managed to locate one parent of each of the girls and they gave their verbal permission for me to borrow their daughters. As I said, things were very different then.

I phoned the show and said that the job was on but the only way we could make it to London in time was by flying down, on what was then a very regular shuttle service from Manchester Airport to Heathrow. The researcher agreed to pay for everything and I booked the tickets.

Anne got the girls washed and polished but it was fortunate that they were already presentable in their green school uniforms because this was all that they had.

One of the girls had never flown before so she was allowed to travel down in the cockpit, alongside the two pilots, and BA loaded both of them up with goodies to celebrate their stardom. Yes, it was a very different world…

A very smart driver, complete with our name boards, collected us at Heathrow and we were whizzed down to Soho for the show. The studio was tiny, tucked away in one of Soho's media streets, but the kids had really enjoyed their trip in a limo, even if was only a modestly sized one.

The researcher met us at the door, naturally clutching her obligatory comfort blanket clipboard, and we were briefly introduced to Frank Bough, who was then one of the big stars of British TV. He was politely dismissive of all three of us because clearly we were only the supporting act to Ken Clarke, who was Secretary of State for Health at the time.

Mr. Clarke was only marginally more interested in us than Frank Bough but made some polished, political cooing noises to the kids, the sort you hear on the rare occasions when a senior politician has to suffer the indignity of meeting any of the general public. He said that if there was anything he could do to help the Project in the future, to be sure to let him know.

Mr. Clarke later became Secretary of State for Education and, as much for fun as anything else, I did write to him and ask for help. The reply was distantly courteous explaining that things were now very different from when we had been on the Frank Bough Show together. As my very wise solicitor always says, "A verbal contract is not worth the paper it is written on…"

The researcher fussed around and told us when our three minutes of fame would be. I replied that this was all very interesting but how were we going to get home? A wave of the hand followed: "Don't worry about all that – we can sort out the details after the show."

This was not going to happen. I had sufficient experience of TV to know that once guests have appeared, particularly microscopically unimportant ones like us, they have the same value to a show as a freshly used paper tissue has to someone with a heavy cold: zero.

No, neither the kids nor I were appearing on anything until the transport was booked for the return journey – and trains were out of the question at this time of night.

There was an avalanche of sighs, furrowed eyebrows and dark looks but I wasn't budging even when the show's producer made a personal appearance. No transport – no appearance. Through gritted teeth, a car was booked.

We did our three or four minutes and the girls were wonderful – absolutely brilliant. I was so proud of them. Despite being tired, and under intense pressure, they conducted themselves impeccably. I was okay too.

Afterwards, we were invited into the show's Green Room for canapes and wine but the girls didn't like the nibbles and I wasn't going near the wine. Another small limo had appeared but I told the researcher it would have to wait because I was taking the kids for a meal in McDonalds - which was just round the corner. Duly fed and cola-ed, we set off for the 200 mile trip back home.

I got the girls settled on to a back seat each and they were soon asleep, whilst I sat with the driver in the front and chatted. By 2am, we were all back home and I had time for three hours sleep before I prepared for the Launch. It had been an interesting experience.

Everything went wonderfully well. Our office was packed with the great and the good and the two local TV stations came down to film, along with radio and the print media.

We involved kids of every age and set them to work on the next issue of the magazine. Every one of them was breathtakingly good – really perfect.

Lots of nice things were said about the Project by important people and I got some compliments too, which I enjoyed.

The only slightly sour taste was left by a BBC correspondent who complained about the "lack of black faces."

I resented this bitterly. Every student, from every background and of every race, had equal opportunity with In Our Own Words and I would have defended their right to participate with my dying breath. Equally, I wasn't going to exclude any black, white or Asian child just to make the numbers add up in an ethnically correct way. To do so would be just as wrong as any other form of discrimination.

This is the problem with the BBC: it has its own, powerful, political agenda. I don't mean that it overtly supports the Conservatives, Labour, UKIP or even the Socialist Workers Party. In some ways, it would be better if all BBC correspondents wore an appropriately coloured rosette on their clothing so that you could tell that they were paid up members of the Lib Dems, Monster Raving Loony Party or whatever.

The BBC's bias is far more insidious and covert and is all the more dangerous for this. In simple terms, it is determinedly left of centre and all that this means in terms of regulation, advice on how to live our lives and the enthusiastic support of "minorities" of every kind.

Even BBC comedy continues the constant drip, drip, drip of the Nanny State where those who are so much better than us know how much, and what, we should eat and drink - as well as when we ought to go to bed.

There is no room in the BBC agenda for kids like me who left school aged sixteen, worked hard all day and all night, took huge risks and succeeded. We don't fit into a convenient box and so are of no interest. How many BBC correspondents, or better still managers, have ever been employed anywhere except in the media, show business or PR? You can probably count the total number on one hand.

This left of centre group also has militantly "champagne socialist" interests. Yes, there's ample coverage of the tennis at Wimbledon, the Open Golf and athletics, but precisely how much time does the BBC give to motorsport of any kind – car or bike? At the time of writing this book I can give you the precise number of hours and minutes, which is zero. In the BBC's eyes, anyone who is passionate about MotoGP, F1 car racing or any other motorsport is a member of a sub-species of humanity – and certainly not worthy of being included in the BBC club.

Except for the tax imposed on us all in the form of the licence fee, none of this would matter. If the BBC was "pay to view", or depended on advertising for its revenue, it would be bankrupt in a year because no-one would give money to such a biased, narrowly focussed broadcaster. However, we do have to pay the tax and still the BBC continually fails to represent the whole of British society – concentrating instead upon that sliver which complies with its own political agenda.

When the BBC bloke had cleared off, I calmed down and got on with the job of tidying up and the final part of what had been a wonderful day. One of our patrons was the Labour MP for Crewe, Gwyneth Dunwoody. She was described by the Times Newspaper as: "Intelligent, obstinate, opinionated and hard-working." I got on really well with her and we had some good fun together. She was a strong supporter of In Our Own Words.

When she came to the Launch, she didn't have a car. I seem to remember that Gwyneth didn't drive or maybe she just didn't bring her car that day. Regardless, she needed a lift to appear on the BBC's "Any Questions" show which was being broadcast from Leek, in Staffordshire, that day.

At the mention of driving Gwyneth 40 miles into the Peak District, all the VIPs suddenly became very busy so I smiled and volunteered. Gwyneth was only tiny, in height, but was not exactly size zero so it was a bit of a job to lift her up into the Isuzu 4x4 I was driving at the time. Regardless, I prised her into the passenger seat and set off.

Following the Frank Bough Show, the long drive home and then the launch, I was absolutely on my last legs and was running pretty well just on strong, sugar loaded coffee and Hedex. Still, Gwyneth chatted away very pleasantly and, after battling with the M6 rush hour traffic, we eventually arrived in Leek.

The BBC researcher was waiting for Mrs. Dunwoody, complete with a solicitous smile. I got the briefest of thanks, the door was slammed and that was me done. I was hungry, thirsty and achingly tired but I was also the driver, not the talent, and therefore of no interest to anyone further up the food chain.

It was a valuable reminder of what I already knew: never, ever start believing your own press releases.

*****

I have talked about the planets aligning, the fates weaving a different pattern into my life's thread and all that good, mystical stuff. The planets lined up again and it was time for a change.

The national politicians in Westminster decided that Cheshire was too big, and probably too powerful, to exist as one huge Authority. It was a vast area but the county was well, and efficiently, run. It was also free thinking. The chances of anyone from Cheshire Education Authority ever reading these words are nano particle small but, if you ever do, thanks for allowing me to lead In Our Own Words and Inside Stories. They were good projects and we can all be proud of what we did and achieved.

So, the big planetary shift was that Cheshire was going to be broken up into four Local Authorities. Warrington and Halton (the artificial construct made from Widnes and Runcorn) would be taken out of Cheshire and the rump of the old county would remain.

This effectively reduced the pool of participating schools by a third.

My nominal manager at the time was Walter Done, the Assistant Director of Education for Cheshire. Walter was a smart, switched on and politically aware administrator who was very supportive of our work. I sent in a one page report every six months, telling him what I had done and what I intended doing in the future, and he protected my back and let me get on with the job.

Walter was retiring when Cheshire was disbanded and the new, smaller Cheshire County had no interest me or In Our Own Words.

Anne was growing up by the day and was, rightly, getting itchy feet. I had taught her a lot since she first joined me and my efforts had been re-paid with energy, enthusiasm, boundless commitment – and the ability to smile whilst working with psychopathic killers. No manager could ever ask for more.

Equally my lovely colleague was changing. No longer the giggly new graduate, Anne was maturing by the second and showing every indication of being a high quality, future manager – which she has now become.

She needed a new environment, with different organisational protocols to master and new challenges to meet and overcome.

I also thought that it was important that she went to a large, formally structured employer where she would learn big company skills. Our projects were fast thinking, ultra-flexible and very much small business in style and ethos. After all, what else would you expect a freelancer to produce? Now, I wanted something more for Anne so I encouraged her to go job hunting.

Everything worked out really well and I was delighted when she got a job in the Press Office of one of largest Police Forces in Britain.

*****

Before Anne left, we had one last go at keeping the Project alive and this involved a visit from an educational consultant. The conversation we had with her was the final grain of sand in making me decide to leave In Our Own Words and Inside Stories. It's a very sad story, but one which has to be told.

Our office was located in a secondary school belonging to what was about to become the new Halton Local Authority. We had a palatial base, fully equipped and paid for entirely by sponsors. It included a state of the art computer suite – probably the best in any educational establishment anywhere in the country – an admin area; design suite; small lecture theatre and even our own kitchen and toilets. It really was a top flight facility, not only for making magazines but for a wide range of other educational, or commercial, uses.

It was also debt free and every single item in it was owned by the Project.

We operated completely independently of the school, but if the Project was moved into Halton, then the new Authority would own this superb infrastructure.

Anne and I trolled off to the Council Offices in Runcorn and made a decent enough sales pitch to the Members. They all made the correct politicians' noises – it's fascinating that these are virtually identical in every democracy in the world, almost like crickets chirping – and it was decided that a Consultant would be hired to assess the Project's potential and a report prepared. When this report arrived – and it had a £5k invoice written all over it – the Members would make a decision regarding our fate.

The Consultant duly arrived and, to be fair, she was pleasant enough and had come with the aim of writing something supportive. Unfortunately, there was a clash of personalities – not exactly a first for me!

The major problem was that she knew nothing about the philosophies which were the driving force of the Project and didn't understand my quasi-religious belief in the democratisation of literature. She smiled politely and explained, as you would to a keen but not too bright Work Experience student, that if you really did give control of the magazine to children, anything could happen. Things could "get-out-of-control!"

I beamed at the very thought of things getting out of control because this would mean that the kids were coming up with new ideas and practices that we – the teachers – hadn't thought of. How good was that?

The Consultant lady looked pointedly at her faux leather bound notebook and made notes with asterisks next to them, using the sort of grown-ups words which go into reports to prove a point. "Mr. Melling said that he wanted the children to be out of control..."

She explained that in order for Halton to support In Our Own Words, there had to be fair representation for all children. I was excited again. Yes, this is what I believed in so passionately. Kids of all ages and backgrounds coming together to choose their own work for their own magazine: the true democratisation of literature. What could be better?

The fountain pen left its trail of destruction once more. "Mr. Melling was not willing to take responsibility for the magazine he managed but instead was prepared for the children to behave in an unstructured and unmonitored way."

Whether she was under some pressure from Councillors, I don't know, but to her credit she persevered.

The true democratisation of literature meant that each school would have a numerical allocation of work which would appear, by right, in the magazine. Children aged 5-7 would have "x" amount of space; 7-11s another block; secondary a further tranche and then the Sixth Form and FE colleges, if they wanted to take part, the final allocation.

Within each age range, the space would be divvyed out to individual schools who were then supposed to sub-divide it into male and female pupils whilst ensuring that every minority interest was represented.

It was an abrogation of everything I believed in and took the magazine back to the worst form of tokenism. Yes, we would say to the kids, you have can full control of your magazine – but only in a way which adults approve. The idea made me physically sick and I wanted nothing to do with it.

Anne smiled the Consultant out of the meeting room and then made me a cup of coffee. She was good in situations like this. We both knew that the job was dead.

Things were made easier by one, more long term, issue. Anne, Marion and the Area Co-Ordinators had all become very good at running the project. Anne could do 90% of my work, Marion was a brilliant Office Manager and the six teachers who worked for me were outstanding in their own jobs.

Everyone knew what to do, how to do it and most of the schools co-operated too. It is wrong, very wrong, to say that things had become easy but they were becoming more predictable by the day.

The Project was now solid, well-managed, with excellent facilities and staff. Gone were the days when the whole of the Project's assets fitted on to the back seat of my car and Bess and I sat up all night making magazines on my front room carpet.

There were no late nights at the Messenger being called a f***wit and having bread rolls thrown at me for being stupid – no giggly excitement at being the first teacher in Britain to use a new piece of software which came in a plain white box with a squiggly note scrawled across it in felt tip pen.

In Our Own Words was now mature and, if it continued, it needed a solid, mainstream, report writing, committee focussed, canape eating manager to control it. I wasn't a grown up and I lacked adult management skills and so was the wrong person, in the wrong place, at the wrong time.

I was also becoming bored and itchy and, ironically, full of self-doubt. I had done wonderful things with In Our Own Words, and Inside Stories, but there was also always a safety net, albeit a fragile one, if things really went nuclear holocaust wrong.

Yes, I would be the laughing stock of the teaching profession – the man who was all big mouth, fur coat and no knickers – but I would still have had a job. Things didn't go wrong and, whatever anyone said about me behind my back, they were never laughing – but this wasn't enough for me.

Now, I wanted to walk across the high wire completely solo and with no safety net of any kind. I wanted the chasm to be lethally deep if I fell into it, and I needed the raging waters to be full of crocodiles, fire breathing dragons and tiger sharks (it was a saltwater river because I do like my fantasies to be technically accurate) and for my broken body to be torn apart and never seen again.

I wanted, needed in fact, to lay absolutely everything on the line with no "Plan B". There would be just one box to tick: failure or success. Done like this, I would really know if I was any good or nothing more than a freelance journalist who could tell other people how to do things. Mirror, mirror on the wall etc…

*****

Before I could do anything new I still had a legal, and moral, duty to In Our Own Words, the kids of Cheshire and the Authority which was paying my salary! I have said many positive things about Anne, and she deserves all the praise I have given to her, but I am conscious that Marion has been somewhat pushed into the background and this is unfair.

Marion was about my age and the best way of describing her, and our relationship, was that if I was on a sinking ship, or in a building collapsing in an earthquake, I would want Marion alongside me. Forget the Emergency Services, the SAS in balaclavas or anyone else – Marion would be the one who was the calmest, most organised and all the time with a lovely smile.

She wasn't as creative as Anne or me, but she was an unbelievably thorough and thoughtful organiser who not only fixed any problems which arose but made sure that the vast majority never happened in the first place.

She was also highly honourable and fair, and I admire both of these traits tremendously. Anne had already left and Marion knew that the Project was closing in a few months' time. A lesser person might have abused the generous sick leave provisions Cheshire offered and been constantly absent – and I knew plenty of people who had actually done this.

A lot more might have been delayed coming into work or found reasons to leave early: Marion did neither.

Finally, many of those employees who didn't abuse the system would not have worked with total commitment: Marion did.

Every morning, she was at her desk smiling and we both decided that the last magazines we made would be as good as anything the Project had ever produced. We both slaved over the publications and, in some ways, tried even harder to produce work of which we were really proud.

Not only did Marion behave with dignity and professionalism but she was good fun too. I was facing a lot of pressures, from many directions, and Marion's smiles and kindness meant a lot to me: no manager could ask for more or better.

On our final day we walked out of the office with our heads held high, knowing that no corner had been cut and no effort spared to do the best we could for the kids and the Authority.

Cheshire was equally kind and I got a very fair settlement for agreeing not to work for them again. If I had walked straight into another job, the payment would have bought a nice new race bike and an exotic holiday but for what I had in mind, it was paper clip money.

When Anne left, she had bought the most thoughtful leaving gift imaginable for me. It was a Saxon warrior, cast in resin, peering out over his shield with his sword raised high. That's how I felt at the time. Watchful, defensive and ready for battle.

Now, I was going to find out if I really was any good – or merely good at writing about how to be a success. The last few months had been like the click, click, click of climbing up the slope of the world's biggest roller coaster. Now I was looking down – and I just hoped that the ride didn't finish in a big hole!

12

You Must be Mad!

As we finally realised that In Our Own Words was going to finish, I began to form an idea - albeit a very nascent one – and it was a sibling of the democratisation of literature. Motorcycle sport was watched almost entirely by enthusiasts – spectators who were either riders themselves or who were actively involved in the motorcycling scene. My idea was to make a motorcycle event which would attract not only bikers but everyone else too.

I didn't say anything to anyone – not even to Carol – but just began doodling ideas on a bit of paper and in my head which, in my case, is almost the same thing!

The first job was to find a form of motorcycling which had universal appeal. During the summer, when we knew for 100% certain that In Our Own Words was going to come to an end, Carol and I looked at a lot of motorcycling events - but this time with deadly objectivity and not at all for fun!

I designed a hypothetical spectator – or, more accurately, a family of them – and they came everywhere with us. However, this was far too serious a matter to be some sort of light-hearted fantasy!

The imaginary couple were both 35 years old. He worked as an Assistant Manager in a Garden Centre and she was a Supervisor in a Supermarket. They had two kids – a boy and a girl. The boy was eight and the girl was ten years old. They had a family car.

They did things together, as a family, on Sundays but had limited budget. When they did visit places, they would spend money on food and maybe things for the kids to do.

The family were not anti-bike but they were not part of the motorcycling community either. None of them had the slightest idea about any form of motorcycle sport. If they came to an event, they would bring no knowledge of what was happening. Everything would have to be instantly comprehensible without knowing a single rider's name, the bike they were using or even the type of motorcycle sport which was taking place.

The Mum I created had a low boredom threshold, as did the kids. She also didn't like getting muddy or dusty, although she wasn't hyper-protective of the kids.

She, her husband and her two children – both the boy and the girl - were our target customers. In Socio-economic terms, they were C1: lower middle class, employed in supervisory or clerical and junior managerial positions. There were a lot of potential customers in this group and market research suggested they usually went out on a Sunday and did things as a family.

The C2 sector – skilled manual workers – were also highly desirable but this group were often already in, or on the periphery of, the motorcycling world and so they were, in some ways, easier to reach - as were the unskilled and semi-skilled workers included in Class D.

If all of this sounds very clinical and forensic, then it was. I was going to make an immense, and potentially life changing, request of Carol and I could not do this without showing her that I was giving the new project 101% commitment.

Using the criteria derived from my hypothetical "Mainstream Family" (MF), motorcycle sport is surprisingly inaccessible and lacking in universal appeal. We went through the options:

Road racing: Clean; good parking; looks great; exciting to watch but the MF had to stay rooted to the spot for a long time to see one race and understand it – and this was unlikely to happen. Spectators were also a long way from the action.

Motocross: Exciting. Big jumps. Visually dramatic but incredibly hard to understand once riders were lapped. Basic car parking and toilet facilities. Often dusty and muddy. No proper grandstands.

Trials: Spectacular riding but no fixed viewing spots, and the observed sections often needed walking to get to them. Mrs MF and the kids weren't likely to tolerate this.

Grass Track: Wow! Spectacular action with bikes broad-side in the corners, generating huge plumes of grass and clouds of dust. Great for hard core fans but no chance whatsoever of bringing the MF in to watch.

Sprints: Straight line or twisty races with one bike on the track at any given time. Very easy to understand and undemanding in terms of commitment. A whole class ran from beginning to end in maybe ten minutes or so. If MF could be persuaded to stand still for this short length of time, they could watch a complete race from start to finish and know who won. In short, it was something which could be made comprehensible to the least knowledgeable spectator in the world.

At the time, sprints usually attracted miniscule crowds. There were many reasons for this. The facilities were usually basic – holes in the ground, hidden behind bits of sacking, for toilets were not going to be acceptable to Mrs MF in particular – and there was no attempt to make the product attractive to all but the most hard core enthusiast.

Commentators were well intended but where was the excitement, the buzz, the show business flair? Where were the kids' rides, and the craft shops for Mrs MF? For certain, they weren't at a sprint. In short, a sprint wasn't a memorable day out.

I sat down and began to doodle again. What about a sprint where the racing was at the core of a great day out but around the periphery there was a whole day of family entertainment?

The truth, the absolute truth, is that at this time I lived in two worlds. My body, and a small part of my brain, was husband, father, Project Director and all the things which I needed to be. However, the majority of me was elsewhere concentrating on the new idea. I thought about the event whilst I was brushing my teeth, driving to work, during conversations with the rest of the world and whilst I was writing letters. It's wrong to say that I was obsessed with the idea of a making a motorcycle event for my MF, because I carried on the rest of my life in a more or less satisfactory way. However, I did take the job very seriously because I had big ideas for the, as yet unborn, concept.

It was one of the most exciting times of my life and I look back on it with intense pleasure even now. The best thing was that I had a completely blank sheet of paper in front of me, quite literally, as well as in my head. It was up to me to decide what went on that paper, with no control or restraint - other than such trivia as no money or staff!

Organising a safe motorcycle race for riders and spectators was not the issue – or even my interest. I had run dozens of events for dirt bikes and had officiated at plenty more. I knew all about normal event organisation.

The challenge was to build a strong brand from the outset – quite literally from day one. I dare not even share with Carol what was really on my mind for fear of her throwing her hands up in despair and leaving me, or maybe even getting me sectioned under the Mental Health Act!

A major road race attracted around 25,000 spectators and a motocross Grand Prix about the same number. I held the figure of 25,000 as the absolute peak of the motorcycle sport mountain with only road racing GPs at the some of the great, international motorcycle circuits doing any better. So, my sprint would have 25,000 spectators.

That was the dream. The reality was different. A typical sprint attracted 50 spectators – a good one, a couple of hundred. These figures were ever so slightly under the 25,000 of which I dreamed!

Why then, did I think 25,000 could be achieved? The answer was simple. Whilst I was full of flaws in terms of running an organisation conventionally, I did have a brilliant track record as a start-up entrepreneur.

At 18 years of age, I got myself hired as a freelance journalist with no training, no experience and not even a single published article. In three years, I had become so influential that the mighty BSA Company sponsored me.

Then I had sold 5,400 Griffin helmets from a two-bedroomed bungalow – and made a lot of money as a result.

Finally, with no funding, staff, support or experience I had developed the biggest children's publishing project in the world.

Not only did iconoclastic ideas not frighten or concern me, they were the very reason for living. The bigger the challenge, and the greater the risk of failure, the more fun I had. Now, with the as yet unnamed event, the difficulties were immense – but the opportunities were limitless.

There was one more advantage with the way I worked and it's worth trying to explain it in a little more detail. All the way back to when I got my first job as a paid writer, my ideas have been so far removed from what everyone else thought was possible, or even reasonable, that the normal reaction was either to laugh at them for being silly, ridicule what I had to say or just walk away because the concept was incomprehensible.

This is hugely helpful, because at the start of one my big ideas no-one really knows what is on my mind and I can achieve many things without interference – simply and quickly. It's a lonely way to work but perfect for me.

So it was with the sprint. Only tiny bits of the big idea could be seen by everyone else and, like an enormous cognitive ice-berg, this gave me time to develop the other 90% of my plans below the water line and out of sight.

The first job is by far the hardest – and it's not the obvious challenges such as finance, venue, staff or vital logistics which create the real difficulties. With any problem, I always work back to front starting with where I want to finish. From knowing very clearly what the finished product will be, I can then work backwards to the start and devise the solutions which will take me to the end. It's the complete antithesis of organisations where following the correct procedures is more important than the end result. I am really relaxed – not disinterested, but flexible – regarding how something is achieved. For me, the final result is the only consideration.

I also see things, very clearly, in moving pictures – not quite a full HD video but still with sound and, of course, smells and tastes. After all, any decent fantasy picture needs the full, all-round sensations package to be any good!

I found quiet places to sit with Bess, half-closed my eyes and looked at the pictures floating in front of me. I looked at the faces of the gate staff as they checked riders' passes. I watched the technical inspection of the competitors' motorcycles and listened to how they were treated by officials. I heard the commentator and studied the spectators' faces as they heard what he had to say. I floated above the chip vans and the floors of the toilets. All these things I could see in extremely clear detail – and without ever having to go near a computer simulation. Every minute detail was important and I had to see, hear, taste and smell it all.

What I couldn't see was where this was going to happen because I didn't have a venue!

The most pressing issue was not the logistics behind the meeting but building the brand. Successful companies spend a fortune working on what are called brand properties. These are the things associated with a particular brand, or even an individual product. Certain symbols, whether they are colours, images or sounds, bring to mind specific companies or products. Think of Apple, BMW or Harley-Davidson and you will get the idea immediately.

I had a huge mountain to climb and, at the same time, an infinite amount of opportunity. The mountain was a triple peak. First, the new product had no history – nothing to support it. Customers would have to be taught about the brand properties of the event by experience.

Second, I had almost no budget. You may remember the Skoda story, where we were all flown to Norway so that we could mess about on a frozen lake and share the excitement with readers. This was a good example of a company trying to re-position its brand.

All this was a very long way from the old Skoda jokes: "Why do Skodas have heated rear windows? So your hands stay warm when you are pushing the car…"

With the Norway story, Skoda was looking for journalists to use motivational words like exciting, dramatic, fashionable, tough, dangerous, and so on. This was great but cost a ton of money – and, by comparison, I had almost no budget.

Finally, the responsibility for all of the marketing and brand positioning was going to fall directly on to me. Win or lose, there would be no-one else to blame. Not that these were even the biggest challenges I faced. Where we were going to hold the event and who was going to work alongside me, were by far the greatest.

*****

Hoghton Tower is a 16th century house which stands on a steep, wooded hill overlooking the village of Hoghton, near Blackburn in Lancashire. It is owned by the de Hoghton family and to say that they are well established is something of an understatement. You know that you are talking to seriously heavy duty aristocracy when you realise that the family changed its name to de Hoghton in 1150 - at about the same time as my ancestors were digging the muck out of some Lord's stable and hoping that they wouldn't get horse whipped for raising a head as the Lady of the Manor rode past.

However, these stately homes are mixed blessings. For a start, they are not cheap to maintain. Nice to look at, most definitely, but you wouldn't want to mow the lawns! This meant that Sir Bernard de Hoghton, the 14th Baronet, was always on the hunt for funds to maintain the Hall.

Sir Bernard faced another problem. With such an illustrious family history he had to do something of note, and preserving Hoghton Tower was a key driving force in his ambitions.

Ironically, in this respect, I had a huge advantage. If I only staggered home drunk and smacked my wife about every other day then I would have been doing twice as well as my Dad. From this base line, it was difficult not to do better!

125

By contrast, Sir Bernard was carrying the weight of 900 years of tradition on his shoulders - and I felt for him.

One of the income streams for Hoghton Tower was a 220 yard sprint, run up the main access road to the hall. In truth, it wasn't much of an event except for the setting. Hoghton Tower is located on top of a hill and, on the right day, the view over the surrounding countryside is spectacular. It was also a very special experience to race up the same bit of road which had seen so much history.

There was some infrastructure already in place in terms of toilets and food sales, and this was going to be hugely helpful in terms of selling the event to non-motorcycling customers.

Finally, and of almost critical importance to me, I could piggy back our new event on to the existing Hoghton Tower brand which already had something of a public profile.

I had ridden at Hoghton Tower in the past and, although I am sure that he didn't know it, I had come into contact with Sir Bernard at prize giving. I think I may have even won the 500cc class at the Sprint but I'm not sure. For certain, I had shaken hands with what was unmistakably an English aristocrat and found him incredibly polite, albeit in the patrician way in which those who have been rich and important for a long time interact with those who haven't!

I often write about planets lining up and fates looking down favourably and so they did at this time. The organisation which had been running the sprint at Hoghton Tower no longer wanted to promote the event and so, when I phoned the Hall, Sir Bernard told me that he was without a sprint for 1998.

Sir Bernard took my call at the first time of asking and I immediately liked him. He was straightforward, courteously direct and very keen to do business. Clearly, Hoghton Tower would get the better end of any deal but he wasn't averse to us covering our costs and making a few pounds as well.

Carol and I agreed to meet Sir Bernard and Lady Rosanna at Hoghton Tower, to decide on the way forward - or not. My Mum looked after Elizabeth and we put Bess in the back of the car for moral support.

I knew that I had to get this job right the first time. Sir Bernard was switched on. He knew exactly how many beans made five and so I had to be professional. The first advantage I had was a name for the new event. You might well be surprised how tightly names are controlled even down to some very common expressions. "Lamb Stew" might simply be a description of something good to eat but, before you could use the name for a product, an IP (Intellectual Property) lawyer would have to check that the name wasn't already being used by someone else for their business.

Almost every single decent name or description associated with motorcycle racing had long since been boxed off and, although this initially drove me to despair, it was actually a tremendous benefit.

When I am in a corner, I first try to analyse whether the job is actually difficult or if I am just being lazy. Choosing a title for the event was a good example of this. The lazy side of me would have preferred just to use the first name which came to mind and avoid the effort of being creative. However, this was just idleness on my part because the actual job of finding a name was only a creative challenge. I didn't have to buy new equipment, pay for an advertisement or do anything other than to sit down with a notepad and pen and play with words. Not only was this not hard but the job was fun: what's not to like?

I was looking for an onomatopoeic name – something which carried ideas with its sound and feel as much as with its meaning. For the reasons I have mentioned, I also wanted to use the established name of Hoghton Tower to leverage my event.

To make the story more dramatic, I should say I toiled for weeks to arrive at the title but that would not be true. I seem to remember that it took two or three half-hearted attempts and then "Thunder at the Tower" arrived.

The "Thunder" element of the name carried with it a sense of drama and action, ideal for pitching to the MF customers as well as bikers. "Tower" traded off Hoghton Tower. I avoided using "Hoghton" for the very good reason that a lot of people can't pronounce the name! Correctly, it is pronounced Horton – but very often I have heard Hogton, Hodgeton and even Hog Horton. By contrast, everyone could manage Thunder!

The meeting with Sir Bernard and Lady Rosanna was fuss free. I had prepared a meticulous event plan with a lot of emphasis on the marketing. This was well received and a deal was struck. It was more generous to Sir Bernard and Lady Rosanna than I wanted but I was pragmatic about this. Sir Bernard had a venue and I didn't. Hoghton Tower had an established name and I had nothing but a dream and a sheaf of ideas written on paper. Viewed objectively, Hoghton Tower not only held almost all the cards but also the table, chairs and refreshments for the game!

For this reason, I remain grateful to Sir Bernard and Lady Rosanna for giving me the chance to run Thunder at the Tower – even if they made sure that they were going to be on the winning side financially.

Sir Bernard also gave me an unexpected gift – and of spectacular value. He arranged a second, follow-up meeting, and said that he would ask one of the people involved with the previous sprint to come along. This was Tony Jones, who proved to be an angel – with a thick Lancashire accent and a heart of gold. Without Tony, making the first event work would have been vastly more difficult.

Once it became known that a professional event organiser was going to be running an event at Hoghton Tower and, heaven forbid, making money – although the chance of that happening looked pretty remote at the time – there was a lot of back biting and petty bitchiness, spiced up with some real sprinklings of nastiness too.

Very often, this amused me. Sometimes I was irritated and, very occasionally, I was actually hurt but whatever was said or done it had no, as in zero, effect on whether Thunder at the Tower was going to happen or not. The event was going ahead and it would be a success – or I would die in the attempt. Nothing which was said behind my back, or to my face, was going to change my plans by one nano particle so all those who tried to cause trouble would have been better served directing their energies to something where there was a chance of success because, for sure, I wasn't going to change course.

Slowly, the momentum built and the brand strengthened – and nothing could stop it.

So far I had a brand, an event and a venue but the practicalities of running the event were now starting to take centre stage. The first problem was a lack of finance. In simple terms we didn't have sufficient money to build the brand to a good standard.

The only solution was to put our house on the line. In fact, to re-mortgage our lovely cottage to the hilt – and then some! Not many people knew how big a chance we were taking and those who did had only one reaction: "You must be mad!"

Why did I want to do this and why, even more importantly, did Carol back me? The answer is simple. We were prepared to commit everything to make the event work, even if that meant losing our house. If Thunder at the Tower failed we had to know, in our innermost souls, there was nothing more that we could have given.

Financial investors always seek what they call "Hurt Money" when they fund a new venture. They want to know that the people receiving their backing will suffer if it fails. In our case, Carol got as far as pricing terraced house, rental properties in Runcorn, just in case the bank and building society re-possessed our house. Now that would really hurt!

Even with this capital, the only way that we could promote the event was by paying ourselves no wages and just scraping by on "Quick Sale" and "Own Brand" food from every supermarket which had an offer. Elizabeth would not know that any of this was happening but it was going to be ten months of the leanest of lean rations in every other aspect of our lives.

The final piece of the jigsaw was who would help me to run the event. In some ways, this was the greatest challenge of all.

*****

I had continued to race in hill climbs and sprints, and the occasional road race too. Road racing was only a minor shift from riding in off-road events, so the change was easy. My ability remained the same as every other form of motorcycle sport in which I had competed. I could ride at the level of a good clubman and therefore never got in the way of the really quick riders – but nor did I give them nightmares about the new super-fast kid on the grid.

I was also enjoying the festivals and their laid back approach to imitation racing and, as my French improved, I was getting to like Continental meetings ever more.

When Carol and I were boyfriend and girlfriend, we had visited France and nearly, but not quite, managed to see the Lascaux Cave Paintings. These are magnificent, pre-historic cave paintings in south western France which were created 20,000 years ago.

The originals are, quite rightly, heavily protected now but the French Ministry of Culture and Communication has created a breathtakingly accurate replica of the art near to the village of Montignac, where the first paintings were discovered.

The murals are both realistic depictions of animals and people, and abstract representations of religious beliefs. Even in our modern world, looking at them is an immensely spiritual and moving experience. They were very much something we both wanted to see.

There was a Classic Festival at Lurcy Levis, only 200 miles north east of Montignac, so the idea was that we would ride there, write an article about the festival and then go on to Montignac.

The event turned out to be very interesting – but in a rather macabre way. I was in the collecting box, waiting for my class to go out on track, when I saw a sidecar passenger berating his driver who had stopped the outfit just in front of me. Seeing passengers get all tense and hormonal with drivers was completely normal but this one was getting really irate and shouty because the driver was taking absolutely no notice of him. In fact, he was simply slumped over the handlebars, ignoring every word which was being screamed at him. There was a good reason for the driver's insouciance: he was dead.

The poor man had suffered a gigantic heart attack, or something, and had died just before the corner. With a self-closing throttle, the sidecar had come to a halt of its own accord. Fortunately, the circuit at Lurcy Levis is immensely wide and so everything had worked out well for the passenger. This was a spot of serious, world class luck for him because I could think of plenty of places where, as a passenger, you wouldn't trust a sidecar to come to a safe stop of its own accord.

I hope that the passenger was suitably embarrassed at berating his dead driver but, from what I know of sidecar crews, he probably wasn't. Death isn't considered to be a valid reason for not finishing a race in the sidecar world!

The rest of the meeting was uneventful and a lot of fun. We entertained French children at our trailer and Elizabeth played with her new friends. Classic race paddocks are wonderful places to grow up – safe, fun and a brilliant way to learn about other cultures and languages.

We all had a great time at Lurcy Levis but Carol and I were both somewhat subdued because we knew that there were big changes on the horizon. Everything was forgotten for our visit to the cave paintings but eventually, when Elizabeth was fast asleep in the back of the car, I pulled up by the bank of the River Vézère and switched off the engine.

In other circumstances, it would have been very beautiful and we would have sat in silence to become part of the environment. To our right, the Vézère wound its way through the heavily wooded countryside towards the Dordogne. The river was purposeful but quiet and peaceful, and had a sense of timelessness. The artists of Lascaux could have well looked at the same river, following a similar path, 20,000 years ago.

On the left, the hills and fields climbed steeply to the same limestone crags from which prehistoric hunters had stared out, searching for prey.

Normally, Carol and I would have held hands and thanked creation for being in such a wonderful place in the flow of time: but, for once, we didn't.

I explained my big idea to Carol as she listened in silence – neither criticising nor showing any sign of enthusiasm. At the epi-centre of her silence was that I was suffering from what is called "I disease" in racing circles, when it is usually applied to star riders.

"I want a better handling bike and I want a faster engine so I can win races and I can stand on the top step of the podium and I can be paid more money…" and so on. You can see why the syndrome is called "I disease".

I wanted to walk across the tightrope so I could find out how good I was, and so that I could show the rest of the world what a clever boy I could be…

Like everyone chasing big dreams I was becoming intensely, and narcissistically, focused on me. In my defence – and it's the only defence – this single-mindedness does lead to results. Don't ever play a game, any game, with a World Champion because they will either beat you or go off in a giant sulk and never speak to you ever again. Truly, second is first in the losers' race.

Now, I not only wanted to risk every penny we had by betting on an idea which was, at the kindest, highly speculative and extremely likely to fail. But no, even that was not enough: I wanted Carol to give up everything to join me.

I know that all husbands are proud of their wives but Carol really was a superb teacher. In all objectivity, I have never seen a better Primary School teacher. She was worshipped by the kids she taught and respected and liked by her colleagues. She taught in a perfect school, with a superb Head Teacher and lovely kids. In fact, things couldn't have been better.

Carol was also prepared to back me putting my dreams into reality. The only thing that she asked was to be allowed to continue in the life she had.

She also knew that Marion would have worked for and with me - and done so with enthusiasm. So why not employ Marion and let her carry on with her perfect professional life too?

The practical reasons were straightforward. I had done the figures and the truth was that we could not afford to run one single event: we just didn't have the money. If I added Marion's salary to the budget, even if she was kind to me, there would be no Thunder at the Tower. It wasn't a matter of debate or checking figures – there just wasn't the money.

Carol's sad face broke my heart. She didn't cry in terms of sobbing hysterically but her eyes were stoically wet and, in many ways, this was far worse. We sat next to each other in the car – but each on the other side of a vast chasm. It was a very sad time because I was distant from the woman for whom I would willingly lay down my life.

We are a very tactile couple but this time, there was no re-assuring squeeze or hand on my knee – simply an acceptance of what I had asked.

For my part, I didn't feel that I had won anything or even succeeded. What I had was a temporary stay of execution. In truth, Carol could have killed the idea stone dead there and then, but she chose not to. The concept was still on Death Row but the firing squad was going to have a coffee break for a few months.

A secondary issue was that Carol's stoicism cranked up the pressure on me immensely. It was bad enough betting our house and financial future on an idea which everyone else thought was doomed. Now, my wife was about to give up the career she loved to stand by me.

Moments like this are rare. So often, I hear people – particularly of my age – say that if only they had taken this chance or been given that opportunity then they would have achieved so much more. This was the time to find out what was in me – intellectually, physically and emotionally. For better, or maybe worse, I had a partner who loved me so much that she was prepared to trust me in making the venture work. Pressure? Yes, but there was also a joy which was almost metaphysical in its purity.

We drove back into Montignac to find a street vendor or café selling frites because eating in restaurants was now well and truly a thing of the past. Carol was very quiet. I showed Elizabeth how to dip her chips into the mayonnaise and taught her the word frites. Then, I wiped her sticky face and held her above the parapet so that she could see the ducks swimming in the river below. I was as completely and utterly certain that I would not, could not, drop her as I was that, with Carol alongside me, I would make the Thunder at the Tower work.

*****

I had one more enormous stroke of luck. After Lurcy Levis we went to another classic bike festival but this time in England. There we met Malc Wheeler,

Editor of "The Old Bike Mart" magazine. OBM, as it is universally known, is in some ways an odd magazine. It is printed on newsprint, like a local newspaper rather than glossy magazine stock, and has a very eclectic, almost odd, mixture of articles. Instead of discussing the minutiae of restoring some piece of motorcycling exotica, OBM was, and is, more interested in reaching out to the mainstream classic motorcyclist. In fact, riders just like me.

OBM readers also do things, and this is reflected in the editorial content of the magazine because it seems that every event in the galaxy is listed in its pages. In short, OBM was the perfect match for Thunder at the Tower because its readers went to events.

OBM's editor was also perfectly suited to us. Malc was one of the best TT racers of his generation and had achieved two second places in the Isle of Man – missing out on a TT win by just a single second. He was not a journalist but had come into the magazine business from Ducati UK where he was a key player in establishing the dealer network. From this background, Malc was much more commercially minded than many journalists and, from the outset, he could see the potential of Thunder at the Tower.

Finally, he was a motorcycle racer and therefore a hard man with no interest in the playground politics of those who were knocking our event. As far as Malc was concerned, we would be judged on what we did and achieved, and that was all. For my part, I wanted nothing else.

With Malc's support, and that of OBM, the Thunder at the Tower brand grew much faster than I could have hoped for. Month after month, at a time when the rest of the motorcycling media had no interest in our event, Malc ran our press releases and these reached precisely the customers we wanted to speak to.

The good ship Thunder At the Tower was well and truly launched and heading down the slipway. The only question was whether she would sink or float when she hit the water!

13

Lift Off

IT is difficult to describe just how passionately Carol devoted herself to Thunder at the Tower. There was no holding back, no caveats or excuses but just an unequivocal commitment. I was very blessed to have her alongside me which made me even more determined not to be responsible for moving us into a rented terraced house with a pit bull, guarding some attractive foil packets, for a next door neighbour.

Tony turned out to be more, and better, than I could ever have hoped for. He was an ex-Manchester Police Sergeant and so was a good, and trained, organiser. Better still, he was meticulously thorough and completely trustworthy. The number of times I was grateful for the broad smile accompanied by the immortal words "Oh, give over...", as I raged over some issue or another, was inestimable.

Now, I had the start of a team. Carol did all the admin for the event, Tony put my ideas into practice and we were on our way.

For their part, Sir Bernard and Lady Rosanna were totally supportive and of course, Malc gave our monthly press release a lot of coverage.

We were able to make so much progress so quickly for two reasons. First, I had a pellucidly clear vision of where I wanted us to be in May, when the first customers arrived at Hoghton Tower. Second, I was able to personally undertake a lot of tasks which, had they been done by sub-contractors, would have cost us a fortune and slowed everything down.

From the time I owned Tsubaki Racing, and later ran In Our Own Words, I knew all about public and media relations and I was good at both. I was also able to design all of our printed material in house and, as someone who been trained in magazine production, everything was done to professional standards. Last, and perhaps most importantly of all, I was comfortable with planning and written documents. I could allocate tasks and see problems before they arose.

A major part of the whole exercise was to appoint staff but the reality was that I couldn't appoint any staff of any sort. We had no money to pay anyone and no full-time, salaried positions to offer. Rather, I had to persuade volunteers that they should work for a few pounds of expenses – but with all the pressures of being paid employees.

Things got off to a bad start – very bad indeed. To launch our event, I took some of the tiny budget we had and spent it on an introductory meal at an Indian restaurant in Winsford. The restaurant gave us a nice meeting room, at no charge, and did a good deal on the price of the meal too. I thought, rightly as it turned out, that people would come along to hear what I had to say - as long as they got free food!

I made a formal presentation and talked about brand properties, service protocols and customer interfaces. Even now, I am ambivalent regarding whether this was the best way to approach the task. For sure, the meta-language was that of a marketing person and so was alien to almost everyone present. I could have easily made the ideas more accessible and used non-area specific language because I am a good communicator and speak well: there would have been no problem in doing this.

Why then, did I choose not to make my ideas easily comprehensible to the whole audience? There was a reason – and it reflected a high risk strategy. I wanted to make it clear that Thunder at the Tower was not just another motorcycle event. There would be many new ideas with challenging concepts to learn and understand.

Yes I was grateful for the experience which these enthusiasts, who had been organising motorcycle events for decades, would bring to our event but equally, they could not just continue what they had been doing in the past. Things would have to be done as I envisaged, or not at all. By the end of the meal, most of those present had taken the "not at all" route!

Elizabeth had been poorly so Carol had not come to the meeting, and when I arrived home she immediately saw that I had taken a battering. She made a cup of milky coffee for me, held my hand and I felt better.

I need to give an example of what I wanted and how great a shift this would be from the way in which visitors and participants were normally treated at many motorcycle events. To see this in context, you have to remember that all of this took place 23 years ago and many of the ideas we used are much more common now than they were then.

The core of my whole concept was that customers were not a nuisance, a pain in the bum or, and this is the phrase I really abhor, mug punters, but rather that we should feel grateful, and honoured, that they would give us their time and their money by attending our event.

That gratitude ought to start with customers receiving prompt and courteous responses to their enquiries and then continue to the gate staff welcoming each and every visitor as they paid their admission fee. Finally, the services we provided during their visit ought to be of the highest quality.

I saw all the riders, every single one, as the stars of the show and I expected them to be treated as such by officials. There would be no "them" and "us" but, rather, officials would work with the riders to make sure that the event ran smoothly, and safely, and that the participants gained maximum pleasure from the event.

Those were my aspirations. Getting them to work in practice was going to take a bit more than clever writing and passionate talk!

Some of the reactions were quite amusing. I spoke to one of Sir Bernard's staff who explained, very slowly and patiently, as you would to a very dim Cocker Spaniel who couldn't find his ball, that there wasn't the time to wish everyone good morning as they arrived because they might need change as they paid their admission fee.

How long does it take to say: "Good Morning. Thanks for coming to Thunder at the Tower."

Far too long apparently.

I also asked for fixed, defined service protocols to be built into the Technical Control process. Technical Control, or Scrutineering as it used to be called, was something of a sore point with me. Riders must have their bikes checked for safety before they can take part in any form of motorcycle sport and this is sensible. If the bike doesn't pass Scrutineering, then the rider can't ride. This gives the Officials doing the job immense power to either enhance, or ruin, the day's racing.

The problem is that a minority, and it is a very tiny number, of officials doing this job become very petty and arrogant with riders and this has always annoyed me.

I was once addressed in the following manner: "Hey you, mate, bring your bike here!"

I pointed out, in a most unequivocal manner, that I was not the Official's friend and nor did I wish to copulate with him, so he was not my "Mate" at any level. If he wanted me to move from one line to another, he should ask me with courtesy. Clearly, this did not make me flavour of the month at that event!

By contrast, our riders would be thanked for coming to Thunder at the Tower and then, when the thorough but courteous Technical Inspection was completed, they would leave with some informal good wishes – along with a little gift, to thank them for riding with us.

Riders were no longer a nuisance, and something to be tolerated, but performers in what was going to be a spectacular show.

Eventually, I did find some Technical Officers who agreed with my big idea and the riders did get the service I wanted to provide for them.

Every single part of the show had to be hewn out of solid granite and sometimes I felt that my only tool for the sculpture was a plastic teaspoon! Often, I was left frustrated and exhausted with just how tedious even straightforward jobs could be. Here's just one example.

I wanted all our customers, motorcyclists and the general public, to have a great experience at Thunder at the Tower. I was determined to have some nice portable toilets because I was certain that we would have too many visitors just to be serviced by the Tower's facilities.

I visited the toilet supplier and inspected the units he was sending. They were in good condition – smart and well maintained. So far, so good. However, I wasn't happy with the commercial soap for the ladies' units and wanted this replacing with some scented soap, which felt nice on the customers' hands.

You would have thought that I had just asked for reactive armour and a .50 calibre machine gun turret to be fitted to the loos. I was battered with a tirade of incredulity.

Didn't I realise that NO-ONE, ever in the history of portable toilets, had ever asked for scented soap?

Didn't I realise that customers never washed their hands at outdoor events?

Why was my show so different that I needed scented soap?

Had I ever run a show before or was I just some wannabee organiser with a big head and an even bigger ego?

I listened, fairly patiently, and explained that my wife did use the soap at events we attended. Further, she did wash her hands and she didn't like industrial detergent. So, put scented soap in the ladies' loos – or you won't get the contract. Can I make it any simpler for you to understand?

We paid a premium and the scented soap did go into the ladies' toilets.

That winter was a tough one in many ways. Just when I didn't need it to happen, work from The Daily Telegraph dried up completely and, to make sure that I really felt the pain, I couldn't sell anything to the motorcycling press either.

I asked a bloke I knew well, and who worked in the burgeoning film industry in the North-West of England, if he would leave my business cards around studios. I hope that maybe he would even put a good word in for me with directors he knew, and so help me get a bit of work writing scripts for cheap TV ads, or company websites, but got a blank refusal. As he explained, he didn't do charity work.

My settlement with Cheshire Education Authority meant that I couldn't even do supply teaching, and I would have starved to death rather than ask Carol to go back into the classroom after having persuaded her to leave.

Elizabeth had a lovely Christmas, and I made a Christmas cake with a big teddy bear wearing a Santa hat as the centre piece, but everyone else was on short rations.

The insidious sniping also continued and this hit us hard. A really nasty rumour was spread saying that we were going to run the event without insurance to save money, and this caused me a lot of problems. When a rider takes part in a motorcycle sport event, he automatically expects third party insurance as part of his entry fee. In the extremely rare case of an accident involving an official or spectator, the rider then has appropriate insurance cover to protect him should there be a claim.

Without insurance, riders were reluctant to enter our new event and I was depending on their entry fees to keep us going during the winter.

Of course, the rumour was a total lie. I would not have put anyone at risk by running the event without everyone, including us as organisers, being properly protected with appropriate insurance. In fact, I was so paranoid about doing everything to the highest possible standards that I over insured everything. Regardless, the whisperers had planted the seeds of doubt and, until I weeded these out, the rumours cost us money at a time when we could least afford it.

Every big show has a trade area. At a bike meeting, there will typically be vendors selling spare parts, clothing and T-shirts. I wanted a wider range of goods on offer and not just bike oriented products but, for a start, I was desperate to have anyone, selling anything, to pay money for a trade pitch.

At the Hoghton Tower Sprint, traders had always paid £15 for the day. I put the price up to £25 on the grounds that Thunder at the Tower was going to be a hugely bigger event – and the traders went berserk! Even now, after nineteen years, I don't want to remember the detail of what was said but being a robber, bully and without any parents were at the gentler end of the comments. I was enthusiastically hated!

At the time, I did not take any of this with either good grace or equanimity but with the benefit of the long view I can now, partially at least, see their point of view. I had never run a big, public event before and there had never been a Thunder at the Tower. What then, gave me the right to nearly double their pitch fees?

This is standard "trader think". Subsequently, I ran another seventeen Thundersprints and at many of the events our traders made a lot of money – and I do mean a lot! Never once have I had a trader say to me: "I've had a brilliant time – can I pay you something extra for my pitch?"

However, if things don't work out right for any reason whatsoever – including the weather – then the show organiser is Satan's favourite son.

Almost every aspect of the event was an immense learning process for me and I made a huge number of mistakes of every shape, kind and form. In fact, I can't think of much I didn't do wrong.

A big challenge was how I interacted with the volunteers who were helping us. I was used to working with teachers who were comfortable with written documents and happy to follow prescribed work schemes. Now, many of the helpers didn't much like things written down and I also had to persuade rather than tell them that an idea was sound and worth doing. I found this to be a very slow process - both difficult and frustrating.

So did a fair number of my informal staff who couldn't, or wouldn't, be persuaded and so left!

It was a big change for me to have to constantly negotiate but this was now a key skill which I had to master, or the event would fail – and that was 100% certain.

Eventually, we did get riders to enter and they did so en masse. The trade

sales area was also massive compared to previous Hoghton Tower Sprints –
although it was still very heavily bike focussed. However, we began to see the
first glimmers of the way things could go in the future. There were a couple of
tiny rides for the kids, and a small Army display where the older children could
play on the armoured vehicles. This was how to make a bike event attractive
to a wide audience.

Finally, we had a star rider. Through a friend of mine in the USA, we were
put in contact with an American called Tripp Nobles who had a done a season
of World Superbike. Tripp wasn't an "A" List celeb but I wasn't paying superstar
fees either! Critically Tripp was amiable, good with customers and was
unmistakably American.

He was also easy going, and good practice for me in terms of learning how
to work with star riders. For example, Tripp arrived a week early because he
had got the dates of our event confused and he flew in to Heathrow, rather
than Manchester, for the simple reason that his travel agent had told him that
we only had one major, international airport in Britain and that was Heathrow!

I needed to learn that star riders think in a different way to clubmen
competitors like me – and their attitude is not always a good thing. Even when
I was sponsored I never had a team to support me. Either I organised myself
or I didn't ride. Stars were, and are, very different as I was to discover in
subsequent years…

I also made one final, philosophical decision – and it might seem an odd one.
At the epi-centre of what I wanted to achieve with Thunder at the Tower was
an event which Carol and I would both want to attend. In reality, we were our
customers. We thought like our customers. We had the same aspirations for
our day out as those who were paying to come to our event, and we were going
to be pleased, or dissatisfied, with the same things.

If we were going to have the best Sprint Festival in the world I wanted to
ride in it. After all, it would be madness not to!

I also wanted not to be a VIP - the bloke who organised the event and so had
special treatment. Carol and I both thought it very important that I should stand
in line along with all the other riders for Technical Control, walk the track and
wait in the queue to ride. In short, we felt that it was very important to see the
event from the inside.

Clearly, the problem was that I couldn't both ride and fire-fight problems on the
day but I had strong feelings in this respect too. If I had done the planning properly,
and all the staff were correctly briefed and empowered to do their jobs, then I should
not be needed. On paper, and with Bess on my knee, it looked beautifully simple
and practical. In real life, things proved to be a little more complex!

Once we had the rider entries, and traders started paying for their pitches, I
was thinking of the following year's event where bigger and better things were
certain to happen. None of the bitchiness had prevented Thunder at the Tower

from happening and there was already a real buzz in the motorcycling community about the event. It had been a long winter but now we were on the attack and, goodness me, did I feel good about the change!

*****

Spring arrived and suddenly the sun was shining – literally and metaphorically. Every weekend, we visited bikers' meeting places and distributed flyers and Elizabeth, at all of four years old, became something of an expert flyer issuer! Who said that Victorian child labour was a thing of the past?

We studied the weather forecasts obsessively and the rain decided that it would go somewhere else for our weekend. Tony, Carol and I toiled like slaves all day Saturday and everything looked good for Sunday.

I didn't sleep much at all during the night before the event and so the 4am start was more of a relief than an imposition. As I drove east into the pale lilac and grey tinted, pre-dawn light I had the same metallic taste in my mouth that was always a certain indicator that I was ready for battle. The flag had dropped. The bulls***t had stopped and now all that remained was to see whether I would be an event organiser the following year – or a "Meeter and Greeter" at a well-known chain of DIY stores!

By 11am, we knew that we were in the event organisation business. The queue of bikes and cars waiting to get in was satisfyingly long and everyone had settled into the day.

Not that things went completely effortlessly. I was so terrified of the event failing that I micro managed everything. One minute, I was with Sir Bernard's gate staff – the next, checking the toilets at the top of the hill. Since the two sites were ¼ mile apart, up a steep hill, this was an excellent way to lose weight.

Then, I was back down to the bottom of the venue to monitor the trade area. My enthusiasm to get involved in this aspect of the event might well have led to a seriously unfortunate result!

Carol had marked out the trade areas with white paint on the grass, in neat rows. Not only was I beginning to think of the future - so was she. We had seen how the big County Agricultural Shows were laid out and wanted our event to look just as professional.

A long wheelbase Transit van had been parked across one of the lanes and was blocking access for every other trader. Not surprisingly, tempers were rising.

I bounced across and told the owners of the van that it had to be moved – and immediately! The three big, tattooed and bulging muscled lads looked at me with a 50/50 mixture of contempt and bemusement. After a few seconds, a girl with spiky orange hair and a large nose ring chirped up. "Look mate, we're unloading so you'll have to wait five minutes. What's the rush?"

Now I know that a better way of dealing with the issue would have been to smile, and calmly explain that they were inconveniencing other traders. That was the correct thing to do.

What can I say in my defence? Viewed objectively – nothing. Equally I was at the end, the very end, of a long road of event plans and persuading staff and dealing with rumours and waking up at three o'clock in the morning wet with sweat for fear of losing our house. Now, these people had become the final straw by parking their van across Carol's beautiful entry road.

At this point, I have to say that I am rubbish at fighting. I am not physically best suited for hurting people and get upset at the thought of anyone being in discomfort. I also have no experience of martial arts so leaping across to the Transit van, which was surrounded by three big blokes and a tough looking girl, was going to have only one outcome.

By this time, I was hysterical – quite literally foaming at the mouth. I could see the keys in the ignition so I dived into the driver's seat and said, bluntly and in rather intemperate language, that not only was I going to move the van but I intended parking it in the bog next to the trade area where I hoped that it would sink out of sight and never be seen again.

Ms Orange Hair was the first to speak. "No, no, no, don't do that. Look love, we'll move it straight away. We will, and no messing." And they did.

Later in the afternoon everything had settled down and great, fluffy white clouds of calm and happiness hung over a peaceful event. I was exhausted, but utterly content, and so I went for a walk through the trade area. A voice called to me: "Hey mate, we want a word with you…"

It was one of the lads from this morning's altercation. My bottom clenched so tightly that it could have cracked walnuts. The last time I had been in a fight was when I briefly – for two weeks actually – joined the school Judo club. I was given a petite girl, two years younger than me, to battle against and she threw me to the floor and then accidently stood on my hand.

That really hurt and she didn't even say sorry afterwards!

I had a strong feeling that what was about to follow was going to be a lot worse than lightly bruised knuckles.

The four of them approached me – slit eyed and with muscles bulging over denim waistcoats. As always, the lady was the spokesperson. "Look, you know this morning?"

I did, and was thankful that I hadn't eaten all day for fear of having an unfortunate bowel movement in a public place.

She spoke again: "Well, this morning, well, we well, we was out of order and we wanted to see you and say sorry, 'cos we were wrong."

Then she held out her hand - and crushed my knuckles in an affectionate act of overt friendship.

I accepted their apology in a sort of bluff, manly, rugby style harrumphing way and we were all best friends.

Then she gave me a real gift. "This has been a decent show. You're a good organiser. Can we come back next year?"

I could have fallen on the floor and kissed her purple Doc Martins, I was so pleased.

*****

The rest of the event went very well, although, and I know that I am in danger of wearing this phrase out, we were learning so much so quickly.

Two of the critical things we learned were that you can't have ladies' loos which run out of toilet tissue – not ever, for any reason. Female customers get very tense when this happens and make their feelings known!

Another deal breaker is a lack of chips. No-one except Carol, Tony and I had believed that the attendance would be as large as it was so everyone, from the toilet supplier to the caterers, had based their estimates on previous Hoghton Tower Sprints. This is why we ran out of key items.

Given decent weather, chips are consumed in vast quantities at outdoor shows and British customers expect their chips as an inalienable human right – and get very shouty when they are denied.

It was not so much the big ideas, like brand properties and customer service protocols, which were challenging for me but a myriad of small things - all of which can cause real problems to an event. If I had gone into event organisation in the conventional way, working as an assistant to an Event Director or as a part of a team, then I would have seen the bigger picture.

Simply jumping out of the aircraft with 20 sq metres of Dacron and a needle and thread, whilst quickly reading the "How to Make Your Own Parachute at Home" leaflet, was always going to be a risky way of getting back to earth in one piece.

At the end of the event, we knew that we had got all of our investment money back and made a tiny profit. This was an incredible achievement for a first event and we both felt so relieved and very proud. We had worked hard, taken big risks and put everything on the line but we had also had one major piece of luck in terms of the weather.

Carol's car was so jammed with equipment that we would have had to duct tape Elizabeth to the roof to get her home. There was a small space in mine – room enough at least for a four year old – so we squeezed her chair in and set off for Cheshire.

Ten minutes after leaving Hoghton Tower, the heavens opened. I stopped the car and staggered on to the grass verge to be sick. I explained to Elizabeth that I had a poorly tummy because I had a cold and she was satisfied. If the same storm, of identical intensity, had arrived eight hours earlier then our dreams of being event organisers would have been over forever and I would have been practising: "Good Morning Sir and Madam, thanks for shopping with us today".

It was a brutal reminder of just how fragile outdoor shows could be in terms of being profitable.

Thunder at the Tower had been wonderful but it was also the end of the road for many reasons. The key one was a lack of space. The effective viewing area at Hoghton Tower is only a little over a ¼ mile – 220 yards on each side of the track – and this had become horrendously jammed with spectators during Thunder at the Tower. If we doubled the crowd in the following year, the hill would have become dangerous.

Another problem we faced was illegal entry. Sir Bernard was scrupulously honest but I saw hundreds of spectators coming into our show through the woods and over the fields which surrounded the Tower, and this cost us a lot of money.

Finally, we ran out of room even at this first event. The paddock was jammed solid and there was no space left in the trade area. So, even if I increased the size of the race entry, and sold space to many more traders, there was nowhere for them to go.

Sir Bernard phoned me a few days after the event and was all smiles. From his point of view, Thunder at the Tower had been a great success and he wanted to discuss the following year's event.

I should have been tempted because there was every reason to stay at Hoghton Tower. Sir Bernard and Lady Rosanna were charming and his staff had been very helpful. We knew exactly how to organise another Thunder at the Tower and there had been very few real problems – chips and toilet tissue apart! The way forward was pleasant, predictable and modestly profitable - and I never considered taking it for a second.

Thunder at the Tower had only given me a craving for the next event – and this one would be bigger, better, more profitable and easier to organise. As things transpired, I was only right on three out of the four counts!

14

Thundersprint on Tour

THE elation following Thunder at the Tower was wonderful – even if it didn't last too long. First, there was the immense sense of relief that we weren't going to lose our house and, even better, we had shown sufficient profit to stay in the event organisation business. I would recommend the thrill of betting your house on a project – then not losing it – for anyone who wants to feel a real sense of relief. For sleepless nights, and stomach churning tension, the experience really can't be beaten!

Also, quite suddenly and for no apparent reason, I was back in favour with editors and taking every assignment which was offered to me. Soon, the cheques would be arriving. A week after Thunder at the Tower we had a barbecue in the back garden. My lovely wife splashed out on a really decent bottle of Australian Shiraz; I cooked, Elizabeth played on her tree swing and Carol was suitably affectionate when our squealing daughter was distracted.

Life was good – but there were still major issues to be resolved. There were two twin sisters to be addressed. We needed a new venue for the next event and, wherever the second sprint was, it had to be re-named.

One of the most difficult jobs in marketing is rebranding a product. This is where a new name, and a fresh identity, are given to an existing product. You may, or probably may not, remember that the iconic "Royal Mail" name was changed to Consignia in 2001. The Royal Mail brand was established in 1635 so changing it to Consignia was something of a bold move – so courageous that it lasted only fifteen months before reverting to its original name.

By comparison our problem was, almost but not quite, non-existent!

Fortunately our informal customer surveys showed that the "Thunder" element of "Thunder at the Tower" was popular whilst "Tower" did not have the same impact. I began doodling again and came up with "The Thunder-sprint" – and it was a name which was to serve us very well in the coming years.

*****

As we were packing up at the end of Thunder at the Tower, Carol and I had an informal meeting which was going to have a big influence on the next seventeen Thundersprints. Colin Rose came across to see us. He was impressed by the event and, if we ran another one, wanted to be involved. I was immediately interested because I knew Colin both as a knowledgeable and enthusiastic motorcyclist and also as a very smart businessman, who had started with nothing and done very well for himself.

Colin is so important to the Thundersprint story that it is worth mentioning how we worked together in some detail because he will appear regularly in the next chapters. My relationship with Colin is a complex one. I could never call him a friend in the sense that we socialised together but, after Carol, he became my closest confidant, my most trusted colleague and, on occasions when things were particularly tough, my psychotherapist too.

He also filled spaces in the event organisation which I left empty. Because of his retail background he had infinite patience with customers when often, by the weekend of the Thundersprint, I didn't. Colin was a skilful negotiator, and placater of egos, whereas I made my feelings known in black and white - as I had done with the traders blocking the access road at Hoghton Tower. Colin's smiles, and ability as a diplomat, both saved and made us a lot of money - as well as making for a better event.

Finally, I trusted him - absolutely and completely, and in every way, from handling sensitive commercial information to making split second decisions at an event. Knowing I had a colleague of his quality lifted a huge weight from my shoulders.

For my part, I backed and supported Colin without reservation. Whatever he decided, in any part of the event's organisation, then that was the end of the matter. It soon became known that there was no sense in lodging an appeal to either Carol or me because to do so was simply a waste of breath. This policy gave Colin the confidence to make big, complex decisions knowing that he always had my full backing.

Finally, he was comfortable with written documents – and a lot of my ideas were in words. My event planning documents always ran into thousands of words – sometimes over ten thousand. I needed a colleague who was as happy reading abstract ideas as I was writing them.

The confidence I had in him also produced an invaluable by-product: Colin could, and did, challenge my ideas. Together, Carol and Colin were an event manifestation of "His Majesty's Loyal Opposition" and I was not allowed to put any idea to the rest of the staff unless I could first totally justify it to my two closest colleagues.

Being challenged, sometimes fiercely, by two highly intelligent team members was incredibly useful for another, rather odd, reason. Knowing that I would get an intellectual kicking from two very bright people made me think harder, and with greater clarity, about new ideas.

Almost contra-intuitively, this system also permitted me to dream up really radical plans which were so innovative that, at first glance, they would seem ridiculous and fanciful. However, I knew that if I did my research well, organised my ideas properly and made a perfect presentation then the ideas would be judged with a wonderful openness of mind. Nothing was off the menu so, conversely, everything was on it.

This mind-set gave me the confidence to have bold dreams which, eventually, would reap big rewards.

*****

Now we had a good brand name and the basis of an excellent team to run the newly born Thundersprint event – but still no venue. The obvious solution was to take Thundersprint to a race circuit and there are some excellent venues in Britain. However, earning a wage from organising an event at a British circuit is so difficult that it becomes almost impossible.

The system works like this. The event organiser, or promoter, hires the track from the circuit owner. He then brings in his own safety staff, at his own cost, and pays for advertising the event – if he does any advertising at all.

The circuit keeps 100% of the spectator income, and 100% of the trader fees, and the promoter has to rely on rider entry fees to cover all of the costs.

This business model works for a not-for-profit club hiring the circuit for its members to race, or for a track day, but it also explains why spectator attendance is so dire at club events because the organiser has no incentive to advertise or publicise the event.

There is always wriggle room in any commercial negotiation, and no doubt we could have done something with one of the big, glamorous race circuits, but I already had in mind attracting tens of thousands of spectators to the Thundersprint – and I had no intention of handing over all this income to someone else. We needed to earn a living from the Thundersprint!

However, as well the huge, international locations, there are second tier tracks all over the country and one of these was the Three Sisters Circuit near Wigan. The circuit is primarily a kart track and twists and turns inside a very tight area. It's not exactly Silverstone or Monza but it was perfect for a short sprint and, of critical importance, there was a huge banked area for spectators running alongside the main straight giving some of the best viewing anywhere in the world.

The two circuit managers were approachable and we struck a deal, whereby we could guarantee them what they would earn from renting the track out for motorcycle or kart racing, plus a bonus, and we could keep the rest of the spectator entrance money – known as the gate fee.

Also, we would promote our new event very heavily and so the circuit would benefit from the publicity.

At the time, Thundersprint was very much an unknown product and so I think that the managers thought they were getting a good deal. From our side, I was certain that we could get a decent crowd because Wigan is in Greater Manchester – home to 2.7 million people. With that number of potential visitors on our doorstep, I could not imagine how we could fail.

Right from the start, we promoted the Thundersprint as if our lives depended on its success which, in a way, they did. Carol, Elizabeth and I gave out thousands of flyers for the new event, starting 10 months in advance, and we sent out a non-stop stream of press releases. However, making every one of these press releases newsworthy was a challenge – and one which led me down a completely wrong path.

The received wisdom at the time was that the more stars a race, or a show, had the better. I was about to discover that more was not always better.

We had a stand at the Manchester Motorcycle Show to promote the Thundersprint and talk to traders. The Manchester Show was good because it was busy and we had some brilliant volunteer helpers. Mike Hunt, Ian Jackson and Chloe Dickinson, who soon appointed herself my unofficial show PA, became superstars at selling the Thundersprint to potential visitors. In every way we had a good time at Manchester.

One of the show's star guests was six times World Champion, and six times TT winner, Jim Redman and I watched with admiration how good he was with customers. If you can imagine a racing version of a rock star, Jim was it.

Hour after hour, Jim was endlessly smiling and clearly gave something of himself to every person he met. The issue for me was that I was in awe of him. As a teenager I had seen Jim battle with other great riders of the day whilst I was standing in the shadows, too shy to even push myself to the front of the spectators - let alone actually ask for his autograph.

I spent two days in Manchester fantasising about having Jim ride at our event but I didn't know what to say to him. After all, why should one of the great motorcycle racers of all time want to ride at an unknown event organised by a husband and wife team? At best, I would be laughed at – if not blasted for being cheeky.

Towards the end of the second day time was running out and so, with Carol's encouragement, I approached Jim more nervously than any teenager asking his first ever girlfriend out for a date.

Jim had been knee deep in fans all day and by 5.45 was pretty desperate to visit the Gent's toilets. I intercepted him by the door and, 60 seconds later whilst he desperately hopped from one foot to the other, we reached an agreement for Jim Redman MBE, six times Champion of the World, to ride at our sprint. I went back to Carol dizzy with excitement. Now we had an "A" list star, whose presence would lend the Thundersprint real status.

In the next seventeen years, Jim did an immense amount for the Thundersprint and its initial, and continued, success owed a huge amount to his efforts.

Jim also became a family friend and, when he was eating with us at home, I sometimes took a second glance as he was chatting to Carol or Elizabeth. Who would have thought a penniless teenage fan would eventually be sitting at the same table as one of his great heroes? For me, it often felt like a dream.

What made Jim completely outstanding was his total and utter professionalism and fiercely protective loyalty to us. These were the same traits which made him such a great rider. Nothing was too much trouble for Jim and there was never a complaint, no matter which job we asked him to do. Some other riders were very different.

Before discussing these I need to make a slight digression to explain the importance of the "Heather Scale" to the Thundersprint. Colin had, and still does have, a lovely partner called Heather. She had a motorcycle licence and was passingly interested in bikes – but not anywhere near to the same degree as Colin, Carol or me. In short, she was just the sort of uncommitted customer we wanted to attract to add to our core audience.

Colin and I used the Heather Scale constantly and it worked like this. Heather can take the Thundersprint or leave it. What will make, not encourage but actually motivate, her to get up early on a Sunday and pay to see the Thundersprint?

It immediately became clear that she wouldn't make the effort to see some second tier GP rider or, worse still, an ex-British short circuit star. It wasn't that she was dismissive of their achievements, or ability, but rather that she was utterly ambivalent. Walk past one in the paddock and smile – yes. Pay to see them at the Thundersprint – absolutely not.

Heather wanted to see a big brand star, with legendary status, and anything less wasn't going to persuade her to come to the Thundersprint. Colin and I used the Heather Scale ruthlessly and continuously over the years to judge which stars we should pay to come to our event.

Not that all Superstars were good news. On the back of Jim's presence, we hired another top rider for one event and he was simply a nightmare. Thundersprints are relentless toil for a solid 72 hours and throughout the event he moaned, complained, treated customers with contempt and then finally demanded cash, rather than a cheque, for his appearance fee. The final straw was when he refused to sign a receipt!

Carol never paid anyone in cash, on the grounds that we were running a business not an Autojumble stall. Then he raised his voice to her - and I intervened. Eventually, things calmed down but all three of us vowed we would never have him back – and we didn't.

The event was sufficiently hard work on its own without having to import problems we didn't need.

From the first Thundersprint, star riders had to be seen for what they are: an expensive marketing tool. It didn't matter who they were, what they had achieved in the past or their apparent status. We were paying them - so they either did a good job for us or didn't come because, for 100% certain, I was not going to stump up a lot of money for someone to cause me problems.

Initially, it was hard for an amateur racer like me to make the change from being a fan to an employer but once I did there was no going back and things worked well. I was always respectful and full of admiration for our stars but, equally, it was our cheque which they were taking home - and not the other way round.

*****

The first Thundersprint was a success - but it wasn't much fun. I created many of the problems through a lack of experience and I failed to take the correct actions which would have ameliorated them. In later events, instead of trying to placate or negotiate with a rider or a trader who was being unfairly hard work, I took a much firmer stand. With the 1999 Thundersprint being only our second event, I tried to fix unreasonable behaviour with reasonable discussion: it was a flawed policy and rarely worked.

I also learnt that the few could spoil the enjoyment of the many. If 99.5% of our customers were having a good time, I owed it to them to ensure that a tiny minority did not spoil their day – whether this minority was a star rider, a club exhibitor or a trader.

Colin and Carol were learning too, so in these early days there was not the same degree of backup for me which I later enjoyed.

We also lost a lot of money through illegal spectator entry. No doubt this was divine retribution for the times when I had blagged my way into events without paying! Colin identified the problem immediately but there was nothing we could do about it. The circuit was used to having a few hundred spectators at most and when we put six, seven or maybe even eight thousand spectators inside – we still don't have clue regarding how many people were actually watching – it leaked like a sieve.

Tony Jones, who had done so much for the event, politely and kindly withdrew. There was too much pressure for someone who was such a thoroughly nice person and, although I missed him, I respected his decision and understood it.

Colin was exhausted at the end of the event but he was used to intense pressure from his own businesses and so he came up with a string of things we could do better the following year. Carol did the same, whilst I had learned so much that I became almost a recluse until I had fitted all the bits together.

The following year we were at Three Sisters again and things were both much better – and worse! The event ran far more smoothly but we hit huge problems in terms of spectator numbers. The Three Sisters Circuit had been

The ebullient, and quite lovely, Anne Bingham Holmes – CEO of Vale Royal Borough Council and mistress of all she surveyed – with Jim Redman. Anne pressed the big "Go" button for the Thundersprint and her Officers made everything happen. I liked Anne a lot.

I didn't much care for media people from outside motorcycling but James May is a hard core motorcycle enthusiast and was lovely to work with. He did have some rather passionate – in every way – fans though!

How many people actually came to the Thundersprint? The official estimates were 145,000 and that might not be far out. Have a look at the size of the crowd in these two pictures. Northwich was packed solid for two whole days.

All our star riders were carefully chosen for being just that – Superstars who could increase spectator numbers and would work enthusiastically with visitors. Here's Cal Crutchlow, smiling as always, and James Toseland indulging in yet more tyre art.

Giacomo Agostini, below, was simply wonderful.

This was about as sane and well-behaved as I ever got the eBike team to be with Alex, Geoff and Jamie being, sort of, sensible for a rare PR photograph. Their good behaviour didn't last long though!

Here's a lovely image of Moz Baines and Peter Jordan, two hard core Thundersprinters, engaging with the crowd. They were as important to us as any of the star riders.

This is the final corner at the Thundersprint. The finishing line is at the bottom of the picture and I am riding the Seeley very hard. The key to doing well at the Thundersprint was to ride every molecule of the track absolutely flat out.

I have included this picture to give an idea of how intense the atmosphere was at the Thundersprint for both riders and spectators, who were within touching distance of each other. The Thundersprint might have been a GP in a Car Park but it was a very special event.

These are two behind the scenes images which we never used for the press or marketing of the Thundersprint. First, there is Jim – smiling as ever despite it being 7am - accompanied by his favourite commentator Garry Gardiner, "The Voice of the Thundersprint", getting ready to entertain the crowd.

The Thundersprint course was only short – but it could bite. This is my life-long friend, Peter Wilson, being helped up by a whole host of stars. Peter has a very well developed sense of humour and wanted the picture to be included in the book. Since he proof read both "Penguin" books I could hardly refuse!

This is Jim's section. Carol and I still can't come to terms with Jim Redman MBE, six times World Champion, riding for us – and becoming a family friend. As always at the Thundersprint, Jim was riding one of Clive Brooker's immaculate Hondas. That's Clive looking after Jim and, as usual, looking focussed. Clive was simply brilliant.

Book signings have been good fun. Here's our sales table at the National Motorcycle Museum Open Day with classic racing tuner Fred Walmsley reading his free copy of "A Penguin in a Sparrow's Nest"!

And here I am back at the beginning where I belong – a natural born freelancer who can't stop writing. Thanks for doing me the great honour of reading my words.

conceived as a recreational facility with the people actually using the track, not spectators, being first in mind. When we brought thousands of bikes and cars into the surrounding area, it was chaos – absolute mayhem.

I went out of the circuit at lunch-time and there were vehicles parked everywhere – all over the verges and roadsides right the way back to the nearby village of Bryn. Now we had the dual problems of illegal entry and masses of fly parking.

We got on really well with Greater Manchester Police, who were always pleasant and tried to be as helpful to the event as possible. However, the Sergeant who was our main point of contact was blunt after the second Thundersprint. He was polite, and even kind, but direct too. "Look Frank, you can't run another Thundersprint at Three Sisters. You've caused traffic chaos in the area. Someone's going to get hurt and that's certain.

"I'm going to tell my bosses that the event shouldn't be allowed – and it won't happen here again so look for somewhere else to hold it.

"But I'll definitely come wherever you go because it's been a great day out!"

Not only was there no point in discussion or debate but I agreed with him: given another year at Three Sisters we would have jammed the A49, a main arterial road, and this would have been asking for trouble.

So Carol and I went on tour, looking for a suitable venue. It needed a short section of tarmac, lots of parking space and, ideally, an established infrastructure because not only had we run out of room for bikes and cars but we had filled every hotel in the wider area around Three Sisters.

We found Victoria Park, right in the centre of Southport, on England's North West coast. The park had a bit over ¼ mile of decent tarmac, plenty of room inside for a paddock and traders, and a vast amount of parking space outside.

Southport is a seaside town and so there are plenty of hotels, plus some excellent restaurants and a superb shopping area. The new venue ticked every box and, better still, had room for expansion.

One of the local Councillors in the town got right behind the event and we enjoyed lovely weather over the weekend. There was the inevitable leakage round the perimeter of the park, and a few teething problems, but by Sunday evening we had covered costs and made a profit. The town had been packed with visitors and everything looked set for the future.

With the next year in mind, we put together a brilliant package for Southport – an absolute world beater. Far more than just the Thundersprint, we offered a whole weekend of entertainment including a beach race, live bands and then the Thundersprint. I had in mind Daytona Bike Week in the North-West of England.

Southport should have been laying a red carpet for the whole 50 miles from our house to Victoria Park. Daytona Bike Week generates around $300 million for the Volusia County area and so a three day Thundersprint in Southport would have produced tens of millions of pounds for the area: that was certain. But this golden opportunity wasn't recognised so the Thundersprint tour set off on what was going to be the biggest adrenaline ride in the event's history.

As the negotiations dragged on through the Autumn I had become ever more concerned that we would never be able to run the event at Southport – no matter how hard we tried. Common sense indicated that I had to develop a back-up plan in case the nuclear option happened.

The Thundersprint's reputation was growing each year and by Christmas we had another offer on the table. This time, Manchester Council were prepared to host the event.

★★★★★

Working with Manchester Council was a real shock. The first thing which surprised us was the immense scale of the organisation. To put this into perspective, Greater Manchester has a bit over half the population of Finland – and therefore a lot of resources.

Officers were enthusiastic and polite but they had bigger things on their mind than twenty or thirty thousand potential visitors to a motorcycle event. 76,000 fans fill Manchester United's Old Trafford stadium for every home game, and this was just one part of the day to day life of the city so, yes, the Thundersprint would be a good event - but Manchester was well used to success and almost on a daily basis.

We were offered the magnificent Heaton Park as a venue for the event – and I couldn't believe our luck. The park is huge – over 650 acres in size – and was well used to hosting big events. In May 1982, a quarter of a million worshippers had filled the park to hear Pope John Paul II preach so I was confident that it was well able to manage the Thundersprint.

We were given an area in the southern corner of the park and it was perfect. I was asked to submit a list of things we needed for the event, all of which were agreed instantly and with good grace.

What I didn't know was that there was trouble ahead. The first warning signs came as we tried to sell trade space. In the simplest terms, traders were extremely uneasy about Heaton Park.

The weather on the run up to the event was wonderful and things started to look good but there was still a huge amount of customer resistance to having the Thundersprint at Heaton Park – and much of it was illogical. Riders in the sprint, traders and spectators dripped negativity for no reasons which I could disprove. There was simply a constant feeling that there would be "TROUBLE".

What form the difficulties would take no-one knew, but there was a certainty that good things would not happen.

From our side everything looked great and, as the sun beat down, we were looking forward to our best ever Thundersprint. Little did I know that all the Gods were seated round their heavenly table, ready for the fun to kick off.

On the Wednesday and Thursday before the event, Carol toiled all day in the Mediterranean sun, marking out the trade area to an impeccable standard. There were also designated camping and club areas and, on Thursday evening, I looked at the thirty empty cans of white, spray-on grass paint and I was bursting with pride at the job she had done: it was superb!

To cure the issue of illegal access once and for all, the whole site was surrounded by 2m high steel fencing and during Thursday this was erected at a bewildering speed. The whole job was done to the highest possible standards, with the fencers working to proper engineering drawings: very impressive.

Then the showers arrived to service the campers and competitors. These were real luxury units and better than the one we had in our own house! The shower contractor had a drawing too. He off-loaded the showers precisely where his drawing indicated, just as the trucks arrived with the fencing. Unfortunately, the showers were 2m on the wrong side of the camping and paddock fence line. With a perimeter fence line of nearly a mile, stretching across grassland, this was hardly a problem. We'll just move the fence a little bit so that the showers are on the right side and the campers don't have to walk half a mile, round the outside of the barriers, to use them.

The response was unequivocal. "No, you won't mate. My drawing says the fence goes here – and that's where it's staying."

"Okay, let's move the showers a couple of metres, please? Really, really, really please?"

The shower man's drawing came out – and the showers were staying put.

That night, in the dark, I took my socket set to the fencing bolts and the fence was subtly relocated…

After the size of the crowd at Southport we had become ever more safety conscious. Working with Manchester's Officers was easy in this respect. They were sensible, helpful and made lots of useful suggestions.

The track in Heaton Park was long and twisting and therefore we needed to protect spectators with a lot of straw bales: 1000 duly arrived on Thursday afternoon for siting the day after. I had never seen so many straw bales in one place and the organic mountain really was impressive. I was also severely worried – not merely sensibly concerned for their safety but dry lip and tummy rumbling stressed.

The scenario was straightforward. Here is an immense stack of highly inflammable straw bales, sitting on a site which is tinder dry and baking hot. Clearly, they needed 5* protection!

The Manchester Council Officer with whom we were working was re-assuring. He contacted two elite Park Security Officers who would be guaranteed to protect the precious bales come what may.

The two lads duly arrived, and were very re-assuring and focussed. I explained the job. The brief was simple. Park your van right next to the straw and don't move, for any reason – not earthquakes, aliens landing or anything else. DO NOT MOVE!

When I come back tomorrow morning, and find the straw bales sitting happily where I left them, there will be a £25, each, bonus for you. Just stay by the bales and don't move.

Elizabeth was staying with her friend and so was safe and enjoying VIP hospitality. By contrast, Carol and I were both utterly shattered, mentally and physically. We shared a single bag of chips in silence and headed for home. I weaved the car messily into our drive just before midnight and we staggered into bed with barely a word exchanged. This was not recreational event organisation.

I could not get to sleep so I was almost glad when the alarm went off at 5.30 and I lurched into the shower. I started to dry myself off and began to feel better. The sun was shining again, I was working alongside Carol and we had done all the hard work. Today, the show would really begin and the fun would start. Then the phone rang.

It was a reporter from the local Manchester newspaper. Did I have any comments about the Thundersprint being cancelled?

In these sorts of situations, I am very good – calm, clear thinking and completely free of panic. The first thing was to find out, for certain, what was happening. Was it just a joke in poor taste and, if it wasn't, how much did she actually know and how much was speculation?

The answers were simple and straightforward. The reporter lived near Heaton Park and had seen the flames pouring into the night sky with her own eyes. She had also seen the Emergency Services rushing to deal with the blaze. It could only be one thing to create a blaze of this size: the straw bales. All that remained was to confirm what had happened with our friends in Manchester Council – not that I needed anyone to check the disaster.

We left for Heaton Park promptly - but not in a panic. No-one's life was threatened so there was no point in screaming down the motorway and collecting a speeding fine. Also, I needed to stand back from the problem and start thinking about solutions. It was truly a case of the SAS motto brought to event organisation: "Slow is smooth – smooth is fast."

When we arrived, the situation was worse than I could have imagined - even in my worst nightmare. There was a huge area of scorched, blackened grass with patches of still smoking straw.

There was no point in wasting a moment's energy on becoming frustrated, upset or, worst of all, angry. History can never be turned back – not by Presidents, Prime Ministers or Popes. Good or bad, what's done is done and one has to look to the future. It's also important to find the positives: I had just saved paying the Parkies a £50 bonus!

The immediate future did not look good. There was a senior officer from

Manchester Fire and Rescue Service and he was black and white clear about what was going to happen next: the Thundersprint was cancelled and we should start packing up immediately.

I forced myself to stay calm because we were about to lose so much money that we would be out of business forever. It was like looking down over the edge of a very, very steep cliff and knowing exactly how much it was going to hurt if I fell over.

This was a time for quiet voices and the utmost courtesy. I explained the crisis to the Fire Brigade Officer and he listened patiently. The huge problem we currently face with the obsessive application of Health and Safety regulations is nothing to do with preventing injuries – but simply a result of Personal Injury Lawyers exploiting the law and putting us all under permanent threat of getting sued. Without the legal vultures permanently circling overhead, everyone would just show common sense and protect themselves and those with whom they work. This is just what happened now. The Fire Brigade was going to find a way of, safely, letting the event go ahead because this was the right thing to do.

Clearly, having smouldering straw and lumps of burning debris blowing all over an area where bikes would be re-fuelled, and spectators would be walking, was unacceptable to both the Fire Brigade and me. The answer lay in the lake a couple of hundred metres from the fire which now, with a bit of wind, had started to produce some cherry flames just to keep everyone happy and focussed. The Fire Brigade laid their hoses to the lake and then the appliances began pumping water – a lot of water – not only onto the bonfire but in a great swathe around the original conflagration. Now we had maybe two football pitch sized areas of black lake which was better than a blazing inferno – but still far from ideal.

The Manchester Council Officers were great – really superb. They were switched on, empathetic and supportive. In less than an hour, the world's biggest skip loader had arrived on site. This is the giant cousin of the JCBs which dig trenches in fields. The skip loader lurched to and fro through the mud which it then dumped into a series of waiting lorries. This was the difference in terms of dealing with Officers who really were on top of their jobs and those who thought that box ticking was their sole purpose in life.

Now we were left with a big, black rectangle – but one which was drying out rapidly in the baking sun. It was safe but still had to be roped off to protect spectators from being covered in the remnants of the stinking black mud.

All that remained was for Carol to re-site over 100 traders, mark out their pitches, move the camp site, re-route everyone to the new areas – and do this in less than an hour because customers were already queuing outside. With Colin's help, she did.

Meanwhile, I was dealing with another quite interesting challenge. There was water on site and it had been agreed that we could use this for competitors and campers. The stand pipe was already in place and connected to the water supply, as per the engineering drawings. So far, so very good.

Unfortunately, the water had to be turned on and to do this we needed an authorisation note. No note – no turnyony, not for me, not for Carol, not for the Arch Angel Gabriel accompanied by a team bus of angels: just NO!

The sun blazed down and soon we were up to Sahara summer temperatures. Water was becoming slightly more than merely desirable.

I called Carol across from siting traders and asked if she could do anything to persuade one of the Officers, who had been particularly helpful, to find a solution. As it happened, in his desk at another depot, he did have an emergency key for turning water off – which, clearly, could also turn it on. An hour later the water flowed...

*****

The best thing I can say about the event is that I learned a lot about organisation and, more importantly, about me. The most important thing was that we had to get the right staff in place and I also needed to stand back and cease micro-managing the project. Trying to control every element of the event was counter-productive. I needed to produce a good event plan, ensure that everyone bought into it and then trust that I had put the correct management structures in place to make the event run smoothly.

Let me give you an example of how bad things were. Everyone constantly referred back to me even when Carol and Colin could have dealt with issues. By Sunday lunch-time, I was suffering from a lack of sleep, too much work, an excess of problem solving and being involved in every conceivable decision which was made.

The commentary caravan was next to the track and had a large, flexible, plastic skirt around its base. This gave me an idea.

One of our caterers kindly offered me a tray of his finest chips along with the comment: "You look dead on your feet, Frank. You need a break." I did – and I had a plan. I would take the chips, and a bottle of cold water, and enjoy my gourmet lunch underneath the commentary van, hidden from view by the skirts.

I crawled into the semi-darkness and inhaled the silence and smell of the chips. There wasn't much room but I lay on my back, slowly chewing chips and sipping the chilled water: it was idyllic. At that moment, there wasn't anywhere else in the world I would have preferred to be. If this is what was on offer in heaven, then you could have signed me up on the spot.

The peace lasted only for a couple of minutes and then the skirt was lifted and a friendly face appeared. It was one of our marshals. "Frank, a post has fallen down on the road up to the trade area. Shall I knock it back in myself or do you want to do it?" I crawled out and went looking for the post bumper to return the errant post to the vertical position.

It was an important moment for me. I needed to take a break from the Thundersprint, look at what was good and bad about the show, and then come up with a clear plan of how we should improve.

I was desperate for the Thundersprint to succeed but equally aware that it would fail without a complete re-design. Although Carol and Colin would support, criticise and advise the responsibility would be primarily mine.

15

Borrowing Magic

WE were lucky to get any wages from Manchester because customers stayed away in bulk. Our costs were just about covered but it was clear that even the keenest Thundersprinters didn't like Heaton Park - and the customer is always right. Carol and I were both really disappointed because Manchester Council, and its Officers, had been brilliant but the hard facts were that we couldn't risk another event at Heaton Park. If we weren't going to get a bumper crowd in perfect weather, it didn't bear thinking about how few paying customers we would have had if it had rained.

Yet again, we needed a new venue but we also needed a long, calm think about the future and so we decided that we would do nothing for a couple of months except concentrate on my writing.

After a break, we were ready to move on. We had learned a vast amount since Thunder at the Tower and Manchester had shown us that we could overcome any problem, short of actually being on fire ourselves. Now we knew – in the deepest parts of our hearts, minds and souls – that we could be successful and that was that. There was no need for pretence, or press release bluff – just the truth.

Equally we needed to stand back from our event and look at what the best were doing elsewhere, not so much to slavishly plagiarise their ideas but to put the Thundersprint up against their scale of excellence and see how we could improve. The best, the very best, was Disneyworld with its Magic Kingdom.

I had visited Disneyworld twice before, and Disneyland in California too, and I was fascinated by the quality of the service provided for customers. I wasn't much interested in fantasy characters, or scary rides, but rather the effortless and meticulous way in which the organisation interacted with its customers.

The Walt Disney World Magic Kingdom had 52,964 average visitors per day in 2014 totalling 19,332,000 for the year and is the #1 theme park in the world, measured by attendance. The really clever thing is that, somehow, Disney manages to make every single visitor feel as if the park has been opened just for them.

One of the ways this is done is by having themed areas. Little ones spend a lot of time with Snow White, Mickey Mouse and other fairy tale characters, whilst teenagers and adults get their adrenaline shots from Frontier Land. There is something to see, and do, for everyone.

It is impossible to take in the whole of the Magic Kingdom in a day - or maybe even a week – so Disney sell extended holidays during which customers do nothing but consume giant helpings of Disney things. I say "things" to be deliberately flippant because, clearly, the Magic Kingdom is a commercial operation which exists to make money. If it wasn't profitable, then the area would still be Florida swamp.

Equally, Disney are fair with their customers. Nothing is cheap, or even a bargain, but nor is anyone ripped off with poor quality products or dodgy vendors offering a sub-standard service.

These ideas fascinated me. If we could get our show to a sufficiently large size, we could offer a micro version of Disney Land with themed areas which would provide a range of options for visitors. Hard core race fans could overdose on the bikes and the track competition, whilst those wanting a day out with the family might spend most of the time at the children's attractions or casual clothing stands.

For her part, Elizabeth had zero interest in market research but she was almost airborne at the thought of meeting Cinderella, Snow White and the rest of the Disney team. Whilst Elizabeth had previously flown in Europe, America was going to be a very different trip. Carol explained the need to be patient on the flight because it was a long way across the Atlantic and to try to have a nap and so on: all the good, sensible things a loving parent should do.

I did my part too – and psyched Elizabeth up at every possible opportunity until she was delirious with excitement: that's the benefit of having two parents with completely different characters!

*****

As well as Disney, I had another idea. I like America a lot. I like the Americans too. Provided you realise that, in America, everyone will push themselves in front of you for whatever they want, and you learn not to be offended by this attitude, then everything is fine.

The reason I like the USA so much is that it truly is the land of opportunity in a way that Britain, and the rest of Europe for that matter, are not. The Americans gave me my first chance to write professionally when I was just 18 years old. I had no experience or training and nor had I any professional or academic qualifications. In reality I had nothing to offer a magazine – except determination and ability. My family background, where I lived and the clothes on my back counted for absolute zero. There was only one question to answer: could I deliver stories and so make money for my employer? I could, and so they paid me well – right up to the point when the magazines I worked for were both closed simultaneously.

From then on, I didn't exist. There was no letter of thanks – no final bonus.

I wasn't even worth the effort of throwing in the bin. As for the money I was owed, well that was lost forever. If you work for the Americans, you have to accept this side of their character too.

I am a bad loser but I can forget the harshness of the American system the instant I take my first step on American soil. This is the land of freedom and opportunity - and the potential fizzes in the air. Get up early, go to bed late, work hard in between and you will succeed. The American system, psyche and emotional make-up are designed for those who will make a greater effort and take bigger risks than their fellow citizens.

Of course, the obverse side of the coin is that if you won't work, and you refuse to push yourself, then you will be allowed to fail – and pay the price for doing so because America is a society which is happy to accept losers as well as winners.

However, there are always exceptions to every rule and some of the kindest, most open hearted people in the world are in America – and I was about to meet one of them.

I had become ever more enthusiastic about road racing and I wanted to have a go in America. Clearly, I could not put the Crooks-Suzuki on a trailer and drive across to America so I needed some help. On the web, I found the contact details for Eric Kalamaja who ran Sundial Moto Sports as a very serious hobby. Eric was, and is, one of the best tuners of Suzuki T500s in the world.

I liked Eric immediately. He was enthusiastic, knowledgeable and keen to go racing. There was a class for Production Racing machines at a track called Roebling Road, in Georgia, which is only 350 miles north of the Magic Kingdom so everything fitted in beautifully.

More than anything else, Sundial raced with good humour. Take the name for example. The in-joke was that Eric was so slow when he first started racing that his friends used to say they would time his laps with a sundial, instead of a stop watch. In fact, Eric was being far too modest because he is a good rider and equally as fast as me.

Roebling Road was an incredible place both to visit and race. In 1959, sports car enthusiast J.C. Roebling, sometime multi-millionaire steel baron from Philadelphia, decided that he would build himself a little race track where he could play with his toys. The result was a superb 2.02 mile circuit which twists and turns through the lush Georgia countryside.

Not that JC did things by half. There's a 60 acre paddock and all the goodies necessary for civilised racing. Not a bad attempt for a hobby.

Transport the track to England, build some serious spectator banking, and you would have a price tag of a solid £30 million. But here, the whole circuit was sold to the Buccaneer section of the Sports Car Club of America at an affordable sum - on the understanding that they would continue to run sports car meetings. The rest of the time, the venue is rented out to like-minded organizations for non-spectator racing.

One of these is the American Historic Racing Motorcycle Association - or as it is more popularly known AHRMA. This huge club exists to promote classic bike racing with a range and complexity which is bewildering. At one end, there are the magnificent hand-change, rigid, side-valve Harleys and at the other are classes for modern classics.

As well as road racing, AHRMA organises everything from observed trials to historic motocross and flat track racing - really catering for the whole of the two wheeled world. When I contacted them with a request to ride at Roebling the organisation could not have made me more welcome.

The all-pervading atmosphere was one of racing for pleasure. Yes, Tech Control was efficient, as was rider registration and so on, but the rest of motorcycling world could learn a lot from AHRMA's approach to organisation. At the time the organisation was run by Jack Turner, a thoughtful and charismatic hard core biker with, by American standards at least, a very well defined sense of humour.

Jack summed up AHRMA's philosophy beautifully: "AHRMA is all about fun. The reason we exist is to give the vintage enthusiast a place to play, with a sensible degree of risk management. We need racing to be safe but we never lose sight of the fact that we're there for fun - and that we all gotta go to work on Monday morning."

Race paddocks are magical places at dawn and none more so than Roebling. There is a heady mix of nervous anticipation and an aching desire to get on with the job. I paid my 31st visit to the toilet and then our class was on the line for practice.

The first thing that struck me was that these Americans were top quality racers - fast, smooth and skilful. I cheated by tagging on to the second Sundial T500, ridden by the talented Todd Brockmeyer, and learning his racing lines. Todd was riding really well but my T500 was newly built and faster, and this was enough to keep up with him. Eric was riding the third Sundial production racer and he simply cleared off and left us.

After practice, there was time to wander around the paddock and enjoy what must be one of the most eclectic ranges of race machines ever gathered in one place. There were the wonderful hand change Harleys and Indians from before the war, all the way through to classic European bikes like Dave Roper's Aermacchi and the B50s tuned by ex-BSA mechanic Ted Hubbard. Finally, there was a mountain of converted Japanese road bikes, ranging from extremely basic to completely stunning.

This was fascinating and confirmed what I was beginning to realise about our Thundersprint paddock. Not only did there need to be a range of different interests for the whole audience but these individual areas also needed to be sub-divided, so that there was something just for fans of Pre-War bikes and something different to interest those who preferred late Japanese modern classics. The way to make Thundersprint really work was to provide an offer which could not be refused by the widest possible range of customers.

Eric worked miracles looking after the three production bikes and a Grand Prix class bike ridden by Joey Naval. Since I have the mechanical ability of a marmoset with a migraine, my contribution was to hang around and make encouraging noises until race time.

I knew that things were going to be tough when the flag dropped and Todd cleared off and left me for dead! This looked like it would be hard work. Eventually, the speed of my virtually brand-new T500 enabled me to scrape past Todd and win the production class which was all very satisfying, and a tribute to the quality of Eric's bike preparation.

Eric had the dreaded ignition problems - reflecting the fact that, like the riders, old ignition wiring isn't as flexible as it was in its youth! If Eric had been running, I don't think that I would have been on the same lap.

There was a consolation prize however, because Sundial Moto Sports won the prestigious award for the best presented bikes - a tribute not only to Eric's skill with the spanners but also his meticulous attention to detail.

My win brought to an end what had been a wonderful day's racing and, of even greater importance, a superb weekend of classic biking. Now, it was time to head south to Disney World.

Eric and I had a long hand shake and he said that if I ever wanted to ride his bikes again I would be very welcome. Inevitably, this started me thinking...

*****

I have gone on at lengths about Disney World and the Magic Kingdom because, from my previous experience, they were the best. With an eight year old as Guest of Honour, we were clearly going to max out on theme parks of every kind – and we did. All were good in their own way – efficient and offering a wonderful experience for a child and her parents. The difference was that Disney not only had the Magic Kingdom but the magic ingredient. Here is one example of the perfection of the offering.

Elizabeth had boundless energy so we stayed all day in the Magic Kingdom – right through to the evening's firework display finale, which was brilliant.

We ended up boarding the ferry boat to take us back to the car park at maybe 10.30pm and the experience was fascinating. The staff were smiling and there were lots of little, personal comments for customers. One of the lads heard Elizabeth's English accent and asked her how she had enjoyed travelling from England. In reality, it was nothing because he must have met a zillion English customers during the year but, regardless, he made the extra effort to make her feel special and wanted. I was fascinated.

The same applied during the day. At home, Elizabeth played at being Snow

White all the time and so when we met the character in person, Elizabeth wanted to speak to her at length and have several rolls of film used in the subsequent pictures. Fortunately, it was a slack day in terms of other children wanting to be with Snow White so we didn't wreck anyone else's visit!

Snow White was impeccable - polite, attentive and endlessly patient. This was how to treat customers. If we could use our star riders in the way Disney used its characters, our customer experience could be hugely enhanced.

The rest of the Park was an equally powerful example of how to give customers a wonderful experience – and make money. There were no bargains at the Magic Kingdom but, equally, no-one was ripped off or scammed. The emphasis was on a sense of fairness, albeit a very capitalist one, which said: "Give us your money and we will give you something of value in return."

I guess that was the same principle which the Greeks used for their coins 2,700 years ago!

With Thundersprint, we wanted to provide a service of real value which couldn't be purchased anywhere else in the world. If we could make our offer with courtesy, efficiency and even kindness, then we could also earn a wage.

This idea really gnawed at me almost to the point of obsession when we returned from America.

As well as the lessons which Disney gave to us, and a lovely trophy from Roebling Road, not to mention the extra inch on my waist, there was another parting gift from the USA: internet publishing.

It wasn't that the internet wasn't widely known in Britain at the start of the 21st century – after all, Sir Tim Berners-Lee had invented it – but rather that in America it had embedded itself much more deeply into mainstream culture. By the year 2000 the internet, albeit still in quite a crude form compared to now, was everywhere. Today, it would be unthinkable for a plumber or builder with ambition not to have their own website but this sort of universality had permeated into every stratum of American society much earlier than in Britain. This got me thinking...

The big breakthrough was the launch of Google in 1998. It was no use having all the information out there if you couldn't access it easily and reliably. Once Google was available, then searching for anything and everything was practical.

Despite getting older – an inevitable result of still being here – I have always been forward thinking. Yes, the past is important but I am more excited about what is going to happen tomorrow than what I did yesterday. This is the key reason you will never see me at reunion lunches and dinners. What we did in the "olden days" is wonderful. What we are going to do tomorrow is even better!

The idea of publishing on the internet was particularly exciting. I was already using the web but knew little about motorcycling websites. There were few about but those which were there looked very rustic and amateurish.

One which stood out a mile in terms of quality was Motorcycle USA.com. The story behind the site is very interesting. In 1996, Don Becklin established a website which was the first cousin of a blog. Don road raced on the West Coast of America and, on his website, wrote about what he did and also about the products he used.

This was two years before the launch of Google but Don was located in Medford, Oregon, only 450 miles south of the Microsoft world headquarters in Redmond, Washington. In short, Becklin was in an IT rich environment.

It looks staringly obvious now, but Don's thinking at the time was science fiction sophisticated. He felt that motorcycle accessories could be sold on the web. To do this, he established Motorcycle Superstore and this went on to be an immense commercial success.

The idea behind Motorcycle USA was that it would bring customers to Motorcycle Superstore - which it did, and in vast numbers too, but not in what might appear to be the obvious way. A lesser man than Becklin would have forced Motorcycle USA to produce nothing more than a series of advertorial pieces, whose sole purpose would be to promote products sold by Motorcycle Superstore. What happened was very different.

Motorcycle USA became a very high quality website with a fierce editorial independence. Critically, this policy attracted a very large audience – millions at its peak – and these fed seamlessly into Motorcycle Superstore.

The website also had a unique voice. Not only was the range of features it carried eclectic in the extreme but the journalism and design was of the highest standards. Together, all these factors gave Motorcycle USA a lot of credibility and, again, this helped promote Motorcycle Superstore because the two products were so tightly linked.

I have praised the opportunities America offers on a number of occasions but the obverse side of the coin is that the country practises capitalism red in tooth and claw. If you won't, or can't, accept the harsh realities of this, then you will be repulsed by the culture. Motorcycle Superstore was eventually sold and Don made a lot of money, as would be expected. Motorcycle USA soon became redundant and, after sixteen years of wonderful times, I was given 24 hours' notice that my services were no longer required.

However, all this was a long time in the future from when I first phoned MCUSA and the phone was answered by Ken Hutchison – a truly fascinating character. At the time, Ken was the website's editor. He wasn't a journalist but he was a hard core motorcyclist who made my interest in bikes look like a passing fad! As a young man, he made and repaired aluminium boats, almost became a lumber jack and then had gone on to do a College degree in Psychology. Throughout, he remained passionate about bikes and was a top quality rider.

Because MCUSA looked so slick and professional on screen, I didn't realise that Ken and Don were the company's only two employees and that they were working from Don's Grandad's loft. What the eye can't see, the heart doesn't grieve over ...

I am not quite sure whether Ken actually knew my writing but he professed to be a Frank Melling fan and so we agreed that I would send him stories about bikes I remembered fondly or which had stuck in my mind because they were so terrible. The series would be called "Memorable Motorcycles". Eventually I wrote just shy of 200 articles and enjoyed every single one. On the way, I had so much fun that I should have been paying MCUSA – not the other way round.

Ken was completely relaxed about what motorcycles appeared in the column. They could be dirt, road or race bikes and I could write as many words as I wished because there was no problem in terms of the pagination – the number of pages in an article. Without having to worry about the cost of printing it was as easy to put 2,000 words on the website as it was 1,000. In short, I had won first prize in the Freelancer's Lottery of Life. There just wasn't a better job anywhere in journalism.

The images were great too. The website had brilliant designers and they used pictures in huge sizes and with a clarity no magazine could ever match.

I was also blessed with Ken as an editor. He knew a lot about bikes and he was also confident and bold in his editorial decisions. This is why MCUSA worked so well. Not only could I write stories with opinions and humour but Ken was also against any attempt at dumbing down, so my pieces, and the rest of the site, developed a unique style which made it both extremely popular with readers and highly respected in the motorcycle industry.

I can't imagine what I have ever done to deserve so much good fortune but, when Ken eventually moved on, my new editor was Bart Madson who was just as keen to maintain the quality of the writing at MCUSA. Bart was an English major at College. He had a very finely developed and, dare I say it, English sense of humour and so we had a lot of fun with quirky, off-beat articles which resonated with readers.

Bart eventually became Managing Editor and the new Production Editor was Byron Wilson. Byron was yet another highly literate journalist who was determined to maintain MCUSA's unique voice, which he did – all the way until he received 36 hours' notice to quit and the site was no more!

I have a real Yin and Yang view of the closure. My immediate reaction was that I was no longer part of a publication I loved. It wasn't so much the loss of income but having the bond with readers broken, developed over 16 years, which hurt so much. I really did feel close to MCUSA's readers - and so I am particularly glad that my last ever piece, on a Mk 1 Norton Commando, was one of my best ever articles. I owed it to my readers to do a really good job as I signed off.

So, there was a real sense of sadness. Then I thought about the obverse side of the coin. For sixteen years, I had enjoyed full editorial backing to write the best, most entertaining stories about motorcycles that I could. My editors encouraged me to take on the establishment when I attacked Dorna and MotoGP and even approved hard core, English satire which must have been challenging for an audience which, although world-wide, was predominantly American.

I wrote about everything from the 1907 TT winning Norton to the 2016 MV Agusta Turismo Veloce and everything in between. Whether it was a dirt bike, road race machine or even a cruiser I was given total freedom to write whatever I wished with just one caveat: make the stories entertaining and keep the readers coming back.

Because of MCUSA's status, I was invited to launches of new bikes and I had enjoyed my status as the token fat, bald, old wrinkly in the midst of all the young journalists.

No freelancer in the world could possibly ask for more and I had a wonderful time.

There was one more thing which gave me immense satisfaction and it probably only came about because of my age. When I first began writing professionally, I sat in my bedroom and typed with two fingers on a manual Adler portable typewriter.

After I had finished a story, I collected the sheets of paper together, marked up the corrections with a pen and then re-typed everything – this time with an extra sheet of plain and carbon paper. The carbon paper made a rather indistinct copy on the plain paper beneath it as I typed.

Next, I put the finished piece, along with the black and white photographs, into a big envelope and posted it to my editor by Airmail. Five days later, the package arrived in America. If the story was a news item, rather than a feature, it could be rushed into the next available issue and just three months after I wrote it, a magazine would come back to me carrying the article.

If the story was controversial or particularly interesting, readers would send in letters commenting on the content and these would appear in the following issue. Within four months, I would know what the readers thought of my work.

But then came Motorcycle-USA.com and the world-wide web. Multiple revisions of a story could, and would, be done on my computer and, when I was satisfied with the piece, a simple press of "Alt" with "S" would transmit the words and images six thousand miles across the Atlantic and the width of America.

If the story was time sensitive, Bart or Byron would have the whole article designed and published on MCUSA within one working day. After just a few minutes of it appearing, comments would be arriving from all over the world.

To have readers, wherever English was read, interact with something I had written in less than 24 hours was incredibly moving for me. In 1970, I was sat tapping away at a manual typewriter with seas and time zones standing as huge walls, separating me from other countries and cultures. Now, just 46 years later, whatever I wrote could be read and commented on instantly - by any person on our planet with internet access.

I am incredibly proud to be English – even more so than British – and I would not want to live anywhere other than our truly green and pleasant land with its grey, storm driven winter rain and soft, water coloured, summer clouds. I remain in awe of, and in love with, English literature from Geoffrey Chaucer to John le Carré and get misty eyed when I hear Land of Hope and Glory sung. So, in every way, I respect and empathise with the need for a myriad of cultural identities in our world if only because I want one of them for myself.

Equally, in this wonderful, magical age of connectivity, where we can all be part of one world which is linked in the most intimate way, I wish that there could be some universal consensus regarding our species' future. No God, of any shape kind or form wants to see our fellow human beings maimed and killed in his or her name. Gods have more sense, and greater vision, than to ask for such petty, narrow minded acts of cruelty and violence – or worse still demand them.

To be a God, you would have to do better than this so I wish that no religious group would inflict such suffering on the world and then claim their particular deity had told them that this was the right thing to do – because it isn't.

We stand on the brink of a golden age for humanity where we can be ourselves, and enjoy the quirks and idiosyncrasies which our geographical location, race and culture have given to us and yet - at the same time - rejoice in being part of the same family of humanity. I hope that we take the right path in the next 46 years.

★★★★★

There was a finale to this American trip and, although it belongs to this part of the story, it happened the following year. Starting road racing in middle-age, actually approaching the time when some people were taking early retirement, I was never going to ride in GPs.

At the same time as being too old, I was also too young to have ridden in the events where my heart lay. Despite the horrendous dangers, my dream would have been to race with heroes from the Golden Age of road racing in the 1950s and 1960s – head buried in the tank of a Manx Norton, battling it out on some suicidally treacherous street circuit where the crowd could reach out and touch me and the bike. That was truly road racing.

Of course, the one event I should have done was the TT in the Isle of Man. Carol and I discussed this when the Classic TT was launched in 2013 but I was already far too old to start learning the 37 ¾ mile circuit which kills people with almost monotonous regularity.

I did manage to fulfil part of my dream by riding in a lap of the course during a Ducati celebration which took place in 2011. In that event, Sammy Miller came within a gnat's whisker of dying, quite literally in front of my eyes, when he had a horrendous accident at Waterworks Corner. This reminded me that the TT was perhaps one thrill I could do without.

However, I did want to race somewhere very memorable and there was no circuit in the world with a bigger status than the Daytona Speedbowl, ironically just up the I-49 Interstate highway from Disneyworld.

There is no doubt that Daytona is a unique experience and the most overwhelming factor is the size of the circuit which you can see in its entirety from almost any place inside the venue. The site covers over 180 acres with seating for 147,000 spectators and a home straight almost 3/4-mile long.

But, more than anything else, it is the 31 degree banking which dominates the Daytona racer's mind. This is steep – as in a hard hill-walking climb.

There is also a ghoulish fascination with the thick, steel guard ropes designed to keep Nascar race cars inside the track and away from the spectators. Everyone who races Daytona has to ride alongside the ropes just to go face to face with the steel which will kill you, should you ever come into contact with it. Dull, grey, weather-beaten and half a wrist thick - no-one is in any doubt about the consequences of touching them whilst on a race bike.

As a young man I had seen the great BSA and Triumph factories battle it out with the Japanese at Daytona and now, I desperately wanted to ride the same track and find out why so many riders came away sighing and nodding their heads in respect.

The speed of Eric's road going T500 got me thinking. How quick could a street legal bike go at a really fast track – and against full blown race machines? There was only one place in the world to find out: Daytona. Would Eric be up for the plan? One phone call later and Eric was in his workshop!

The plan was both extremely simple – and very bold. Eric would take a T500 Suzuki street bike, tune it very mildly and then ride the Suz from his home in the mountains of West Virginia to Daytona – something in the region of 700 miles. It would make a great story – quirky and a dream which a lot of riders would like to fulfil.

Over the phone everything looked simple. As the Daytona Bike Week kicked off, Eric would bolt on three race plates and I would cruise round at the back of the field. Then we would all retire to the "Red Lobster" for an American-sized, seafood meal. I would have lived out my dream, Eric would have had some fun racing and then we could all relax.

In order to be safe at Daytona, the standard T500 road bike did need some modifications – but surprisingly few. With the angle of lean it is possible to achieve on modern racing tyres, the standard exhausts are lethally low and drag on the floor, so these were replaced by Suzuki TR750 pattern expansion chambers.

For my comfort Eric fitted a long, narrow, racing fuel tank and clip-on 'bars. The T500 would be flat out at Daytona and hanging on to road 'bars would be hard work.

Stopping a big, heavy bike like the T500 at the end of Daytona's west straight was always going to be marginal with the standard tiny, 8-inch drum brake – dangerously so in fact. The cure was a GT500 disc – the model immediately after the T500 – which fitted perfectly. Eric also used the GT500's front forks.

We ran standard T500 carburettors, and barrels which had only been mildly ported because Eric was going to have a long ride down from Virginia and needed a user-friendly road bike: Daytona here we come.

Eric and I stayed in touch throughout the winter and, as the weeks went by, the bike took shape and started to look really tasty in the style of a classic café racer. The yellow, red and white colour scheme was taken, more or less, from the legendary Barry Sheene's Texaco Suzuki factory bikes and our bike looked every inch the super sports road bike it actually was.

The day before I left for Florida, I phoned Eric to discover that we faced a serious problem. Eric lives on top of a full blown Virginian mountain, with his wife Julie and their extended family of Malamute dogs. Malamutes are best known for their ability to pull sleds through the Alaskan wilderness, so they were fine in the hurricane which was blowing as Eric prepared to head south. Eric wasn't nearly so enthusiastic and so the T500 went in the back of his truck as he slid down to drier and warmer climes.

As things turned out, this was a smart move because the rain was torrential as Eric crawled along the I-95 towards Daytona. Despite what the Floridian Tourist Board will tell you, Florida can be a miserable place in early March. Forget the bikini clad babes: you need serious winter gear!

We met for breakfast in "Wendy's" and 5000 calories later, things were looking better. AHMRA do a truly wonderful job for American classic motorcycle racing, in all its many forms, and their tech crew couldn't have been more helpful.

Yes, we both needed sympathetic psychiatric medical care for even thinking that we could race a road bike at Daytona but Eric had done a wonderful job in terms of machine preparation, so the tech inspection stickers went on without a problem and we were ready for action.

The bike was truly surprising – almost to the point of disbelief. We took it out into the countryside around Tomoka Springs for a shakedown session and it was as docile as a 50cc scooter. However, when it hit the power band at 5500rpm everything became really frisky. Beneath its road bike skin, I was beginning to think that Eric's T500 had some hidden secrets.

After the standard struggle with Daytona security staff – uniforms do have a seriously negative effect on the personality of otherwise pleasant people – I smiled and grovelled my way into the access tunnel which runs beneath the north banking. Coming out of the tunnel at Daytona and into the circuit is always an awe inspiring experience. The word vast is accurate but does not do justice to the sheer immensity of the speed bowl. It stretches out on to the far horizon like some alien planet and trucks, bikes and people are simply swallowed up.

Eric had brought his own race bike but, as always, was more concerned about my needs than his. Despite not being in the VIP part of the paddock, I couldn't have had better treatment if I had been riding for a full factory team. Another wholly positive factor was that parked quite near to us was top British classic racer, Les Trotter. Les was vastly experienced at Daytona and had won the 1976 Manx Grand Prix as well as being a top TT racer.

Trotts kindly agreed to let me follow him round the Daytona Circuit for a few laps to ensure that I knew where I was going, and so that I didn't throw Eric's lovely T500 up the road. Les was a good tutor and I came back to our truck with a big smile. The bike was sweet and fast, and the track wasn't hard to learn. Things were looking good.

The second practice was even better – much better in fact. It was one of those wonderful racing days where everything is perfect. Not 99% good, but absolutely perfect. Eric had built an absolute rocketship and I had never ridden a better race bike in my life.

Everything was easy – almost too easy – and that should have been the warning. Towards the end of the session, I truly eased off and things were still going sublimely well. Eric had got the handling absolutely on the money and the big bike stopped well too.

The motor, tuned for torque, was a dream. Pulling stupendously high gearing, the T500 was cruising round the banking at over 130mph – with speed still in reserve. Now, touring round at the back of the field was forgotten. Those AHRMA trophies looked good!

Coming off the north banking, the big twin was ambling along at 7000 rpm in top and I was line perfect – and catching everyone. Then, in a fraction of a second, came the dreaded chirp from the back tyre that said one thing: seizure. I had the clutch in with a reaction time honed by years of racing two-strokes and so stayed on the bike.

Back at the truck, we all knew that there were big problems. Eric had the cylinder head off the bike in seconds and found a grape sized hole in the left-hand piston. The absolute despair which a rider and team feel when they meet a situation like this is impossible to describe: it is crushing. We simply sat, drained and useless. Then, Trotts wandered across to see why we were looking suicidal.

Trotts, being an old school racer and a fine tuner in his own right, had a very different view of our predicament. It wasn't so much a disaster as a nuisance and, in a flash, Eric and Trotts attacked the T500. GP mechanics eat your hearts out: we had the "A" team!

The barrel was hammered off the piston and the crankcases filled up with what was going to be the first of many pints of neat race fuel, which then drained out of the bottom of the crankcase, taking with it lumps of alloy from the melted piston. Let's just say that I'm quite sure the patch of Florida grass underneath the Suzuki wasn't very verdant in the following months!

Trotts' sponsor donated a brand-new piston to the cause whilst my job, as the mechanical moron in the team, was to clean the aluminium smeared cylinder liner with coarse emery paper.

Meanwhile, Eric had found the cause of all our troubles. A tiny fleck of grass had been pulled up against the main jet and, with the engine gobbling up fuel at 12 miles per gallon, that was enough to instantly melt a piston.

Meanwhile, the seconds ticked away…

How the dynamic duo achieved what they did is still a thing of wonder to me but as they called my race to the grid, Eric cracked the T500 up, and off I went to the start line. I knew that this was going to be an interesting experience – with a break-in period of about 200 yards and three minutes!

With a brand new piston, there is always a strong chance of seizure but Eric and Trotts had worked so hard that I was happy to take that chance, or any other, rather than let them down by not riding.

I have always been a fast starter and this was no exception. In the first three yards, I was right on the pace with the leading bunch. Then came the realization that instead of having 8000 rpm to play with, there were only 5000 revs in the engine. The new piston was just too tight in the bore and was acting as a huge brake on the motor. Heaven alone knows what temperature it was running at, as the good side of the motor tried to drag its reluctant twin sister into action.

The first three laps were frustration after frustration. I would make suicidal passing manoeuvres on the brakes through the infield, only to be passed on the straights. If only, if only, if only… The mantra of frustrated racers world-wide.

Then coming off the north banking, where the bike had originally seized, the big twin gave an enormous cough and suddenly 7000 rpm was available. By the south banking, a further 1000 revs had appeared.

Now, bikes in front simply disappeared as Eric's flying machine gobbled them up. The north banking was particularly memorable. Daytona has since been re-surfaced but in 2001 the track was very uneven. The T500 was pulling 8,300 rpm which equated to something around 135 mph. Going this fast with no fairing, it was a question of just hanging on as the combination of speed, rough track and g-force tried to part me from the bike. Daytona truly is a special place to race a motorcycle.

On the last lap, I was in eighth-place as we entered the east straight. The next four riders were bunched in a group and I was catching up at a rate which would have seen me comfortably past them on the next lap – and fourth-place would have been a good result on a road bike.

But there was an even worse sight another 100 yards further on, where the leading three riders were battling it out for the outright win. I was catching them fast too.

If only the bike hadn't seized. If only we'd had the chance to break in the piston. If only the race had been two laps longer. But "ifs" count for nothing in racing.

What I did win was the privilege of riding for Eric Kalamaja – the sort of person who, if aliens ever visit our planet, will get the human race a first class review. Would I have traded a Daytona win for the chance to ride with Eric? Not for a second. We came, we saw, we raced, we surprised a lot of hardened racers with the speed of our road bike – and we had a great post-race meal.

I was disappointed - but only for a surprisingly short period of time because the Thundersprint was standing on the brink of a chasm. In the next three months, I would find out if I was going to crash or fly…

16

The Right Place at the Right Time

ON a number of occasions in my life, I have been in precisely the right place at the right time – and in 2003 I really was. This was very fortunate because I did need an elephant sized slice of good fortune at that point in time.

After Manchester, we didn't have a venue for the next Thundersprint. It was all well and good coming back from America loaded with clever marketing ideas but none of these would be any good if there was nowhere to run the event.

Then I read our local newspaper and suddenly, the sun came out – or at least I thought that it did. First a short – but very important – digression to explain something about the history of Northwich. The town is located on what, 200 million years ago, was the bottom of a sea. The water evaporated and the salt was left intact – and in immense proportions. It has been produced commercially in the region for at least 2,000 years and maybe even more.

By Victorian times, salt production had reached epic quantities. In one mine, the great cavern was over 30 feet in height and these spaces were a real tourist attraction, with over 1000 visitors a day at peak. The Victorians loved the show, reporting that the caverns were: "Thoroughly illuminated, with long streets being fitted up with stalls and refreshment bars.

"Music is also plentifully supplied and as many as 400 persons have been known to join in one dance in the crystal halls."

Unfortunately, the mines leaked water and the salt pillars, which supported the caverns, eventually dissolved. This led to gigantic, water-filled holes beneath Northwich - and endemic subsidence throughout the town.

I have to say that I am not a fan of John Prescott, Tony Blair's Deputy Prime Minister from 1997 to 2007. He comes across as a coarse person who should have stayed at sea handing out drinks, instead of being given the power to ruin people's lives, but he did do one good thing: he funded the stabilisation of the flooded mines.

This was an incredible, and successful, feat of civil engineering and the area's Chief Executive, a lovely lady called Anne Bingham-Holmes, wanted to publicise the success.

At the time, Northwich was in an administrative area called Vale Royal, right in the centre of Cheshire. Vale Royal had two main towns – Northwich and

Winsford – and neither had a high profile nationally or internationally. This was an important factor too.

The story I read was that Anne was looking for ways to promote Northwich. I contacted Vale Royal Borough Council and spoke to Andrea Peattie, another very pleasant and open minded Council Officer, and soon we had an agreement to bring the Thundersprint to Northwich.

The speed with which things happened was due to a number of factors. First, and most importantly, Anne wanted the Thundersprint to happen. Once anything had her thumb print on the job, things moved very swiftly in Vale Royal, and her Officers got on with the job without debate or discussion.

There was strong, cross-party political backing for the idea too. Councillors of every political persuasion supported the Thundersprint enthusiastically because they, as much as Anne, wanted something big for Northwich and Vale Royal. I have stressed these points because, ironically, they will explain why the Thundersprint eventually left the town when Northwich ceased to be important to the new Local Authority.

Then, there was the support of top quality staff. Andrea was a superb fixer of things and an excellent problem solver, both formally and informally. Richard Hallows, Vale Royal's Director of Social and Community Services, made sure that big, key issues were addressed properly and correctly because what we had in mind was very different from a conventional motorcycle race.

Finally, Vale Royal's manual workers put their hearts and souls into the event. I could always ask one of the lads to prune an extra bit of tree or fill in a pot hole – work which wasn't always on their job list. It was dramatically different from the engineering drawings and formality of Manchester because there was a very real sense of personal ownership regarding the Thundersprint in Northwich. All the staff, from Anne to the lads with the chain saws, lived in the area and wanted something good for the town.

However, what Anne and everyone else in Vale Royal expected and what I had in mind were two very different things. I was becoming increasingly sceptical about the attraction of actual racing for the wider public. MotoGP, with the best riders in the world competing on the finest machines, was one thing but away from this top level, watching motorcycles race was of interest only to real enthusiasts.

I was very heavily influenced by what I had seen at the Magic Kingdom and for the new event I wanted to turn the Thundersprint racers into a Disney World style cast where, although they played themselves, the riders became part of the show in the same way as Mickey Mouse and Snow White were at Disney.

The Disney parade was also deeply attractive. Thousands of customers lined the roads to see fantasy characters wave as they drove past. If we could replicate this in Northwich, with race bikes, the spectacle would be fantastic.

It is important to remember what a quiet little town Northwich was at the time. For example, the bigger of the town's two football clubs usually attracted maybe 300 spectators to a home game. Northwich Carnival had a few thousand. With Southport still burning in my mind, I was sure that a free to view Thundersprint would bring 25,000 visitors to the town.

In some ways Vale Royal was a wonderfully old fashioned area and so everyone was far too polite to actually laugh in my face, but I was very well aware that no-one believed we could attract such a huge number of visitors. Later, I heard that the figure being knocked around the Council offices for a successful Thundersprint was 2,500 spectators. At this point, I was the one who was doing the laughing. We had doubled this number for Thunder at the Tower and there was no way the new event would ever do this badly.

Our idea was that we would run the Thundersprint right in the centre of the town and that it would have free admission. Vale Royal would give us the town, and some infrastructure free of charge, and cover some of our expenses.

The big problem was the stupidity of British mainland law. In simple terms, it is impossible to run any form of motorsport on a public road in England, Wales or Scotland. In theory, you can have your own Act of Parliament to permit the use of some highly specified bit of highway but, in practical terms, it can't be done. This is why there is motorcycle road racing in the Isle of Man and Northern Ireland but not mainland Britain.

When the Thundersprint was at its peak, I had a meeting with a wonderful, free thinking politician called Stephen Ladyman who was Minister of State for Transport. Stephen was a keen motorcyclist and a fan of all motorsport – so much so that he had starred on Top Gear. He wanted the Thundersprint, and other well organised events, to run on public roads.

The meeting went very well and the Civil Servants did what they always do in these situations: nod, make encouraging noises and take notes.

Stephen left the room for some reason and the Senior Civil Servant looked at me through ruthless eyes and said: "I don't give a f**k what the Minister thinks or says. There'll only be racing on public roads in England over my dead body – so forget it.

"And I'll be here long after he's gone."

And that's why every country in the world can enjoy the economic benefits of motorsport in city centres and yet the English, who have the best and most safety conscious organisers anywhere on the planet, can't! Is it any wonder the public become cynical about the way we are governed?

The regulations are, allegedly, on their way to being changed at the time of writing but I still wouldn't hold my breath at the thought of seeing racing on English public roads. I guess the Whitehall Civil Servants are still fighting a rear guard action to stop this happening and believe me, it's the London based apparatchiks who rule the country, not the politicians.

There was an unlikely fix in Northwich but only someone like me, who at best is very loosely attached to reality, could ever have seen it. Right in the centre of the town was a big car park. Not immense by any means but still large. Around the edge of the car park was an access road.

As the New Year began, I was still struggling to find a solution to running the event in the town centre without using any public roads.

One evening in January, I drove across to Northwich on my own just to think entirely without distractions. I needed the town to be empty and to have no company. This was a solo job.

The weather was abnormal with a fierce, Arctic wind whipping huge, surreal clouds of luminescent, freezing fog across Northwich. It was just what I needed as a stimulus to see the area in a totally different way. The fog charged across from the River Weaver in sparkling, vertical sheets alternately exposing and hiding the whole area and making me concentrate hard just to see anything at all.

I stood in the gale on the high grass banking overlooking the town's biggest car park. My eyes were streaming with tears from the icy wind and I could barely stand. Then, without any thought, the whole solution appeared almost instantly and with complete clarity.

One moment, I didn't have any idea of what to do – and the next minute, everything was obvious. It was possible to run a sprint inside the car park.

I slid down the grass and began pacing out the length of the access road. Give or take, I could mark out a 400 yard course. The car park was owned by the Council. It was therefore private land and racing on private land was legal!

Everything except the actual track would be located on the public roads and this was legal too. All over Britain, Christmas fairs and the like were held in town centre streets so this was possible.

All that was needed now was for Vale Royal to agree to what was a very, very radical idea.

Even with Anne's backing for the event, the Council's agreement was not a foregone conclusion. I could see perfectly well where the track should run but convincing everyone else was not straightforward, not least because the car park roads I wanted to use were full of enormous pot holes. In fact, these turned out to be a huge help. They were so bad that the roads were already scheduled for re-surfacing on Health and Safety grounds. I made the case for using a slightly different type of Tarmac, called Prixmat, for the job. This was a specialist surfacing material providing high grip, and was extremely fast draining, so for the 364 days of the year when the car park wasn't a race track, the good citizens of Northwich would have the world's safest access road to their parking spaces.

Yet another wonderful Vale Royal Officer called Don Patterson, a Civil Engineer who had worked on building Hong Kong airport, planned and controlled the job and, out of no-where, we had a raceable, albeit very quirky little track. I was thrilled.

A high grass bank formed one side of the car park. This was perfect for spectators, and the Council brought in temporary grandstands on another two sides to create a fantastic arena.

The run up to the first ever Thundersprint at Northwich had been the hardest ever. To be honest, we had become a bit of a joke by continually moving from one venue to another and, after Heaton Park, customers were starting to become a bit wary. The traders were the same. They trusted us as an organising team, but they wanted to come to a show where everything was familiar and they could settle down to making money.

By May, we were exhausted. With the help of some wonderful volunteers, we had given out 75,000 flyers, attended shows and spent every weekend meeting customers at bikers' meeting places throughout the country. The riders and traders supported us and had given us their money, along with their best wishes. Now, all that we needed were the spectators.

The team had also been strengthened by the addition of Martin Crook who, although he was nominally in charge of Technical Control, became an excellent manager able to make critical decisions on the spot and without consultation. Running the paddock area was David Lawton, an engineer, who was also able to act independently. Carol led a team administering the whole event.

The Thundersprint was now far too complex for me to even attempt to micro-manage and so we hired Eddie Nelson, a very experienced race organiser, along with the Darley Moor Motorcycle Road Racing Club, to execute the racing element of the event for us. Being able to leave this critical part of the Thundersprint to someone I trusted was a huge relief.

Finally, Garry Gardiner, who was nominally our commentator, took on a far greater role than just telling spectators about the riders. He became "The Voice of the Thundersprint" and I could leave Garry to interview our star riders, politicians, sponsors, Councillors and guests, knowing that the job would be done perfectly.

In management terms, the system is called a flat management structure where each area of responsibility overlaps the one next to it. My job was to produce a really meticulous event plan so that all of my managers knew precisely what needed doing, and most importantly, when and why.

*****

We were in Northwich at 5am on the day of the Thundersprint. It was cold, with light drizzle falling from a slate grey sky. Carol and Colin had done a wonderful job setting out all the trade stalls and they sat in long, neat, empty rows. Water dripped gently from the plastic roofs. I could almost hear their soft breathing as they slept undisturbed by their owners or customers.

I walked through a gap in the fencing and stood, completely alone, on the track. No-one had yet ridden a race bike on it. It's fine writing an event plan and then selling an idea but, in the early dawn light, I felt very lonely and vulnerable – but not frightened.

If I was right, if my dreams, ideas and doodles were worth anything then the event would be a success. If I was wrong then I would be found out. There would no committee to blame – no system to hide behind, no wall of anonymity. Vale Royal had backed my ideas. Carol and Colin had put them into action and now, all that remained was the test.

Strangely, I didn't want any support, kindness or re-assurance – not even from Carol, Colin or my managers. I was completely and utterly certain that everything I had conceived would work in practice and that the event would be a success. This state of mind is difficult to explain. It's nothing to do with bragging or showing off, and nor is it some false idea of one's ability. Rather, it comes from a certainty that you have meticulously planned every detail of the event and therefore success must follow - almost automatically – if everyone does what is required of them.

So, I experienced the intense loneliness of being at the end of the command chain, and the vulnerability of knowing that everyone in the team had to do their part, but not for a second did I have any doubt.

This state of mind was essential – vital even. Once I doubted my decisions, even for the merest blink of time, then so would everyone else and the whole edifice would come tumbling down. At 5am, in the drizzle and half-light, my willpower and confidence had to be rock solid.

By 7am, everything was in place. I always took sole responsibility for allowing access to traders and riders on the morning of the Thundersprint. Regardless of the tension as the queues grew ever longer, not a single person was allowed on site until Carol, Colin, Eddie, Martin and David were absolutely happy that their individual elements of the event were in place and settled. It was essential that the management teams were calm and relaxed because the very moment that 220 riders, and about the same number of traders, came through the barriers they were all going to want instant and individual attention.

Rather than radioing the staff on the main access gate I jogged up there, to personally supervise the checking of passes and to make sure that the entry was calm and controlled. I always found this operation the most emotional and moving part of the whole event. All the thousands of words of planning notes, the months of giving out flyers, meeting traders and talking to riders, the meetings and phone calls – everything in the Thundersprint Universe met at this one singularity point - the end of the event and its beginning.

The barriers were pulled back and I stood at the side of the road, proud and almost tearful, as the first van rolled up and the first access pass was checked.

There were smiles and waves from riders and traders who had become personal friends during the last five Thundersprints and icy, hostile glares from first timers who thought that they had been kept waiting for too long. Regardless, each pass was checked individually because it is easy to stop a problem at the access gate - but virtually impossible once a vehicle is inside a show.

As the riders and traders streamed in I began to get the wonderful, dry, metallic taste in my mouth which showed that I was on the very edge of my performance ability with nothing left in reserve and no more to give. It wasn't just excitement - but totally committed focus. If a group of marauding aliens, melting the Northwich buildings with their death rays, had turned up at the gate I would have still made them stop and show me their passes.

After the initial rush I jogged back to the paddock which, in this first Thundersprint, was located on one of the public roads. Riders were still unloading their bikes. There were smiles, jokes about starting so early and the lovely paddock banter about my lack of riding ability: it was great.

The drizzle had stopped and now the pale grey sky was beginning to show dappled patches of the softest, powder blue. This could be good...

The traders pulled back their overnight covers and started hanging goods on the frames of their stands – busy, focussed and hopeful. Given good weather, they might earn back their pitch fee or even take home a day's wages. The constant threat of bad weather dominates show traders' thinking. Rain and wind will keep the spectators away and ruin stock: it's a perilous way to earn a living.

Traders who didn't know me, barely acknowledged my greetings. I was just another show organiser and, at this stage, the Thundersprint was just another show, no different from the dozens of other minor events scattered up and down the country. Those who had been with us for years shook my hand, teased ruthlessly and wished me good luck. As one of our Asian friends said as he grasped my hand: "Insha'Allah (God willing) we'll all make a few quid." They were my thoughts exactly.

Everything was going exactly to plan except for one really odd thing. There were a few spectators sitting in the grandstands. How weird was that? Spectators at 7am, sat down and unpacking their breakfasts: this was odd. I couldn't imagine why they were there so early.

Martin's team were in full, polished, technical control mode by the time I got to the paddock. Jimmy Aspinall, Eddie Griffiths, Les Trotter and Bill and Pam Redmayne were impeccable – friendly and welcoming but completely thorough. This is what Technical Control should be like.

Carol and her team dealt with the paper work, and gave the riders a gift to thank them for riding with us. Elizabeth acted as everyone's PA – and got a lot more exercise than she ever did in her PE lessons!

Jim Redman was our rock because he led by example. He had his protective clothing checked, waited politely in line for his souvenir t-shirt and was a model of modesty and professionalism.

All riders were required to walk the track before they could ride. Because the Thundersprint course was a car park access road, riders needed to be aware of the special challenges it posed and so it was a condition of riding that they should inspect the track for themselves before riding it.

Most riders took this in good part and Jim helped tremendously in maintaining rider co-operation. Not that this was totally straightforward. On one occasion, two riders who were new to the Thundersprint stood at the entrance to the track and really let fly with their mouths at the thought of walking the track. One of Eddie's marshals was taking the verbal diarrhoea so I intervened personally. The conversation was short.

"See that bloke there (I pointed to Jim), walking the track? See the care he's taking? He's won six World Championships and six TTs. When you've won seven World Championships, come to me and tell me that you don't need to walk the track and I might listen." They walked the track!

Interestingly, later in the day they sought me out and apologised for making such a fuss - which was a gracious thing to do on their part. I put their reluctance down to the early start and we exchanged a good humoured smile!

By the time practice had started, everything was running beautifully – but we had a problem on our hands: spectators were pouring in.

I had predicted around 25,000 spectators, a figure which everyone else thought was manically optimistic, and that these would be spread throughout the day. In fact, fans simply invaded Northwich Town Centre in numbers I never expected - and from extremely early in the morning.

This meant that the paddock, the trade areas and the spectator banking very quickly became crowded. In short, I had not used the available space effectively simply because I never dreamed we would have such a huge crowd.

This is where the Flat Management system proved its worth. Without the need to follow a rigid system, Carol, Colin, Martin and David fixed issues as they arose and the event carried on, albeit with a bit of a bumpy ride but still safely.

Just how big the attendance was became apparent during the Cavalcade. Jim and Claudio Castiglioni, the owner of MV Agusta who had become a personal friend of mine through my work as a journalist, led the parade and the pavements were jammed with cheering fans. We may not have been in Disney World but as the race bikes boomed and roared round the town centre, it was clear that we had a hit show on our hands.

I have a vivid imagination but I simply could not have dreamed of how enthusiastic the spectators were and how well everything ran.

If the parade was Disney World then the rest of the event was straight from the Magic Kingdom too. I was determined that the Thundersprint would be far more than a race because, as just a motorcycle competition, it was never going to be world class.

To do this, I pulled some purely theatrical stunts. As the start time of 1.30

got nearer, Garry would whip up the crowd through interviews with the stars. At precisely 13.18 – only 120 seconds before the commencement of the display – a Battle of Britain Memorial Flight Spitfire would do its sighting pass. Just as accurately, 13.20 would see the start of its five minute aerial display – and there wouldn't be a dry eye in the stadium.

Immediately following the Spitfire, came the blessing of the event by one of our friends from the Salvation Army. This was a time for quiet and reflection – but I also wanted the tension and excitement of the crowd to be bottled up almost to the point of exploding.

Finally, we played the National Anthem and everyone stood dutifully singing as if they were representing their country. It was pure theatre and I loved playing with the crowd's emotions.

As the last words of the National Anthem faded away, Garry hit the rev limiter in terms of excitement. In just a few seconds he had the crowd cheering, doing Mexican waves and getting ready for what we called – with complete justification as far as I was concerned – our "GP in a Car Park."

The absolute truth is that there were two ways of looking at the Thunder-sprint. The factually objective analysis would conclude that amateur riders rode round a narrow car park access road at, by road racing standards, slow speeds. In empirical terms this is what happened.

The other interpretation, and the one which even our most illustrious stars followed, was to accept the event for what it was: the world's best motorcycling theatre. If you watch Shakespeare's Henry V being performed live on stage you clearly aren't seeing a real, medieval King facing 10,000 French Men at Arms at Agincourt. It would be stupid to think that you are. But if you want to be moved by Henry's passionate urging to his troops then you can be, and you will be. If you permit yourself, it is possible to stand in the mud and ache to be one of his "...band of brothers."

So it was with the Thundersprint. Yes we were riding a bit of road, in a town centre car park, but when the Spitfire had roared away, the re-assuring words of prayer had been spoken and we were standing straight for our National Anthem - goodness me, it felt like a big something. A GP? I don't know, but for sure it was memorable – whatever it was!

As for the track, the least likely race circuit in the world worked wonderfully well. By the time of the Thundersprint, I had ridden the ¼ mile of tarmac at least 10,000 times – albeit only in my head – but it was still a strange experience to come to the starting line.

I loved the gladiatorial atmosphere of the Thundersprint – the spectators pressed up against the safety fence so near that you could see the colour of their eyes. The scent of the race fuel and the aroma of burnt castor racing oil was nectar to me. The Thundersprint was never a real Grand Prix but it was a great experience.

Here's what it felt like.

Once my class was called to the starting area, I pushed everything else out of my mind – Carol, the next job I had to do - simply everything.

With the noise of the unsilenced race bikes booming round the arena, and the spectators cheering, I move into a quiet, peaceful place with just me and the bike.

Garry is whipping up the crowd but I never really hear him, except as the faintest of background noises. The crowd stop being individuals and blur into a single mass of spectators, like the toy people Elizabeth used to play with as an infant.

Before I can race I have to be sure that the engine is running cleanly so, in the last few seconds before I am called to the start line, I blip the throttle to clear out any excess oil which has built up whilst I have been in the collecting box. Now, I am certain that the engine is running sweetly and the bike is eager for battle. This increases the calm and makes the inner silence even more pronounced. All the time, I am emptying my mind of everything except the bike and the track. Nothing else in the world has any relevance.

I roll the bike up to the start line, where it is positioned precisely in front of the timing beam by the marshals. They are very strict regarding where the bike should be because even a tiny run up to the timing light will dramatically decrease the overall lap time.

My Seeley Suzuki makes maximum power at 8,300 rpm but I want the most torque – the pulling power which provides the best acceleration – and this comes at 7,000 rpm. In the silence and calm which is inside my head, I bring the big, two-stroke twin up to 7,000 rpm.

Every class in the Thundersprint is won, or lost, by fractions of a second – and I always want to win at what, for me, is the best event in the world – so every particle of my being is condensed into the throttle in my right hand, the rev counter needle in front of my visor and the clutch lever in my left glove. Nothing else exists in the world.

Once the starting lights flick out, I am free to go. My whole world becomes even more tightly, intensely focussed. There are no distractions or wasted thoughts. Simply me and my bike. My eyes are fixed on the first 90 degree corner, just 100m away.

With the rev counter needle hovering at the 7,000 rpm mark I feed in just enough of the clutch so that the bike accelerates very hard but the revs don't drop at all. Although only taking a couple of seconds, it is a gentle, delicate operation working co-operatively with the bike rather than insisting on making it obey my commands. 7,000 rpm, and the maximum pulling power, is going to give me the acceleration I need and the Seeley must be on my side to deliver this.

In the best starts I can balance the bike with the clutch and throttle, and the front wheel just hovering over the track for the first 30m or 40m.

Using the low gearing which is essential for the Thundersprint, the acceleration of the Seeley is vicious. Just as the clutch is fully home, second gear has to be popped in – all the time whilst watching the right-hand corner which is now accelerating towards me very quickly. How fast? Maybe 60mph, which is pedestrian slow by real racing standards but impressively quick in a car park!

Now, it's a question of how late can I brake? The first corner always sees riders on the deck through braking too late or too hard so it's a fine judgement call. I go into the corner with the rear wheel pattering in complaint and then it's maximum acceleration out of the bend, and a tiny bit of opposite lock with the handlebars to correct the inevitable micro-slide as the tyre fights for grip.

Another short straight and then a long, double apex, right hand bend - the highlight of the lap for me. The key is to turn at the second apex which means heading directly towards the steel fencing - right up to the point where I am certain it is impossible to turn – and then flick the bike in hard. There is no run-off and all that I can see is a wall of faces pressed hard up against the mesh.

I am one with the bike. The Seeley is tiny and I am wrapped around, and in, it so tightly that we become one with no separation between where man finishes and motorcycle begins. The relationship is intensely symbiotic. I need the Seeley to win – the Seeley needs me in order to be a racing motorcycle and justify its place in the multiverse.

Getting the power on hard is vital but at the same time I can feel the rear wheel scrabbling for grip. Too much power and there will be a slide, which will slow me down – or worse! Not enough, and the time will be too slow.

Now there is the final straight – only 70m or so – and I can sense, rather than see, the spectators facing me as I scream towards them, flat out in second gear with the engine running on past the 8,300 rpm red line. Yet again, 60mph isn't quick but it is a big thrill inside this intense and restricted bowl.

I only see the blur of spectators for a fraction of a second because my eyes are now fixed on the final left-hand bend. Wait, wait, wait until there is no possible chance of stopping the bike and then lay it hard down and run wide into the disabled parking bay to get the maximum space for the final 20m of flat out acceleration.

22.4 seconds of very intense riding and I am panting hard. Now, I can see and hear the spectators clearly again and I smile inside my helmet because I have set a time fast enough to win my class.

Yes, if you want to believe that the Thundersprint is a GP in a Car Park it can be - and that's real magic!

No-one knows how many spectators came to that first Thundersprint in Northwich except to say that the figure was enormous. Not only was the whole of the town centre crammed absolutely full of people but the huge crowd watching the lunch-time cavalcade was an indication of what was to come.

I had made mistakes, and significant ones too, but my managers had solved the problems as they occurred and I was extremely proud of both them and the systems which I had put into place. It was important to learn from the mistakes but it was also absolutely critical to learn from what we had done well. From my point of view, it was as if the first five Thundersprints had been practice for Northwich and everything came together beautifully at this event.

Things were just as good with Vale Royal Borough Council. Anne Bingham-Holmes had a great time. She was delighted with the attendance and was kind enough to say so. This meant that Richard Hallows and Andrea Peattie could work with me to make the following year's event even better.

The political support was there too. Lots of Councillors came to the event and had a great time. We also enjoyed the active support of Mike Hall, the town's MP, who right from the outset was a great fan of the event.

There were lots of smiles and encouragement to do even better in the future – and we did!

17

The Big One

THE Thundersprint really deserves its own book but in "The Flying Penguin" there isn't sufficient space to include anything but some postcards of the event. I hope that these will give you a taste of what it was like to be at the centre of this fireball of an event.

Apart from the crowds, one of the things which Thundersprint fans remember most is the star riders who appeared – and we really did have some big ones!

We followed a policy based strongly on the Heather Scale and hired major household names who would bring in visitors. This policy often caused friction with second level "stars" who felt that we had a duty to pay them so that they could enjoy themselves at the Thundersprint. Typically, these riders would ask for £500 which was ludicrous when they would not bring in a single extra spectator.

If we had gone down the route of having lots of minor stars there were many, insidious, hidden expenses which bumped up their total cost to us as organisers. For example, the rider would want meals and drinks – usually with his wife. Add a few free T-shirts – few means there is no limit to the number demanded by the guest star – and the £500 appearance fee has become £600 or more. That £600 doesn't come out of fresh air and takes a lot of earning.

This is why we had a firm policy of paying riders who would show us a nett profit – after all their expenses!

The big names were the ones we needed and we had some of the most important riders of the time. It's not really fair to choose one above another because they were all right at the top of the Heather Scale and each one was good in their own way. For example, we had double World Champion James Toseland ride with us in 2010. The deal for James to ride was arranged through Toseland's manager, Roger Burnett, an ex-racer who – very unusually – has gone on to have a successful career away from the track. I like Roger a lot and, despite having a laser sharp business brain, he was very fair with us.

James duly arrived, and did a good job, but I felt that he was somewhat distant from the event and us. Certainly, he had no time for idle conversation with Carol, Colin or me. Against this, he was meticulously professional, and the crowds loved him so, as far we were concerned, this was perfect. I didn't want James' autograph and a souvenir picture – I wanted him to please the crowds and he did this very well.

I think James felt that the highlight of the weekend was when he, and his band, played to a packed house at the Northwich Memorial Hall theatre on the evening before the Thundersprint.

We also had a special memory of James' visit – and it wasn't his Memorial Hall gig. Cheshire Police were always very supportive of the Cavalcade – really superb. The Cavalcade was led by Police Outriders and there were Police bikes at the rear too. Their job was difficult. The Cavalcade had to go quickly enough that the engines of the race bikes didn't overheat - but it couldn't be allowed to become a race demo on public roads. The Cheshire Police riders judged the speed to perfection every year.

For our part, we had an agreement with Cheshire Police that all the riders would be on their best behaviour. A key part was that Cavalcaders would not, for any reason, "high five" spectators as they rode along the two and a half mile route - every inch of which was packed with cheering fans.

The year James rode with us things got off to a challenging start from the moment we began gathering riders in the collecting area. In some ways, the Cavalcade was the most difficult part of the whole event. In addition to 120 race entrants, another 100 or so riders took part in the Cavalcade so we had the rather interesting job of corralling over 220 extremely excited riders into a very tight area and then getting them to start, together, precisely on time.

Why the need for military precision? The Cavalcade route used the main arterial road through Northwich and this had to be closed for the absolute minimum of time. When the Police outrider left the paddock area, everyone had to follow otherwise the timetable would sink out of sight and we would be in big trouble.

Once the last bike had joined the Cavalcade, the barriers were drawn across the road to allow the thousands of spectators to cross safely.

My job was to film the Cavalcade from a bike and so the responsibility of deciding which rider would be the last to join the Cavalcade fell entirely on to Colin. It would be badly wrong to think of this job as nothing more than an administrative task – because it was so much more.

First, Colin had to take sole responsibility. It couldn't be a shared decision, because this would lead to confusion and doubt which would have been a certain precursor to a real safety issue

Next, the Cavalcade collecting box was very long and narrow and the far end finished, out of sight, in the paddock some 200m away from Colin.

Finally there was a huge emotional, as well as practical, pressure on Colin. For many of the Cavalcaders, as well as the racers, the Thundersprint was the highlight of the year – and I don't say this lightly. For example – and I promise you that all these examples are completely true – we had wives who induced births to get the baby out on time for the Thundersprint. There were plenty of examples of divorces being pushed through just to get the job out of the way before the Thundersprint and a few cases of break ups being delayed, and then abandoned, because the two battling lovers had such a good time at the event.

Relatives were buried with haste and holidays booked to avoid the Thundersprint weekend.

Marriage proposals were made and retirements celebrated. There was even a foal named Thunder because it was born on the morning of the event. This was particularly lovely for us.

Clearly, customers had a lot invested in the event. Therefore to miss the Cavalcade was a big issue. Colin understood this, not only as a manager but also as a motorcycle enthusiast who loves bikes and riders. Equally, the Cavalcade had to run safely and smoothly.

In the whole event, it was the one judgement call which I would have run a mile from – and then hidden under a hedge!

The first 99% of the Cavalcade pulls away easily. Now Colin is left with four, five or six bikes which won't start or, worse still, are coughing and banging towards the exit. At some point, he has to make the horrendous decision of closing the barrier. How many more seconds does he give that rider to coax his bike into life?

The Police outrider controlling the tail of the Cavalcade is gesticulating and so the barrier is pulled across – and Colin has to deal with genuinely broken-hearted riders. Someone had to do this tough job – but I'm glad that it wasn't me!

Not that things always went to plan when the Cavalcade did set off. On this occasion, James led the riders away, down the hill and towards the Memorial Hall and crowds cheered and waved like mad things. It was a wonderful spectacle – round the Bull Ring, past the Police Station and the town's Royal Mail Sorting Office and back up the hill.

The road we used was a dual carriageway and the roads were separated by a narrow central reservation. Standing in the centre of this was a young lady, clutching a very tiny baby. Instantly, I knew what had happened.

Before the event, Vale Royal Council had been contacted by a Mum whose baby was being christened at the Church adjacent to the dual carriageway. The proud mother was concerned that she, and the rest of the family, wouldn't be able to reach the Church conveniently, and precisely to the schedule she had worked out so meticulously because the Cavalcade was in action.

The Council was very good in situations like this and it was kindly suggested that perhaps Mum, Dad and baby could arrive five minutes early rather than keep to their pre-planned timetable. Alternatively, maybe the christening could be delayed by a very short time or perhaps family and guests could park on the same side of the dual carriageway as the Church.

None of these options was acceptable. Mum was determined that she would keep to her plan – and that was that!

Just before the Cavalcade began, she somehow pushed past the Council's marshals, complete with baby, and managed to reach the central reservation – in perfect time to see 220 bikes come down the hill. I suppose the good thing is that she had an excellent view of what was always a fantastic spectacle. I checked on the baby as I rode past on each of the three laps, and it seemed relaxed too so it must have been a calm and happy infant who clearly had an interest in motorcycles.

Meanwhile, my pleas to James regarding "High Fiving" had fallen on deaf ears. Star riders really do like to be worshipped and Toseland was no different, letting thousands of fans feel his glove as he rode past. Of course, the lesser mortals saw what was happening and so they joined in too. Now we had a mass "High Fiverthon" taking place - and everyone was having a great time. The Health and Safety fun would have really started when someone mis-judged a spectator's hand and broke their wrist: fortunately, it didn't happen.

Not that James was finished. The Cavalcade route was almost two and a half miles long but at one point, it passed directly in front of Northwich Police Station. Clearly, this was the place where James decided he would put on a show. To be fair, the smiley face – complete with glasses – which he drew on the road with the smoking rear wheel of his bike was of exemplary quality. It was such a good job that it was still perfectly clear six months later and in full view of every Police Officer who visited the station!

Unfortunately, Northwich Police were not best pleased with James' efforts and were on the radio instantly to make their feelings known. Colin was good in these situations and smiled the tension away, finishing with one of the great killer lines of the event when he was told about the road and rubber artwork. "He's double World Champion. What do you expect? That's what we pay him for!"

Which in truth it was…

We had many other seriously star riders and they joined in, heart and soul, with the event. I was particularly fond of Leon Haslam, and his lovely wife Oli, who were both models of courtesy and kindness and a big hit with the fans.

Steve Parrish really understood what was needed of him and made life very easy for me, as well as opening a lot of doors because he was so highly regarded by other star riders. Steve Plater was another model of professionalism and enthusiasm, and did a brilliant job for us.

On a personal level, I liked working with Cal Crutchlow simply because he was such good fun. It's a real shame that MotoGP keeps Cal locked away because he is a thoroughly nice person and a real bike fan. Over the weekend, I asked him what he would do if he wasn't riding MotoGP and he came up with a very telling answer: "If I didn't ride professionally, I'd be going club racing and sleeping in the back of the van every weekend. I love racing."

We changed our star riders every year but we kept Jim Redman for a range of reasons. First was out of loyalty. We had traded off Jim's reputation a long time before the Thundersprint was huge. The second reason was that he was endlessly patient and kind with fans, and we respected him tremendously for this. Jim had the magic knack of making every fan feel as if they were the only person in the world when they were speaking to him – and he could do this endlessly, for hour after hour. It is a wonderful gift.

Finally, Jim was superb away from motorcycling. He could meet sponsors, politicians and Council Officers and make them all feel valuable and wanted.

Jim was able to work so well because we had the good fortune to form a relationship with Clive Brooker, who not only supplied Jim with motorcycles to ride at the Thundersprint but also acted as his PA.

Because he was so busy for the whole weekend, Jim needed the administrative burden of being in the right place at the correct time lifting from him. Clive was a good classic racer in his own right, as well as being a superb mechanic, so he understood all the racing elements of the weekend to perfection.

In some ways the PR and public elements of the event were harder, and more important, than Jim's time on track and Clive, ably assisted by his son Lee, made sure that these flowed smoothly too. They also both did something very difficult. Although Clive was a star in his own right, he was always willing – insistent even – that Jim took all the limelight. It took a lot of self-confidence to stand back and do this : only the best facilitators can manage the trick.

In our eyes, Jim was right at the top of the motorcycle stardom tree. In classic racing terms, he was almost on the final leaf, on the very last branch, at the top of the tree. Almost? There was only one rider in the world above him – fifteen times World Champion, Giacomo Agostini.

It was all well and good having Cal Crutchlow, James Toseland and a galaxy of stars at the Thundersprint but Giacomo? Even with my imagination, this was a step too far. But, as I have said on a number of occasions in this book: *wyrd bið ful aræd – fate is inexorable.* And I really do believe this to be true.

In this case, I was riding in the fabulous St Cergue Hill Climb in Switzerland - as was Giacomo. One of the better parts of my character is that I have never had any illusions about my riding ability – or lack of it! So, I have deliberately not said that I was riding with Giacomo – because I wasn't. Well, almost but not quite I wasn't...

Wherever Giacomo rides he is the star attraction. After all, he is one of the greatest motorcycle racers of all time. At St Cergue, I was writing about this legendary event and was a guest of the organising team. The stars, and me, were put at the front of the collecting box at the top of the hill. That was the first bit of fate.

Purely and utterly with no input on my part, I was shooed to the front of the line by a marshal trying to make room for the increasing numbers of riders behind. I ended up squashed next to Giacomo Agostini: fate #2.

Whilst we were waiting for our second run, there was a big accident with a sidecar and everything was delayed: fate #3.

It was baking hot and so Giacomo and I both removed our helmets: fate #4.

Giacomo had a long look at my Seeley-Suzuki, which really is a lovely bike, and smiled: fate #5.

Somewhat tentatively, I told the great man about the bike. The key thing in these situations is never, ever, bluff, exaggerate or bulls**t. In the racing world, these super riders have seen vastly more than anyone else, have done more, know more and achieved things we mere mortals can't even imagine. The only thing to do is be completely honest because, that way, you will never be found wanting.

So we chatted about the Seeley, somewhat guardedly but still sharing the common ground of two motorcycle racers – albeit several light years apart in terms of ability and achievement. As we were preparing to put our helmets on for the ride down, I also told Giacomo about the Thundersprint and, in an instant, the roller shutters came down across his eyes. The reaction was wholly understandable. Giacomo is an "A List" Hollywood grade celeb and wherever he goes there is a constant queue of people who want a piece of him. Now we weren't talking about bikes but having a slice of a legend – and he wasn't interested.

As we were packing up after the event, I couldn't wait to tell Carol that I had been chatting to the great Giacomo Agostini and she was all giggles and excitement. People queue up for hours for an autograph - and her husband had been in personal conservation with the greatest of the racing deities.

Then Carol spoke in the same quiet and gentle voice she always uses when she feels strongly about a subject: we should have Ago at the Thundersprint. I rejected the idea outright for all the sensible reasons. First, and most importantly, Giacomo was expensive. As the Superstar Act in the Classic Racing Circus he demanded superstar money and this was going to be far too much for us. Then there was the Thundersprint itself. If Giacomo did come to Northwich, I wanted him on the track with Jim - not sat in a tent signing autographs.

This was a man who had won everything, on every great circuit in the world, and now he was going to be asked to ride round a car park. From every point of view, it was inconceivable.

Then Carol squeezed my hand and said: "Forget the money. We can always make that another year. You have been an Agostini fan since you were a boy and here's the opportunity to have him at our event. Let's get him there."

And this is why I love and admire my wife so much: there is no mountain too big for her to conquer. Fate #6.

So we decided that we would have Giacomo at the Thundersprint. The only thing left was how to get him there!

That evening we were in the same celebratory, post-event dinner as Giacomo
– but clearly five tables down from the great and the good. Waiting for a gap
between courses, I approached Ago and made a 30 second sales pitch – whilst
his hosts gave me looks which would have drilled holes in titanium.

Giacomo said not quite nothing, but the three words he did speak were
important: "Meet me afterwards." Where or how I didn't have a clue!

Towards the end of the meal, Giacomo walked past us and flicked his eyes
towards the door. No words were spoken. Everyone had been enjoying the
wine, as well as the food, so for once Giacomo's exit wasn't noticed.

Next to St Cergue's Community Hall, where we had been eating, was a park.
In the dark, beneath a tree, Giacomo sat on a bench. We approached him like
two agents in a John le Carré spy novel. I made the pitch and Carol joined in
enthusiastically.

Giacomo spoke very little and then asked for a written proposal. We were
both riding at the Bikers Classics event, at Spa in Belgium, the following
weekend and he would give us his decision then.

I wrote a detailed offer and sent it to Giacomo – but without any mention
of a fee. Instead, I wanted to tell him about the unique nature of the event
because whatever else he is and has become, at heart, Giacomo is still what he
started out as: a motorcycle racer.

The following weekend at Spa, we stood in the long line of fans waiting to
see Giacomo and eventually we were ushered into the inner sanctum for a
private meeting with the great man. Carol got a hug and a big smile: I didn't.

The good news was that Giacomo was agreeable to the idea. Now, there
was only the money to discuss. We did our "Good Cop – Bad Cop" show and
Carol negotiated a fee which was both impressively high – and incredibly good
value. Wow and then a lot more wows! We had Ago as our star rider.

I mentioned earlier that the cost of the rider was not just the appearance fee and
this was brought home to us in high definition with Giacomo. As things eventually
transpired, we had a good laugh but at the time what happened brought a lump to
my throat – and a sharp pain in a more sensitive part of my body!

First, Giacomo was given his own dedicated driver and car for the weekend.
This was necessary in order for him to get from Manchester Airport to the hotel
and then on to the track the following morning for 7am – a time that had the
great man throwing up his hands in sheer horror.

Vale Royal Council helped with accommodation, so Ago was in the area's
poshest hotel – a real 6* establishment. I had worked all throughout Saturday
at the event and, on my way home, I called in to check that Giacomo had settled
in - at a hotel where I could never afford to stay.

To be fair to the Manager I must have looked a bit dishevelled when I arrived
and no doubt smelt as bad as I looked. When I asked whether Ago was dining,
I got the icy stare received by peasants through the ages. Translated, it said:

"You disgusting creature, get round to the stable door and you might get a stale crust and a bowl of gruel – if I'm feeling kind."

This was not a good time to play the role of a snotty dictator to a very tired, and somewhat emotionally drained, event organiser – red rose in his dinner jacket button-hole or not. In summary, I was exhausted, hungry, thirsty and more than a little irritable. I asked to be shown to Ago's table and was told that I should wait whilst it was ascertained if Mr. Agostini wished to see me or not. This was the comment I least needed in the world.

I made very direct eye contact with the Manager and spoke: "Look sunshine. Mr. Agostini is working for me. I'm paying his wages. I'm paying for his meal and I'm paying his hotel bill too. What else do you want to know?"

The change in attitude was impressive and instant. Now, instead of looking down his nose, the Manager was in full Basil Fawlty mode – including holding the chair out for me to sit at Giacomo's table and insisting on a complimentary drink.

Ago was having a great time. Rather than dine alone he had invited his driver, and his driver's girlfriend, for dinner and the table was loaded with four bottles of wine. Our superstar hadn't been best pleased with the first three bottles and had kept ordering until he found one to his liking. I felt as if I had just been kneed in the man bits as I calculated the bill. Ago had eaten and drunk the profit on a lot of trade stands! This is what a total price means in reality.

There is nothing I can say about Giacomo's attendance at the Thundersprint except that he was great. He was professional, enthusiastic, helpful and good fun too. He walked the track and attended the riders' briefing, as he was required to do, and joined in with all the peripheral activities.

MV Agusta enthusiast Ben Shaughnessy, and his Alto Racing team, supplied Ago with a lovely bike and he rode round the track and put on a great show.

In every way he was perfect and, as the crowds poured in, good value for money too.

Ago was also gracious. Wherever he goes, Giacomo carries the #1 plate on his bike but I would not have this happen at the Thundersprint. In our eyes Jim was #1, and always would be. Jim who had ridden, and still put on a brilliant show, even though he was staggeringly ill, at Southport. Jim who had stroked sponsors' egos and chatted up Councillors. Jim who was fiercely loyal to us and savagely protective if we were ever criticised in his presence. Jim who had sat in our lounge with his shoes off and cuddled our infant daughter.

So, Jim carried the #1 plate and Giacomo #2 – and both did so with the good grace that comes from genuinely being the best.

Not only did we have the greatest riders at the Thundersprint, we had some of the most exotic bikes in the classic racing world. Many of these came through the kindness of Sammy Miller.

From being the finest trials rider of his generation, Sammy had applied the same determination and ambition to his Museum as he did to motorcycle competition. Now, the Sammy Miller Motorcycle Museum, in Hampshire, is one of the foremost collections of motorcycles anywhere in the world.

The great joy of the bikes in Sammy's Museum is that they all run – and well too. As one might expect from Sammy's competition background, there are a lot of race bikes in the collection.

So, in a paddock located in a Council car park spectators could walk round and see four cylinder Honda GP bikes, the legendary eight cylinder Moto Guzzi and, my favourite of all, the 1957 Gilera Four. Later, I rode this bike and I still get dizzy thinking about how lucky I was.

Sammy, and his mechanic John Ring, were endlessly patient and it was wonderful to have these great riders and their iconic bikes in the open for ordinary people, just like me, to see and touch. This is what made the Thundersprint great.

Finally, we had guests from outside the biking world but these produced mixed results.

At one end was James May, at the time not nearly so well-known as he is today. James is a hard core bike fan and pobbled round the track waving to the crowds and having a good time. In the paddock, James was patient with the fans but did not have the same commitment as Jim, Cal or Giacomo who seemed to empathise with Thundersprinters much more. Maybe James was still coming to terms with stardom or perhaps he didn't see cuddling spectators as part of the job specification - because he is very charming on a personal level.

We had other TV people come along too and basically they were a pain in the bottom, with a grossly inflated idea of their importance or value to the event. Without any debate at all, Carol, Colin and I all decided that we were best staying away from them.

*****

I can never decide which was the biggest single attraction at the Thundersprint – the star riders, the incredible range of bikes on the track or the actual size of the show. However, if it wasn't the bikes then a strong contender for the big draw had to be the Spitfire display.

The word unforgettable is much over used but to see this near mythical aircraft display right over the centre of the town was a truly unique experience. It's also something which I'm sure will never, ever happen again because, following the disaster at the Shoreham Airshow in 2015, regulations have been tightened so much that no aircraft would be permitted to display in a town centre.

I had done some flying as a young man and was a bit of a Battle of Britain junkie. As a Hippy pacifist, I remain very much anti-war but if I ever had to fight anywhere it would have been flying a Spit to defend England from invasion – and this was a very credible possibility in the summer of 1940.

The RAF has a collection of historic aircraft to celebrate this victory: the Battle of Britain Memorial Flight. They have a number of Spitfires at their disposal – and some fantastic pilots to fly them. However, because they are the best aircraft and the best pilots, getting a BBMF aircraft at a show is not easy.

The system works on a bidding process and is quite bureaucratic. The organiser makes a bid to the RAF Selection Committee, explaining why the BBMF should supply an aircraft and then supports the request with an explanation of the nature of the show, why the event would be good for the RAF and, most importantly, the predicted attendance.

If the bid is successful, then the BBMF are allowed to consider allocating an aircraft. This is another hurdle to jump because, quite rightly, the BBMF are very careful where their aircraft display.

We always took meticulous care with our bid and spent a long time preparing it. Perhaps this is why we were successful every year. We were also suitably well-mannered and grateful to the BBMF and became quite good friends with the Officers in charge of the flight. Certainly, the BBMF were high on our list of recipients for Thundersprint goodies.

Carol, Elizabeth and I also visited the BBMF in Coningsby to personally thank staff for the support we were given. This was much appreciated and we even got a behind-the-scenes, VIP tour of the unit to acknowledge the effort we had made. Now, in addition to her three Brownie badges – Elizabeth really wasn't aspirational in terms of gaining Brownie awards – my somewhat eccentric daughter was able to add a short session in the tail gunner's turret of a Lancaster bomber to her CV!

The warmth of our relationship encouraged me to push the boundaries of what the BBMF would do for us, to the outer limit. Working with the RAF is easy in terms of timing. These military pilots are used to turning up at a point in the middle of nowhere, exactly on time.

Because we explained the critical importance of the Spit arriving before the blessing and National Anthem, the RAF co-operated fully with us. This meant that I knew for certain that the aircraft would be over the show at 13.18. The timing also meant that I knew exactly where the sun would be. Both facts were important because I had an idea.

I did my homework and checked where the sun would be at 13.25 and then drew a reverse course away from this. The idea was that the Spit would fly away from the show on this track. That was the first part of the finale. Now I needed the pilot to waggle the Spit's wings in salute to the crowd, so that the sun would catch on the wing tips. That was the second part.

Finally, I needed the aircraft to climb away from the crowd so that the Rolls Royce engine was under load and the roar of the supercharged, 12 cylinder engine ricocheted off the spectator banking like cannon fire, whilst the aircraft was silhouetted against the sky.

At its best, when we had perfect weather at the Thundersprint, there was no better finale to an aircraft display anywhere in the world – and that's the objective truth.

I was very proud of the display, particularly so because no-one knew how much planning went into it. Like all good magic, the audience could never tell why the trick worked. It was attention to detail like this which made the Thundersprint very special.

★★★★★

I can't write this series of postcards without mentioning the Thundersprint's sponsors because without them the event could not have happened as it did. The event was expensive to organise and promote and, with free spectator admission, we could never have earned our wages without sponsorship.

Our most important sponsor was Vale Royal Borough Council because they provided a modest grant, vital infrastructure and staff support for the event. The bottom line is that without the enthusiasm of the Council there could never have been a Thundersprint in Northwich.

We also had the active and enthusiastic support of the area's MP, Mike Hall. Mike was a true man of the people. He was also very well connected in the North-West of England and a really cute navigator through the byzantine complexity of Local and National Government. We liked, and respected, Mike a lot. Through Mike, we received a one-off grant from the North West Development Agency.

We didn't take a single penny of this money for ourselves but, instead, spent it all on turning the Thundersprint into a two-day event. Bizarrely, for internal political reasons within the town, we had to put Saturday's show on one side of the town and Sunday's on the other. This meant that everything had to be packed up on Saturday evening and moved a mile and a half to the new site. Organising the Thundersprint was never easy!

We were fortunate to have some great commercial sponsors for the Thundersprint and these included the three big insurance companies of Bennetts, Carole Nash and e-Bike. The relationship with Bennetts and Carole Nash was very much a commercial one. With e-Bike, things were very different!

e-Bike had been conceived by Arron Banks, who is now better known as a key financial supporter of UKIP. His idea was both wonderfully bold and, at the time, very innovative. It was this. Customers would purchase insurance products directly through an interface with a very clever website and have minimal contact with actual human staff. This would reduce premiums and so make e-Bike a market leader. Now everyone is comfortable with never having human contact but, fifteen years ago, it was a truly radical idea and e-Bike needed a very high public profile to promote the concept.

I had spent a long day at the Birmingham Bike Show selling trade stand space, getting material for articles and taking pictures: three jobs for the cost of doing one. It was the end of a nine hour day, plus the travelling, and I was dog tired. On my way out, I passed a small trade stand where staff were getting ready to pack up. I really didn't want to speak to anyone but we didn't have a sponsor for the following year's Thundersprint so I thought I would have one last go, just to finish off the day. It was the best decision I ever made.

e-Bike was run by Geoff Derham and Jaimie Hanley. They both had job titles but, regardless of what it said on their business cards, the two of them were the ones who pulled every handle at e-Bike. They were switched on, fast thinking and dynamic – and both were blessed with a truly manic sense of humour.

e-Bike came on board with a substantial amount of sponsorship for the Thundersprint and this allowed us to have star riders like Jim, Ago and the modern aces. They also supported our ordinary riders with generosity and enthusiasm. As Geoff once said to me: "These blokes are the customers who pay our wages – not the stars." And of course, he was correct. With e-Bike, the riders' goodie bag was of spectacular proportions!

In fact, things were even better than this. When Vale Royal saw the commitment e-Bike were making, they chipped in with some pressies for riders too, so a Thundersprint goodie bag was more like the gifts given to stars at the Oscars than a bike meeting.

Most importantly, e-Bike believed in the concept of the Thundersprint and took part in the event with commitment. Their Bristol offices were stripped bare of staff as everyone came up to the Thundersprint and turned Northwich into the centre of the e-Bike universe.

Not that they were easy to control. Working with free-wheeling, anarchic maniacs is fine but getting them to follow an event plan was not easy. Still, it was fun.

Probably the highlight of e-Bike's sponsorship was the time when Jaimie was leading the Cavalcade in the e-Bike pick-up truck, just behind the Police bikes. Our Guest of Honour from Vale Royal was a senior Councillor and he wanted his constituents to see how much he supported the Thundersprint. As I have noted, the event was loved locally.

The Councillor decided that the best way to do this would be to stand in the back of the bright blue and yellow truck and wave to the crowd. Jaimie shrugged his shoulders and said that if this is what the Councillor really wanted, then he was good with the idea. Jaimie was always fond of anything which was edgy!

However, Cheshire Police weren't - and put an absolute veto on the plan. It was at this point that Jaimie and I turned away, as the Councillor explained to the Officer who had banned his road trip that this was Vale Royal, he was at the top of Councillor tree and he would stand in the pick-up – or be arrested.

Of course Jaimie loved the idea of being rammed off the road by a Police car in order to bang up an errant Councillor, and so off he set.

We have lots of images of the Thundersprint but, in act of extreme kindness, the one I will never publish is the glorious, full colour pic of Jaimie, one elbow out of the pick-up window and in tears of laughter, as the Councillor stood proudly in the back of the truck giving a straight arm salute to his adoring constituents. The Nuremberg Rallies had nothing on the Thundersprint Cavalcade!

*****

Almost the first question we are asked about the Thundersprint, even now, is how many spectators actually came to the event. Throughout this book, I have stressed my attempts to be as honest and objective as I can – and I will be as truthful as possible now. The facts are that no-one knows the precise attendance at the Thundersprint but I can give you some indications.

The first one is based on Economic Impact Surveys carried out by Cheshire West and Chester Council, who succeeded Vale Royal in administering the Northwich area. These were expensive affairs, paid for by the Council, and we had very little to do with them. They were a second cousin of a VAT or Tax Inspection where the person being investigated has no say in what information is being sought but is merely required to provide it.

I am stressing this point because, whilst the company conducting the surveys was neither hostile nor discourteous, they were certainly not there to represent the Thundersprint or to show the event in a favourable light.

This is the Executive Summary for the 2011 event and it's worth quoting verbatim:

Executive Summary

This report sets out an evaluation of the economic impacts of Thundersprint 2011. It includes an analysis of the gross and net visitor expenditure impacts on the Cheshire sub-regional economy and a summary of findings from a visitor survey conducted at the event.

Economic Impacts

The table below summarises the net expenditure impacts of those attending, participating and trading at Thundersprint 2011.

Gross Direct, Indirect	Gross Impacts	Deductions	Net Impacts
Attender spend	£12,580,925	63.0%	£4,654,942
Attender spend	£7,978,294	67.5%	£2,592,946
Participant spend	£17,227	63.0%	£6,374
Participant spend	£27,730	39.1%	£16,888
Trader spend on-	£25,853	63.0%	£9,566
Trader spend off-	£32,988	25.0%	£24,741

- The gross direct expenditure impacts of Thundersprint 2011 are significantly higher than in the previous two years at £15.4m, made up of trader, participant and attender expenditure at and as a result of the event. This is some £5m higher than those reported for 2010.
- When accounting for the expenditure that would otherwise occur within the economy in any event, expenditure displaced from other activities and leakages (directly and through trader supply chains) the net expenditure impacts directly attributable the event account for just over £7.3m. This represents an increase of 14% on the previous year and is largely attributable to a hike in the average attender on-site expenditure from £52.17 in 2010 to £81.63 in 2011.

Visitor Impacts

Thundersprint 2011 attracted an estimated 145,000 attenders across the two days of the event. Of these, 67,600 were from outside Cheshire and 30,500 from outside the region. An estimated 1,500 of attendees were international visitors.

- Whilst the event continues to draw visitors from across the UK and overseas, the majority reside within the North West, Staffordshire and east of the Pennines.
- As in previous years a significant proportion of those attending have been to the event in previous years. The proportions of those attending just once is declining suggesting that event has a loyal market and is successful in retaining newcomers over the years.
- The range of groups attending is diverse with equal proportions of attenders visiting with friends or part of a couple. The proportions of those attending alone has increased and whilst there has been decrease in the proportions of families attending, with more than a quarter attending it is clear that event caters for family groups.
- Almost a fifth of respondents indicated they were staying away from home overnight on their visit. Of these, the significant majority (84%) indicated they were staying in Cheshire. The average number of nights staying the area was 2.6 nights. These results suggest that local accommodation providers derive considerable value from the event.
- It is clear that word of mouth and past experience are the key influences on attenders decision to visit. Notwithstanding this, the findings suggest that a proportion of those outside the region rely on other channels and particularly newspaper and magazine articles, websites and blogs.

The expert assessment was 145,000 spectators and I don't think that this was very far out. The Cavalcade route was just under two and a half miles in length and it was lined with spectators, in some parts five deep. This meant that we had five miles of spectators – plus those who preferred to stay in the town centre because watching the Cavalcade meant getting next to the route early for a good view – a bit like seeing a Royal visit but with race bikes instead of the Queen in a horse and cart!

Another piece of information, this time more anecdotal than empirical, is the distance away from Northwich customers had to stay. In later Thunder-sprints, we were finding accommodation for visitors all over the North-West of England – as far away as Manchester which is 25 miles from Northwich.

Finally, the crowds in the town centre were enormous with every street packed tight with fans. No-one can ever put an accurate number on how many people there were but something in the region of a mile and a half of streets were jammed solid – as anyone who visited the event between 10.30am and 2.30pm will testify.

The people of Northwich were wonderful – welcoming and very tolerant of the invasion of their town. Cheshire Police were exemplary too with a highly intelligent, light touch approach centred on keeping a low profile and a watchful eye on proceedings.

In short, the Thundersprint worked incredibly well. That the event was promoted and largely organised by just two people – Carol and me – supported by a tiny team of part time assistants, made the achievement all the more remarkable.

Both we and the Thundersprint were highly regarded in the community too. We won numerous business accolades in the area including Travel and Tourism awards in 2005 and 2006; Business of the Year in 2007, along with Best Customer Care, and, to my blushing surprise, I was voted Business Person of the Year in 2008.

We were going to so many posh ceremonies that Carol and Elizabeth ended up with some nice new frocks – which they loved – and I was told to go out and buy a decent dinner suit, which I resented!

So with all the success, and from every direction, why isn't the Thundersprint still in Northwich, bigger and better than ever?

There are a number of reasons and each is both very different, whilst being complementary. First, and most importantly, are the problems everyone faces in working with me. Freelancers are odd beasts and we are not team players. Self-motivated, self-reliant and self-monitoring people can't be compromisers for the greater good, or willing to agree with a consensus view just for the sake of harmony.

Good freelancers, and I do claim to be very good indeed, don't need help or support because they will deliver - regardless of the circumstances. Equally, we are highly intolerant of those who can't. In terms of the Thundersprint, I had bet our house, and our future, on my idea and won. Therefore, I was only going to take criticism or advice from someone who had done equally well or, ideally, better.

The Thundersprint was also highly eccentric – as was I. The motorcycle industry was deeply suspicious of someone who thought of motorcycle stars as Disney World characters and believed that racing in a car park was more theatre than sport.

Finally, I was – and always will be – painfully shy. Waiting outside a pub for your Dad to stagger on to the pavement and then collapse in a pool of vomit does not build elegant social skills in an eight year old and so I have always been deeply uncomfortable in networking situations. Where I should have been attending Chester Races, or motorcycle industry dinners, and gossiping to the "right" people, I avoided these situations like the plague – and I still do.

As I have intimated, the motorcycle industry did not support the Thundersprint and in so doing it missed a golden opportunity to reach out to new customers. This was unforgiveable.

Regardless of the fact that I was not an industry insider, and had no desire to be, the Motorcycle Industry Association (MCIA) should have embraced the Thundersprint because it offered a wonderful opportunity, not only to sell bikes at the event, but to bring new customers into a market which is shrinking every year.

We did have some exemplary support from individuals such as Simon Belton from Yamaha and Honda's Neil Tuxworth. Dealers, like Wigan Yamaha, Aprilia Merseyside and Knutsford Honda, were great too but on the whole, the Thundersprint was neither understood nor appreciated and this was a marked failing on the part of the MCIA.

Next, there was the murder of Vale Royal Borough Council – and I have used this emotive description deliberately. From 2007 to 2009, Hazel Blears was Secretary of State for Communities and Local Government in Tony Blair's Labour government. She rode bikes and came to the Thundersprint in her riding gear. On a personal level she is lovely – very smiley and fond of giving hugs. However, like all politicians, she was focussed on political ends. The sun is hot, water is wet, sharks eat fish and politicians are always obsessed with the next election: that's the way of the world.

Despite what anyone says, I am convinced that this is why she insisted on scrapping Vale Royal Borough Council - in the hope that the new Council would be weighted towards Labour.

The whole exercise was a shambles from start to finish. The first idea was the only practical one and this was to combine all the individual council bodies within Cheshire into one Super-Council but this would not have given the political benefits which were desired. Instead Vale Royal was forced – kicking and screaming – into a shotgun marriage with Chester City Council and Ellesmere Port Council. The city name of Chester was incorporated into the new Authority's name because there was no way this side of the universe closing down that Chester was going to lose any status in the new Council.

This was the problem the Thundersprint faced. Chester is a very beautiful, culturally important and high profile city – and Northwich isn't! In the simplest terms, this was the root of the issue.

Chester West and Chester (CWAC) offices were in Chester, the contacts were in Chester and the power was in Chester. We still live in the area and the local joke is that the Council should be re-named "Chester and Suburbs" because all the action is in Chester and what happens in the rest of the area really isn't of any consequence.

Because of our extended contract with Vale Royal, the new Council was initially stuck with the Thundersprint and there wasn't much that they could do about it. So, in the best tradition of English bureaucrats through the centuries we were slowly, carefully, and ever so politely, choked to death.

Instead of Anne Bingham Holmes' smiles and urging to do ever more and better things with the Thundersprint, CWAC Officers bombarded us with demands to reduce costs and cut corners. It was a wearying experience, devoid of smiles or encouragement.

Had the Thundersprint been located in Chester, I remain 100% certain that it would be still be in existence – probably bigger, if not better, than ever. Maybe if I had been more willing to kiss bottoms, nod in agreement and sip warm white wine it would still be there. But none of this was ever going to happen in reality and so, with aching sadness, we said goodbye to Northwich.

We ran two more Thundersprints and in both cases Carol, Colin and I got the strong feeling that Wyrd was sending us unequivocal messages.

The Anglesey Circuit is located on the western edge of the island, facing the Irish Sea. It is one of the best tracks in the world to ride and, on the right day, is breathtakingly beautiful. But on the wrong day, the south-westerly winds whip in with gale force and the location is grim. For the weekend of the Thundersprint, we had the wrong two days!

Anglesey is also a long way from the big centres of population and this makes attracting a good crowd to the track hard work. The location, and a hurricane, combined to cost us a lot of money.

Darley Moor has a much better location, right in the centre of the country near to many major cities. The circuit was the right length for the Thundersprint and the whole setting is very pretty with acres of immaculate grassland and woods. We also knew and liked Eddie and Chris Nelson, from the Darley Moor Motorcycle Racing Club, who had expertly run the racing element of the Thundersprint in Northwich for many years.

Trade sales were excellent for the Darley Moor event, as were entries for the Cavalcade and the actual sprint. In fact, everything looked certain for a real super success. Then it began raining – and continued to pour down in quantities which would have put a decent sized monsoon to shame! The parking and paddock was turned into a quagmire and event was an utter disaster.

Carol keeps an hour log of what we do, so that I don't fritter away all of our working time on speculative ventures, and our income for the Darley Moor event made interesting reading. She calculated that we earned £3.51 per hour – split two ways! We weren't getting rich from the Thundersprint!

After Darley, we decided that enough was enough. Wyrd had been whispering in our ears for a few years and had now started shouting!

The reasons for our decision were not as straightforward as they might seem. It wasn't simply a case of the money, or lack of it. Sixteen years earlier, when we were hungry, we would have taken the £1.75 an hour wages in good part and come back harder and stronger for the following year. But 2014 was not 1998. We had been careful with the money we had made and, in the simplest terms, we were no longer hungry.

We were also tired. Organising the Thundersprint was always brutally hard work. My normal – and note the word "normal" – working day was from 5am until 10pm, six days a week from November until June. After the event Carol and I were always really ill, for two or three weeks. £1.75 an hour was not much compensation for this much effort.

The final factor was that we missed Northwich and Vale Royal Borough Council. We missed the encouragement from Anne. We missed the help given by Richard and we missed Andrea's smiles. When we looked for the lads who would cut an extra branch from a tree to make the event better, they weren't there. No longer would we walk through the town centre and be thanked by the people of this wonderful little town for bringing something important to them – an event which made them proud to live in Northwich and to be part of the Thundersprint.

So, for all these reasons we decided that we would not run any more Thundersprints and instead, remember all the good times – and there were many.

I had walked the high wire, crossed the chasm, and reached the other side. Carol and I were closer than we had ever been and had grown to respect each other even more. Wyrd had told me that it was time to move on. And so we did.

18

Full Circle

SOME of my very earliest memories as an infant were telling stories to anyone who would listen. Then I lurched, chaotically and erratically, into literacy and began to write in a turbulent, untidy scrawl which was often illegible, even to my kindest teachers.

When I was eighteen years old, I sent a story to Motorcycle World of 357 Park Avenue South, in New York. They liked it so much that they paid me: this was rather good!

I had no training as a professional writer, no experience as a journalist and no knowledge of what I should or should not say. There was every reason not to accept my work and only one thing in my favour: I could tell stories which readers enjoyed.

From then on, there was no turning back. I would be a freelance journalist forever.

More than any other of my numerous careers, and the successes they have given to me, I am most proud to be a writer.

So, when we decided not to run any more Thundersprints, I wasn't left with the empty void felt by a lot of 65 year olds whose working life has just ended. On the contrary, I was pretty well flat out writing for MotoUSA and Classic Bike Guide.

This was great – unbelievably so – but I also needed another project, something which would stretch me and cause a pleasant degree of stress!

There were two driving forces for the start of my next adventure and they came from completely different sources. All parents love their children but, additionally, I like my daughter Elizabeth. We have been friends since before she first offered to share her baby bottle with me – and she was only five months old then!

On the way back from race meetings, Elizabeth used to sit behind me in the car and we would talk – for hours. These conversations would put Carol to sleep almost instantly but Elizabeth and I would chatter and debate and swap gossip for hundreds of miles.

A regular topic was racing stories, tales of battles won, bones broken and bikes of near mythical beauty and performance.

I had to be very careful with these anecdotes and not indulge, well not too much, in: "The older I get the faster I was…" fantasies. Elizabeth had a razor sharp brain and almost total recall of each story. If I made an error in a second telling of the same epic then I would be brought to justice – and instantly too.

As she grew older and eventually left home, Elizabeth asked me to jot down the stories for her along with some memories of my childhood. To please her, I began to write what would be nothing more than a collection of informal notes to be read just by the two of us.

I started with my earliest recollections but this was the wrong thing to do. Lots of kids had sad childhoods, and I wasn't in the worst position by any means, but I didn't have anything happy to recall for Elizabeth until the time when I took control of my own life.

The second attempt began just with racing stories, many of which she knew off by heart. The problem with these was more a technical one. All writers need what is called a voice – the way the reader is addressed. The stories I told to Elizabeth in the car were full of giggles, hesitations and pauses and when I tried to replicate this voice in the written form it was a real mess.

At the same time as Elizabeth was pleading for stories of the olden days, and not just racing, every time I saw Harry Moffatt at a race event he was pressing me for the bike memories I was always gossiping about in the paddock.

Harry is a wonderful person – kind, enthusiastic, highly literate and an arch motorcycle racing fan. Together, Elizabeth and Harry persuaded me that maybe I should try to write a few stories in a coherent manner. Now, almost without realising that I was doing it, I began writing as if the stories were a paid commission.

In some ways, this was a relief because I had found the voice I wanted to use and I had an audience – even if, initially, it was just two people.

So, depending how the project was viewed, this was either the third version of what was to become a book – or the first proper attempt!

I showed the draft to Elizabeth and Harry and neither was happy: they're not easy customers! I knew what the problem was immediately. Any story has to be constructed so that the reader is led through highs and lows in order to retain their interest. This is a story telling trade skill, and you can see it in action in everything from Beowulf to Coronation Street.

The stories I wrote for Harry and Elizabeth weren't yet unified so the reader wasn't encouraged to find out what came next. By now, this was the Mk IV iteration!

I had another go because, by this time, I was beginning to really enjoy the job. It had now shifted from just being a bit of fun for me and Elizabeth, to a real challenge.

I showed the work to Carol who is not only my wife, best friend and business partner but a brilliant editor – and that's not just a proud husband speaking!

She read the stories with interest and then came up with the killer line: "You know, this is good enough to be a book…"

We sat down and had a formal meeting which, despite there only being two of us in our business, is the best way we always make big decisions.

Carol interrogated me hard. Critically, were there sufficient stories to make a whole book and was there the breadth of material in addition to the racing tales I used to tell to Elizabeth? There was no point in launching the project and then me turning round after ten chapters and telling Carol that I had run out of things to say!

With Carol's hand on the tiller, the book now took a different direction. I'm not sufficiently important, in any way, to write a conventional autobiography but maybe I could write a collection of my memories.

I also wanted to write more than just my story. Autobiographies are, inevitably, the history of what happened to the great and successful people in every society throughout the world.

I wanted to tell the story of an ordinary person – someone brought up in a Council house, with no contacts or social advantages of any kind.

I ached to share the feeling of winning ten shillings (50p) at a grass track meeting, and then nearly wetting myself with excitement, so that the reader could see the world through the eyes of a clubman racer.

As I did, they also had to know the fear of failure which the British class system imbues in kids from my background on their first day of Higher Education.

This led to the Mk.V version – and some serious debate between Carol and me. In our relationship, "serious debate" is translated as verbal, mixed martial arts cage fighting! I wanted to call the new book, "A Penguin in a Sparrow's Nest". The title was to reflect that, in my eyes, I was the wrong kid, in the wrong place, at the wrong time. I wasn't so much a cuckoo in the family nest but a giant, half ton penguin which ate fish instead of bread and seeds!

Carol came up with all the correct reasons why this was a wholly inappropriate title – and she was right in every respect. Book titles are supposed to lead the reader into an understanding of the content. What was the new book about? Penguins? Sparrows? Birds nesting? A fantasy about a lost penguin who found himself washed up by a storm and ended up in a little bird's house? For sure, there was no clue that the stories were about motorcycles and growing up in the 1960s and '70s.

Eventually, I compromised and added the sub-title of "The Story of a Freelance Motorcycling Journalist."

Of course, the moment her back was turned – actually, she went into the village to post some letters – I added the lovely Old English "Wyrd Bið ful Aræd" to the front cover and insisted on having an image of a very confused and stressed penguin. As an aside, Elizabeth says that this is a perfect avian representation of me and my normal state of mind!

Now we had a title with 75% of a book, and could show the project to commercial publishers – who promptly, and universally, rejected the idea. Just like Carol, they said that the title was inappropriate for a book about motorcycling – and "inappropriate" was the kindest comment!

Occasionally, someone read the text and they were horrified. Instead of story after story about motorcycles there were diversions into teaching, social comment about the late 1960s and early 1970s, and topics which were so personal that no-one with a grain of brain would ever go near them. The bottom line was that no-one was going to publish "Penguin".

For my part, I had now become obsessed with making the book honest. I wanted, needed even, for the title to be "A Penguin in a Sparrow's Nest" because that was what I was.

The book had to tell stories which showed my innocence, and often sadness, as well as the manic fun and success I enjoyed. I wasn't a World Champion, or some Media Superstar, but only a clubman racer who could touch-type and I wanted to tell history from this viewpoint. So, we decided to publish the book ourselves.

The current myth is that this is an easy thing to do. Anyone can write a book, stick it on the web and make a fortune. Unfortunately, this is one of the biggest mis-representations ever. A successful, self-published book sells around 250 copies – a self-published autobiography half that number!

Clearly, self-publishing Penguin was a certain way to lose a lot of money!

In this case I wasn't betting the family house, as I did with the Thundersprint, but to print 3,000 copies of Penguin, and undertake the associated marketing activities necessary to have any hope of selling the book, was not a cheap exercise.

Carol made the payments eagerly and with enthusiasm because she was committed to making Penguin a success. However, the sums involved showed that we were playing this game for real: failure was going to be an expensive undertaking. Just how serious became apparent when I personally unloaded 1.4 tonnes of books – the delivery driver had unfortunately developed a bad back when he came to us. Now, we realised we were doing this job for real!

We sent a zillion review copies out to the magazines. Reviewers were kind to the book and gave it glowing reports. However, what caused the book to sell really well was word of mouth. There were some lovely reviews by readers which both helped sales and also brought us lots of smiles. Here are just a few:

> *"This is a wonderful autobiography of someone who really is just like us. Someone who, from humble beginnings, has made an interesting, exciting and successful life for himself."*
>
> *Frank is a talented writer and draws the reader into the narrative of his life so successfully one finds it difficult to put the book down."*
>
> Scott S

"We are a mature motorcycling family. My wife and I loved this book. Then I lent it (sorry, Frank) to our life long female motorcycle friend. She ended up burning her husband's tea to a frazzle as she couldn't put it down and was determined to get to the end!"

Michael Knowles

"A life of sunny grassy plateaus and a succession of jungles', to quote the author. This is an exhilarating account of one man's determination to make the most of a life and to excel wherever his heart, or sometimes necessity, leads him.

"Frank is not afraid to speak his mind with caustic comments about aspects of modern life, which many of us can tune in to."

Wendy Moleas

The constantly recurring theme was that the story was told by someone just like the reader and this is what made it attractive. And, of course, this was true: I was, and remain, my readers.

Penguin was also popular with an audience far outside the motorcycling world – and was especially well liked by female readers.

It's not impossible to get a self-published book stocked by one of the big book sellers but nor is it actually impossible for a club racer to beat Marc Marquez: it's merely very, very, very highly unlikely.

In 2014, there were 184,000 new or reprinted books published in Britain so you can see that statistically the chances of a self-published autobiography making it on to the shelves of a commercial bookshop were remote – as in an ice-cream looking forward to a long and happy life on the equator.

We did try with the book trade, we really did, but we were met with a wall of practised, professional apathy – and still had a pile of books in our garage the size of a small car. This was not good because I couldn't get at the bikes!

The solution was three fold. First, we had a really nice website designed by Tim Wright at Tantrum Media. The first plan was for me to do a home-built website but this would have looked exactly what it was: a DIY effort produced by an amateur. By contrast Tim is a fine designer, and the site worked well especially in key things like taking payments. Potential customers could sample the book, read the reviews, and make a smooth, transparent and honest purchase through the website, if they liked what they saw. This made Tim's fees very good value!

Then we put the book on Amazon and sales began almost immediately. Amazon's bureaucracy is hard work but the site does give a book an international presence.

Finally, and most importantly of all, we set out to sell the book personally at bike shows and in bookshops. This was the most important sales avenue and was also the best fun because, for both Carol and me, it was a completely new experience.

What became clear is that customers wanted to speak to me directly and to share a writer's experience of making a book. I tried to learn from Jim Redman, to make sure that every experience was special for a customer and to ensure that I reacted in a way which met their needs. Compared to Jim, I am a real amateur at this job but I least I knew what I was supposed to be doing!

We were learning with every single event and, in the early days, I did learn a lot. We did the LlanBikeFest in the lovely Welsh town of Llangollen. Our pitch was next to David Hailwood, son of the legendary Mike Hailwood. David is good company and we were having a great time chatting to him and selling a few books as well.

In one of the quiet moments, a gorgeous – as in jaw droppingly stunning – ash blonde girl approached me. She leaned over our table and I could only admire the quality of the stitching on her white blouse as the buttons strained desperately to escape their holes.

She spoke – in a voice like warm honey:

"Are you Frank Melling, who wrote the Penguin book?"

It's really difficult to look cool and attractive if you are fat, bald, and wrinkly – but I did give it my very best shot.

"Yes, that's me. Is there **ANYTHING** I can do for you?"

Of course, Carol was in hysterics at this point and on the point of falling off her chair laughing.

The lady stood - and now it was her jeans which were under strain…

"Do you do photographs? Like, will you have your picture taken with people?"

Did I do photographs? Did I do photographs? Did-I-do-photographs!!! Well, yes actually – and this photoshoot was looking like the most desirable since we launched the book. I confirmed that indeed I was happy to be photographed with Penguin fans. Just step this way…

With a Hollywood smile brighter than the sun she spoke again.

"Oh great, because my Nan wants her picture taken with you and she's too shy to ask…"

And in came a lovely, cuddly replica of the Fairy Godmother from Cinderella and we did have lots of pictures taken – all by her granddaughter.

Book signings are very much a two-handed job and I always work with Carol. On these occasions, Carol takes the money and sometimes, at the busiest shows, chats to customers whilst I am signing a book for someone else. Very occasionally, she can fulfil another vital role.

At the Brackley Festival of Motorcycling everything was going swimmingly well. I was riding in the event and we were also selling a few books. The whole day had been excellent, chatting to customers who had read Penguin or who were thinking of buying a copy.

A beaming lady, wearing a Thundersprint T-shirt from Darley Moor, approached our table clearly with a mission on her mind.

She had already bought a copy of Penguin and had loved the book. So far, so good. Despite the rain at Darley, she had a great time there too. This was all good.

Now she had come to Brackley for me to sign her t-shirt. Better still, she wanted a customised job with "Frank" arched over one side of her chest and "Melling" over the other. I wasn't happy about this at all. For a start, I had never signed any part of a lady's body and didn't much want to start learning the technique now. The other problem was that signing her t-shirt would be much more like truck sign writing than a conventional autograph because there was an awful lot of room available!

In a flash, Carol smiled her way into the conversation. What a great idea to have Frank sign the t-shirt, and thanks so much for asking, but the signature would look so much better on the back where everyone could see it.

The lady agreed. I dug around in our show box for our biggest board marker and the lovely customer went away happy.

*****

As a local author, I approached the Chester Literature Festival but didn't make any progress. It was just like the school nativity plays I used to write – with absolutely no room at the Literature Inn!

In some respects, I could understand the organisers' point of view – although I hardly agreed with it. Penguin was self-published, an autobiography, had a motorcycling theme and I was not part of the arts community so there were four reasons not to have either me or the book at their Festival!

Against this Penguin was selling extremely well, with a mountain of positive reviews, and was sometimes the best-selling book in its category on Amazon's site.

Regardless, having been rejected for 2015, I simply left the Festival exactly where it was and sold books in the city another way.

Chester has an enormous WH Smiths' store and the manager was very smiley and proactive. Yes, we could do a signing at his shop and would we please bring a race bike into the store and make a real show? So we did - and had a very happy Saturday, just before Christmas, selling books and entertaining customers who wanted to sit on a racing motorcycle and have their photographs taken.

We did another signing at the Chester branch of Waterstones and this was good too. Waterstones' book loving staff were very welcoming and customers were eager to chat to an author about the writing and publishing process.

The WH Smiths' show led us into one of the most interesting events of the year. WH Smiths has a concession inside Bridgemere Garden Centre, near Nantwich, and the idea of taking Penguin to a brand new, non-motorcycling audience, was fascinating.

There needs to be some explanation about Bridgemere because this is not a normal pot-plant-and-plastic-gnome set up in a shopping arcade. For a start, the site covers 50 acres and grows over a million plants a year, making it arguably the biggest garden centre in Europe.

As well as plants, there is a huge restaurant, delicatessen, butchery, house-hold furnishings department and much, much more.

Carol and I did a recce to Bridgemere and drove home, culture shocked, in near silence. Bridgemere was immense – more theme park than garden centre. Despite its size, the staff had a corner shop style of warmth and informality which made us feel very welcome.

The following day, we wheeled the Suzuki to the WH Smith concession, set up our table and talked to people about bikes and racing – in between being brought cups of coffee and slices of home-made Christmas cake. We also sold plenty of books. If this was work, then I have had many worse jobs in my life!

Perhaps best of all was the warmth of the welcome given to motorcycling. Frozen's Princess Elsa came across from her magic cave to sit on the Suzuki and the cast of The Wizard of Oz, who were also appearing at Bridgemere, were all over the bike.

It's events like this where the motorcycle industry should be – reaching out to new customers instead of continuing the incestuous relationship it has with existing bike enthusiasts. It might be much easier, and more familiar, to take your products to a bike show but to build a long term future for motorcycling, the opportunity lies in Britain's Bridgemeres.

Good as Bridgemere was in terms of making Penguin profitable, the big event of the year was the International Classic Bike Show at Stafford in October. This is a monster of a show and we took the job very seriously with the aim of selling a serious quantity of books.

In this respect we were helped tremendously by two brilliant reviews. The first was written by Rowena Hoseason of Classic Bike Guide and Real Classic magazines. Rowena is a very literary reviewer and wrote an insightful assessment of Penguin which really engaged her readers.

Once more, as had happened with the Thundersprint, The Old Bike Mart turned out to be a huge help to us. OBM's Editor, Pete Kelly, was a Warrington lad who empathised with some of the stories of growing up in the town during the 1960s. Pete's review brought us a different group of readers.

With their help, and the rest of the positive press coverage and reviews we received, sales at Stafford were excellent and Carol's handbag travelled home with a very pleasant bulge in it.

★★★★★

Directly after Christmas 2015, Carol sat down and went through all the costs of Penguin meticulously. She also worked out how much we had earned and came up with a clear conclusion. Just six months after we had sold the first copy of "A Penguin in a Sparrow's Nest" we had covered all our costs and the project was in profit – and that was 100% certain.

We had achieved this in our own way and had a lot of laughs on the journey. Regardless of what the mainstream publishers, book shops or literary festivals thought about the book, its title or its content, readers liked it. We had a success and there was no denying this.

Better still, we were receiving a steady stream of requests for "Penguin #2" – which is the book you are reading now.

"The Flying Penguin" is necessarily a very different book from "A Penguin in a Sparrow's Nest". I can't continue to tell the story of a penniless, sixteen year old kid still living in a Council House because I was already 38 when the book starts and I had achieved a lot of success. So, Penguin 2 could never be Penguin 1A with more stories from the classic era of motorcycling.

What it could be is honest and the continuing story of a clubman racer who can touch type and, I hope, who can tell stories.

There are also a couple of last minute post scripts to the story and I want to include them because, at an age when many people of my age are thinking of retiring, or have actually given up work, I am looking forward to an exciting new future.

First, although Carol and I decided that we could no longer run the Thundersprint, we couldn't stay away from event organisation - it is truly an incurable addiction. To give us our fix, we now we run a lovely little event called Thunderfest which is a time trial held on tarmac.

Thunderfest has a small entry, and none of the glitz and glamour of the Thundersprint, but our colleagues and the riders are wonderful. At the last Thunderfest, which was held at the Darley Moor Circuit, I was truly touched, almost to the point of tears when, just as everyone was packing up to go home, Oliver Presswood – who rides in every Thunderfest - presented me with a magnificent wooden penguin to celebrate the success of the first book. The spontaneity of the gift, and the smiles of the riders when I received it, meant a lot to me.

Then, quite literally as this book was hours away from being sent to the printers, I was approached by a new American website which wants me to write a monthly column. How good is that? Forty-five years after my first story was published a brand new magazine, staffed by dynamic young writers and editors, want me to join them. I simply cannot believe my good fortune.

So, from the bottom of my heart, thank you for joining me on the journey and maybe, at some time in the future, I will write some more of the tales which haven't made it into the first two books.

Thanks once again from a penguin who has learned to fly.

A Penguin in a Sparrow's Nest

The Story of a Freelance Motorcycling Journalist

"A Penguin in a Sparrow's Nest" is the best selling, first part of Frank Melling's memoirs. It recounts the inspirational journey of a sixteen year old who left his Council House to become a shelf painter and went on to be one of the most prolific motorcycling journalists of his generation with over 1200 articles and 14 books to his name.

This true story could almost be a fictional novel because it is an epic tale of overcoming adversity, avoiding death on many occasions, huge efforts – and a lot of success.

On the way, Frank was fortunate to enjoy a good night's sleep in a brothel; learn about the dangers of asking for breakfast on his first day at the Isle of Man TT races; discover the delights of skiing on a motorcycle and appreciate the benefits of not listening to paramedics discussing his imminent death.

Every page is filled with warmth, humour and highly original stories which are a wonderful window on growing up in the 1960s and 1970s.

The voyage Frank takes you on during "A Penguin in a Sparrow's Nest" is unique but one always driven by passion, determination and boundless optimism.

A Penguin in a Sparrow's Nest has become a best seller with over 75 five star reviews and over 2,500 copies sold.

Signed copies are available now from:
www.frankmelling.com for £12.99
including free post and packing